Between Fitness and Death

DISABILITY HISTORIES

Series editors: Kim E. Nielsen and Michael Rembis

Disability Histories explores the lived experiences of individuals and groups from a broad range of societies, cultures, time periods, and geographic locations who either identified as disabled or were considered by the dominant culture to be disabled. Conceiving of disability and disabled experiences broadly, and spanning a range of embodiments, the series highlights innovative approaches to disability history that deepen our understanding of the past.

Between Fitness and Death

Disability and Slavery in the Caribbean

STEFANIE HUNT-KENNEDY

UNIVERSITY OF
ILLINOIS PRESS
Urbana, Chicago, and Springfield

Cataloging data available from the Library of Congress
ISBN 978-0-252-04319-2 (cloth : alk.)
ISBN 978-0-252-08506-2 (paper : alk.)
ISBN 978-0-252-05207-1 (ebook)

What is remembered in the body is well remembered . . .
—*Elaine Scarry,* The Body in Pain

Contents

Acknowledgments

This book has been a labor of love. When I set out to try to illuminate connections between disability and enslavement in the Caribbean, I could not have anticipated the twists and turns the task would take me on. But as I continued down that path, I have benefited from stimulating conversations with colleagues and from the emotional and practical support of friends and family. It is an absolute pleasure to express my sincere gratitude to each one of them here.

During my research and writing, I have had the good fortune to receive financial assistance for which I am very grateful. At the University of Toronto I received financial support from the Ontario Graduate Scholarship, the Kathleen Coburn Graduate Admission Award, the Jerome Samuel Rotenberg Memorial Graduate Scholarship, and the New College Senior Doctoral Fellowship. This funding greatly facilitated my research at the British Library, the Library of the Religious Society of Friends, the Royal College of Surgeons, the National Archives at Kew, the Faculty of Law Library and the Main Library at the University of West Indies at Cave Hill, the Barbados Museum and Historical Society, the Bridgetown Public Library, the Barbados Department of Archives, the National Library of Jamaica, the Massachusetts Historical Society, and the John Carter Brown Library. The staffs at research libraries and archives kindly tracked down manuscripts for me and helped me tackle a question central to my project: Where is disability in the archive of slavery? I am grateful for their help. At the University of New Brunswick I received funding from the Busteed Publication

Grant and the Harrison McCain Foundation Grant in Aid of Scholarly Book Publishing, which helped defray the costs of permissions and indexing.

While it is difficult to pinpoint exactly when I began to see this project as a book, friends, colleagues, and editors helped immeasurably along the way. First, I wish to thank Melanie Newton for her remarkable and unfailing support. With the heart of a true mentor, Melanie has deepened my understanding of the larger processes and movements of history and refined my skills as a scholar. Over the years, I have benefited tremendously from her intellectual generosity and unceasing kindness. She will always be my role model. Nicholas Terpstra and Madhavi Kale read and reread the original manuscript; they provided models of scholarship and clarity, and the kind of advice and encouragement every writer should have. Ryan Perks read an early draft of the manuscript, and his edits were incredibly helpful. Vince Brown offered his ideas, critiques, and most of all his encouragement at every step. Several people generously shared their research and helped me with the management of my data. Linford Fisher shared his unpublished work and archival transcriptions with me. My graduate student, Carlie Manners, collected valuable data used in this project; her enthusiasm and passion for Caribbean history rekindles my own. In her commitment to discovering disability history in the archives of slavery, my friend Jenifer Barclay was an ever-present reminder of the importance of the work we are doing. For their advice and support at critical moments in this long process, I also thank Anne McGuire, Sean Hawkins, Natalie Zemon Davis, Tara Innis, Kathleen Brown, Rod Michalko, Marisa Fuentes, Ruma Chopra, Pedro Welch, Laurie Bertram, Shaun Grech, and Karen Soldatic.

I owe many thanks to the hardworking folks at the University of Illinois Press for their efforts to make this book into a reality. For sharing their perceptive questions and their extensive knowledge, not to mention their time, I would like to thank my editors Kim Nielsen and Michael Rembis. I first met Kim when we were paired through the American Historical Association's Disability Mentorship Program. What started as an online student-teacher relationship blossomed over the years into a friendship made of long Skype calls, cross-country road trips, and handmade gifts. The manuscript has greatly benefited from the suggestions of my readers, Jenny Shaw and Sasha Turner, who provided praise and encouragement as well as rigorous critique of the book. In his careful attention and enthusiasm, James Engelhardt made revisions and other final details pleasant rather than onerous. I have also enjoyed working with copyeditor Deborah Oliver and production editor Tad Ringo.

Parts of this book were published, in somewhat different form, in the journals *Social Identities* and *Slavery & Abolition*, and the edited collection *Disability in the Global South*. I thank the editors of these titles for the opportunity to publish my work. Thank you to the participants in several academic conferences and seminars in which I took part, especially Celia Naylor who first took an interest in me and my work at the 2011 AHA.

I am fortunate to have the support and friendship of colleagues in the History Department at the University of New Brunswick. Lisa Todd answered my numerous questions about the publishing process and provided me with advice and friendship. Sasha Mullally has been a valuable mentor to me, motivating me to reach my goals and emboldening me to push beyond them. I am indebted to conversations, intellectual commentary, and guidance from Gary Waite, who has demonstrated and taught me the power of mentor relationships. Jeff Brown, Sean Kennedy, Janet Mullin, and Funké Aladejebi provided their support during the writing process. And to all the colleagues who helped create a positive community in which to work and live, thank you. Our department administrators, Elizabeth Arnold and Misty Sullivan, helped me keep my head above water in an academic environment ever more inundated with administrative work. I am especially grateful for the students I have taught over the years at UofT and UNB, whose passion for social change and courageous questions about the silences of history has been a constant inspiration for my work. My thanks to all of you.

To those special friends whose wit and humor made it all worthwhile, my deepest thanks: Frances Timbers, Ryan Kohls, Katie Pezoulas, Monique Boissiere, Sarah Kastner, Amy Scott, Matt Sears, Jenny Denault, Kat Segesser, and Alisha Julien-Reid. Bethan Fisk's friendship has been immeasurable. Together we set goals, shared resources, and offered comments on each other's work, all the while sharing in the joys and challenges of navigating motherhood and academia early in our careers. Chris and Moira Fleming offered their ongoing love and support, kindly inquiring about my work at various stages of its production. Special thanks to Benjamin St. Louis, who has supported me through many meaningful periods of my life. Thank you for continuing to call and for your prayers, steadfast support, and practical advice. Tristana Martin Rubio, you have been my tower of strength since undergrad. Thank you for your good humor, love, and intellectual comradery. You are without equal.

This project owes a great deal to my soul family, who encouraged me through my struggles and successes. Christina, Ben, Mike, Becca, Anna, and Chamel: thank you for the most amazing babysitting co-op, which enabled me to write and not break the bank. Andrea and Liam provided countless dinners, parties, cakes, and laughs. And to our little ones—Sullivan, Viola, Sabina, Breza, Lawrence, Clara, Amelia, Lincoln, Elouise, Ry, and Jules—thanks for putting it all in perspective.

My family has proved an incredible source of strength through often fraught times. I sincerely thank the many who have held me close to their hearts and loved me from afar, including the entire Hunt, Edwards, and Kennedy families. To my siblings-in-love—Raechelle, Jenny, and Ryan—thank you for your fierce friendship. Steve and Colleen Kennedy welcomed me into their family and kept me in their prayers. Thank you to my late Nanny and Poppa Edwards and the many extended family members everywhere.

To my siblings for providing laughter and many pleasant distractions along the way: Jessica, Linz, Ali, Andy, Blue, Kyle, and Abbie. Special shout out to Linz for driving me to Toronto for library runs, accompanied by shopping trips and good food, and to Ali for reading first drafts. To Ali and P.A. for letting me room with them. All of you have inspired and infuriated me, and I love you all the more.

The love and support of my parents, Ellen and David, are as essential to my work as they are to my life. My Marmie has given me the courage to believe in myself and my place in the world of academia as a first-generation university student from a working-class family. She has been my most ardent champion and greatest benefactor. Her love and encouragement spring from every page. My dad looked forward to my book with great anticipation; he passed away weeks before it went into production. I thank him for taking an interest in my research and immersing himself in historical fiction about the period I study— even if this book doesn't exactly put me in the same league as Dan Brown, as he so proudly liked to think. I know, with certainty, how delighted he would be to finally see my book in print. "Too cool, Stef. Too cool."

To those who have lived intimately with this project, I owe a special debt of gratitude. My three children have seen this book come to fruition from its earliest beginnings. I began writing the first draft after the birth of my first child, Elouise, and defended my dissertation four days before my son Ry was born. I submitted the book manuscript a few weeks before my third child, Jules, was born. You are the source of overwhelming joy. . . . And while my debt to you can't be expressed in words, I nonetheless want to thank you for the beauty and wonder you bring into my life every day. The greatest debt is to Graeme Kennedy, whose love sustains me and who has shared fully in the making of this book. I am wholly grateful for the endless hours of discussion, research, and travel he contributed to this project and for his many sacrifices to make the research and writing of the book possible. I dedicate this book to him.

I am grateful for God's provisions of joys, challenges, and grace for growth.

Between Fitness and Death

Introduction

In the 1690s, the editors of the *Athenian Mercury*, a popular London periodical, delved into the question of whether Africans and blacks would ascend to heaven on Judgment Day, and, if they did, whether their blackness would ascend along with them. The editors asserted that Africans' ability to "rise to the last day" was really a question of "whether *white* or *black* is [a] *better colour*?" Although they conceded that notions of beauty were somewhat relative, in the end the editors maintained that the meanings behind black and white were not subjective but rather natural. They explained that "Black is the colour of Night, frightful, dark and horrid, but White of the Day and Light refreshing and lovely." The "blackness of the Negro . . . [is] an accidental Imperfection (the Cause whereof see before)," therefore, "we conclude then, that he shall not arise with that Complexion, but leave it behind him in the darkness of the Grave, exchanging it for a brighter and a better at his return agen into the World." God's "merciful" correction of imperfect bodies was not only reserved for people of African descent, however; other supposedly "deformed" and "monstrous" individuals—giants, dwarfs, or those "born with six fingers or one less than he ought," to name a few—would ascend to heaven "at the greatest *perfection* of their *natures*."[1] This view of blackness as a physical and moral ill that could be fixed only by supernatural transformation after physical death mirrored historical understandings of monstrosity and deformity: both conditions were thought to be unnatural and a sign of God's disfavor.

The *Mercury* editors speculated that, like other so-called monstrosities like lameness and blindness, blackness was caused by a pregnant woman having aberrant thoughts that then imprinted on her developing fetus, to the detriment of the infant's appearance.[2] Employing colonial references, they explained that "the Featus in the womb is sort of a vegetable, joyn'd to the Mother as a Branch to the Root, or rather as the Plants of the Indian Figg-tree to one another by a small string or ligament." This attachment, the editors professed, meant that "the Mother seems to have as much power over the Child's Body, nay, more than she has over her own." The editors held mothers responsible for the appearance of their children since, as they put it in 1691, the mother's soul, "its passions, its joys and pains . . . and accordingly, any object being strongly fix'd on the Mother's fancy, 'tis thence transferr'd to the Childs Body." According to the *Mercury*, the innately monstrous mother passed deformities and defects, like blackness, to the child, even if the deformity was the father's in the first place.[3]

Suggesting that only the divine could "cure" the so-called monstrosity of blackness was not unique to the *Athenian Mercury*. Indeed, as Africans became more important to Britain's empire, the English drew on existing notions of monstrosity and deformity to understand the place of blackness in their expanding world. Old World concepts of disability, which had been used to produce and reproduce hierarchies of power and justify the unequal treatment of individuals in English society, were then being used to articulate an antiblack racism intertwined with ableism. What made the *Mercury* unique in its discussion of the preternatural cure for the monstrosity of blackness was its suggestion that enslavement was the conduit through which blackness could be most efficiently and effectively cured, that is, die. The editors of the *Mercury* called enslavement "the greatest *kindness*" since it saved Africans from being "*killed* or *eaten*, or both, by their barbarous conquering Enemy" in their home continent. Slavery, therefore, was the "means to save their [African's] *souls* as well as *Lives*."[4] Simply put, slavery generated salvation and salvation cured blackness. While not the only argument proffered in defense of slavery at the time, it further illustrates the intersection of blackness, monstrosity, and enslaveability in the seventeenth-century English Atlantic world. The *Athenian Mercury* articles were published at the height of the metropolitan debate over the Royal African Company's monopoly on the slave trade, and such debates gave rise to a new understanding of slavery's significance to the English economy. The *Mercury*'s discussion of blackness as a collective, inheritable, and racial monstrosity, one that could only be cured through slavery, reflected a turning point in how English elites understood their relationship to Africans, slavery, and empire.

The discussion in the *Athenian Mercury* of the origins of black skin color throws into relief questions that so far have received relatively little attention. How does colonialism—specifically slavery—challenge the way we think about histories of disability, race, and labor? In what ways might slavery and the expansion of the slave trade have transformed English understandings of supposedly defective bodies and minds in the metropole and colonies? How did disability, disfigurement, and deformity among the enslaved—whether transient, permanent, natural, or inflicted—influence English understandings of race and ability in the colonial period? How did slavery-induced disability shape the embodied reality of enslavement in the British Caribbean? How did the specific disabilities wrought on the enslaved relate to a broad continuum of capacities and abilities between the extremes of helplessness and absolute power? These are among the questions this book sets out to answer.

Between Fitness and Death looks at the relationships between disability, antiblack racism, and slavery in the British Atlantic world from the early days of colonization in the sixteenth century to the abolition of the slave trade in 1807. The historical intersections between racism and ableism show that the English held antiblack attitudes from their very first contact with Africans in the sixteenth century.[5] Many sixteenth- and seventeenth-century English writers argued that Africans were neither fully human nor fully animal; they were monstrous beings who inhabited a space on the outermost limits of humanity.[6] This distinction between animal and human meant that Africans were "monsters" in the eyes of the English, which had a lasting impact on English colonists' treatment of Africans in the Caribbean and the US South.[7] The English notion of African monstrosity became explicitly gendered by the seventeenth century in the context of England's imperial and economic expansion in the Americas. Gender, sexed bodies, and monstrosity were at the center of Europeans' anxieties and struggles to understand Africans and their place within the emerging Atlantic World.

The decades leading up to the abolition of the slave trade, known as the first phase of amelioration (1788–1807), represent a crucial moment in the history of disability and race. During the last decades of the eighteenth century, with the legal end of the slave trade in sight, planters and parliament supported a plan for the amelioration, or improvement, of the system of slavery through legislative reform. Many of these laws centered on making slavery less physically destructive—notably not out of a new concern for the well-being of the enslaved but out of the self-interest of planters, whose need for a naturally reproductive labor force became essential with the end of the slave trade. I focus on the 1780s to 1807 because of the political fervor of the antislavery campaign

and because abolitionists' use of disability and the figure of the broken, supplicant bondsperson became an emblem of the inhumanity of slavery; that image
powerfully influenced public opinion in this period. This is not to say that the
campaign to abolish slavery in the nineteenth century was not compelling,
but rather that the arguments for abolition had fallen on the side of concern
for the security of the islands due to the slave rebellions that swept the British
Caribbean following the Haitian Revolution. Thus, the abolitionist campaign
to end slavery became less about humanitarianism and more about the political imperative to end slavery for the sake of preserving the empire.

My analysis of disability in the context of Atlantic slavery is threefold. First,
I explore representations of disability as they connect with enslavement and
the development of an English antiblack racism from the sixteenth to the eighteenth centuries. This book explores the notion of disability in the writings of
English travelers, slaveowners, lawmakers, and abolitionists as a trope used to
denigrate Africans and their descendants to the status of subhuman beings.
Second, I move between the realms of representation and reality in order to
examine the embodied, physical, emotional, and psychological impairments
produced by the institution of slavery and endured by the enslaved. British Caribbean slavery produced a factory of violence in sugar production. Life spans
for most of the enslaved in the Caribbean were brief, and the physical distance
of imperial control allowed for particular types of atrocities on enslaved bodies. Third, I examine slave law as an institutionally driven system of enforced
disablement. *Between Fitness and Death* explores not only disability rhetoric
but how disability functioned within the law to disable the enslaved, to limit
their mobility, freedom, and political autonomy. By reading travel writers and
commentators works, legal codes, runaway advertisements, and antislavery
and proslavery writings through the lens of disability as well as through the
lens of race and gender, *Between Fitness and Death* suggests that we look at the
archive of slavery anew.[8]

• • •

Between Fitness and Death begins by discussing the way race and disability
were entwined in the sixteenth and seventeenth centuries. Long before the English became involved in the slave trade, they were exposed to ideas of African
monstrosity from ancient texts and fifteenth- and sixteenth-century Spanish
and Portuguese travel narratives. By the seventeenth century, ideas of an African form of monstrosity served as a timely justification for the enslavement of
Africans in England's expanding empire and for the wealth this generated. Thus,
African monstrosity became part of the logic of English capitalism. The political

activities of certain mid-seventeenth-century English individuals greatly shaped the creation of a metropole, a colonial *England*. In other words, the colonizers were no less colonial than the colonized. That metropole emerged in the context of the transatlantic slave trade, the racialized boundaries of which came to define the difference between freedom and enslaveability, making clear who was on deck and who was in the hold. The making of race was a process, one that involved ableism.

By integrating a disability analysis into historical understandings of the development of English antiblack racism and slavery, my approach goes beyond earlier studies by demonstrating that disability was a factor that shaped both the lives of the enslaved and the meanings of enslavement.[9] British and African diaspora scholarship has noted only in passing the intersections between slavery and disability, discussing European views of Africans in isolation from wider discussions of "monstrous," "deformed," and disabled bodies.[10] The term *disability* was not widely used until the mid-nineteenth century, but historians have applied the concept to ancient, medieval, and early modern studies in order to reveal the discourses that revolved around physical signs of defect, deformity, and monstrosity. In both the medieval and early modern periods, the categories of deformity and monstrosity overlapped in several ways; neither was fixed. But the concept of monstrosity contained elements that anticipated later forms of racist thinking. In the specific historical context of the establishment of England's early Caribbean colonies—St. Christopher, Barbados, Jamaica, Nevis, Antigua, Montserrat—the introduction of sugar to the European economy, and the expansion of the transatlantic slave trade, English elites increasingly spoke about black skin color as a form of monstrosity. Thus, the development of modern understandings of raced and disabled bodies were inextricably bound together during this period of England's imperial expansion.

The English perception of African women's bodies as deformed and monstrous and yet somehow fit for hard labor and enslavement shows how discursive violence was inextricably intertwined with the material violence of slavery. Contemporary understandings of racial formation and disability are incomplete without an understanding of the ideologies that underpinned slavery and in turn how the conditions of enslavement produced disabled bodies and racialized ideas about disability. In the 1660s the legal principle of maternal inheritance—that the mother's status determined the child's status irrespective of the father's status—was applied throughout the Anglo-Caribbean. The concept of maternal inheritance positioned Africans and their descendants, and in particular African women, in the liminal space between human and animal and made their supposedly monstrous or disabled bodies available to suit new purposes. However, one of the paradoxes of the institution of slavery was that without the *abilities* of the enslaved, the entire sugar industry would fail. The ways in which whites conceptualized the terms of slavery projected a complete loss of liberty that was brought about by an institutionally driven process of enforced disabling.

Between Fitness and Death offers a historiographical intervention by arguing that slavery disabled (discursively and materially) the human, rather than created a dehumanized object. It is widely assumed that systems of mass slaughter and exploitation, like slavery, were also systems of dehumanization.[11] I argue, by contrast, that in order to justify the systematic exploitation, persecution, and murder of an entire group of people (blacks, in this instance), the perpetrators of systematized racist violence constructed a danger based on anthropological uncertainty. According to such an ideology, the monster was dangerous because of their potential to reproduce their own "race" among themselves and with other "normal" humans, turning all of humanity into a race of monsters. Enslavement, violence, and forced labor were therefore both a means of controlling and punishing the monster and a method of exploiting the monster's only useful human quality—its capacity for hard labor.

The slavery system worked only because the enslavers recognized Africans' humanity—people capable of both laboring and reproducing. The English distinguished Africans as an especially deformed and disabled group of humans who could not be useful without European intervention; slavery thus became necessary to put to use an otherwise useless group of humans. By selecting disability as its frame, this book therefore presents an important conceptual shift that centers the human, while showing how the conditions of slavery undermined Africans' abilities. By showing how the discourses of disability justified slavery, the disabling conditions produced by slavery further allowed Europeans to bolster their own argument that the African was suited for nothing but brute labor. These framings also set the stage for the reform movements of late eighteenth-century abolitionists who viewed slavery as problematic but were not quite willing to embrace black equality. Depicting enslaved people as disabled humans, rather than as dehumanized objects, allowed reformers to elicit sympathy for fellow human beings without committing to deeming them worthy of being British subjects.

This book illustrates that disability categories related to labor predated the Industrial Revolution and sheds new light on the timeline of modern ideas about working bodies and impairment.[12] When Caribbean sugar production developed in the seventeenth century as an industrial enterprise, the enslaved body was defined by its relationship to an economy driven by production and profit. As the Trinidadian scholar C. L. R. James argued, "from the very start [the enslaved] lived a life that was in its essence a modern life."[13] The division of labor by skill, age, gender, and physical condition that characterized Caribbean plantations, together with the emphasis on discipline, organization, and timekeeping, made the production of sugar a precociously industrial and modern undertaking. Plantation slavery was a necessary precondition for both industrialization and the emergence of modern concepts and displays of disability.

Comparing and contrasting the figure of the free, wage-earning metropolitan worker in England and the enslaved, non-wage-earning Caribbean laborer shows that colonialism, race, and specifically slavery are key to understanding the intersections between the commodification of the laboring body and disability. Factory workers in the metropole required wages to purchase products that fostered their continued participation in the capitalist economy. These products—the sugar that extended working hours, the cotton for their work clothes, the coffee and tobacco for leisure time—were produced by enslaved laborers.[14] The logic of Atlantic capitalism had created a wage economy in metropolitan England; applied to the Caribbean, the same logic determined that it was more economically efficient to work enslaved laborers to death than to treat them well and so prolong their survival.

Having been worked mercilessly, the enslaved suffered and endured disfigurements, disabilities, and deformities that were then described in detail in runaway advertisements placed by slaveowners and overseers whose enslaved property had gone missing. The enslaved body was most often described as injured, branded, whipped, and otherwise marked by slavery's disabling violence, demonstrating the prevalence of disability among the enslaved; the specificity of these descriptions were intended to aid in the identification and apprehension of the fugitive bondspeople.[15] Runaway advertisements provide only part of the story, for the enslaved also suffered abuses not always outwardly visible—high infertility rates among female captives and psychological and emotional disabilities are just a few examples of the inconspicuous afflictions of enslavement. To the extent that they were an institutionally driven method of reactive and precautionary control, the advertisements disabled bondspeople by limiting their movement and perpetuating the longstanding European notion that Africans and their descendants were deformed and disfigured beings whose corporeality reflected their supposed inner degeneracy.[16] Descriptions of fugitive bondspeople in such advertisements reveal the various ways in which slavery-induced disability systematically disfigured, dismembered, and impaired black bodies. Slavery is therefore key to understanding not only the corporeality of disability but the conceptual and interpretive meanings ascribed to it in the sugar-producing colonies of the British Caribbean.

Changes in the runaway advertisements as time went on suggest that slave-owners were conscious of how abolitionists utilized the descriptions of disabled and injured enslaved bodies in runaway advertisements in their attack of the institution of slavery. In the last decades before the abolition of the slave trade, runaway advertisements in Barbados and Jamaica show a remarkable decrease in mentions of branding and marks of the whip, both of which were corner-stones of the abolitionist attack on slavery. Despite representing enslaved people in debilitated physical states, runaway advertisements suggested that fugitive bondspeople were a threat to white society. The advertisements discursively disabled the enslaved by limiting their autonomy and freedom of movement.

Once the abolitionist movement gained strength in the late eighteenth century, the British continued to draw on disability to support both antislavery and proslavery arguments. Supporters of slavery decried the idea that Africans were monsters and instead argued that Africans were more akin to animals than humans. Anti-abolitionists drew on developing pseudoscientific arguments to suggest that Africans and their descendants were a species other than human. Abolitionists, in contrast, emphasized the figure of the broken, beaten, and disabled bondsperson. The image of the disabled bondsperson appealed to both British Christian sympathies and a growing charitable culture toward the disabled in metropolitan Britain. It also served to curtail the other competing image of black slavery—the armed, able-bodied, threatening, and specifically male rebel of the Haitian Revolution. The maimed bondsperson represented a way in which abolitionists could frame abolition in nonthreatening terms. In representing the enslaved as debilitated victims of slavery in need of white support, abolitionists blunted the emancipatory potential of the enslaved and extended humanitarian ideals toward the enslaved while rejecting the very notion of human rights. The disabled black body, thus, haunted both antislavery and proslavery writings and was a significant theme in debates over the end of the slave trade.

The book calls attention to an underexplored aspect of British abolition, namely the distinction between human rights and humanitarianism that shaped English conceptualizations of black citizenship in the world of the Haitian Revolution. Proslavery writers emphasized the gendered image of the rebel—an able-bodied, armed, and threatening black male—whereas abolitionists envisioned a black, suffering but supplicant, bondsperson. The place of supposedly "disabled" and "able" bodies as the basis for competing modern ideas about citizenship was rooted in a sharp distinction between two models of emancipation: imperial humanitarianism and subjecthood on the one hand, and revolutionary human rights and citizenship on the other. *Between Fitness and Death* contends that it is historically significant that efforts to relieve the suffering of disabled and enslaved people were not framed in terms of human rights but humanitarianism. Abolitionists often linked the social, economic, and political oppression of the disabled to that of the enslaved; in so doing, they yoked humanitarianism to Britishness but remained silent on, and implicitly rejected, the idea of *human rights*. Humanitarian *ideas* of citizenship were what abolitionists offered to the enslaved, predicated on the assumption that theirs was a "crippled" form of citizenship.

. . .

Slavery created a world with historically, culturally, and ideologically distinct and often competing understandings of disability and ability. In Atlantic slavery, impairment was produced by the violence of colonization—the dispossession of land, the physical enslavement, and the control of resources perpetrated by European colonial powers. In what follows, I draw on Neloufer de Mel's definition of "disablement" as "the deliberate, wilful maiming of abled and physically strong" individuals in war zones. By doing so I aim to recognize the violence inherent in slave societies.[17] This study focuses on how slavery produced disability and how it ascribed a specific meaning and context to both acquired and congenital disabilities, which were determined by the reality of enslavement. Disability, then, was, a defining feature of this violence and the antiblack racism that undergirded it.

The idea that blackness has an essential, historically rooted relationship to disability is central to the story told on these pages. In the world of Atlantic slavery, black bodies were systematically disfigured, dismembered, and impaired, and this production of disability was in large part predicated on the European and capitalist notion that black bodies were made to be destroyed. Today, many writings about disability are politically invested in demonstrating that impairment is not a personal tragedy to be prevented or cured but a universal condition to which we are all susceptible.[18] While this is both true and meaningful, especially in the context of the contemporary global North, it does not help us understand the historical relationship between disability and colonialism. Thinking historically about disability among a population of exiled and colonized people ruled by a European plantocracy, a population whose impairments were "produced" by the violence of colonization, requires a set of methodologies different from those formulated in the northern metropole. Disability in the colonial Caribbean must maintain that the production of impairment through slavery was tragic and involved incredible levels of violence—we must not ignore this fact. "Tragedy" and disability are, therefore, historically produced and must be understood in specific historical contexts. The violent production of disability is at the heart of the histories of blackness in the Atlantic World.

Ability itself has a raced history. According to early modern Europeans, Africans and their descendants were intellectually and physically "deficient" and, therefore, ideally suited for physically taxing and ultimately destructive labor. Africans' physical and intellectual deficiencies, in other words, *enabled* them to perform such labor. In the context of Atlantic slavery, "ability" was not measured solely in terms of productivity: the concept as it was applied to enslaved Africans differed drastically from that of free Europeans. For instance, while enslaved laborers were defined by their physical health, well-being, and age, their acceptance of or compliance with enslavement was equally important. The notion of an "obedient" labor force as a key defining feature of "ability" existed beyond the period of Atlantic slavery to greatly influence the mid-nineteenth-century industrialization of Europe and North America. Plantation accounts further illustrate that slavery shaped meanings of ability. Plantation owners and managers categorized incorrigible runaways (individuals who frequently ran away from the plantation) among the "useless"—those whose physical impairments or diseases made them unfit for plantation production. Individuals labeled as incorrigible could have very well been physically, intellectually, and psychologically fit, but white authorities perceived their desire for freedom as a limitation on their status as productive laborers. The very notion of ability, thus, has a very different historical meaning for black people—one that was decidedly shaped by the experience of slavery. With these points in mind, *Between Fitness and Death* draws on the tradition that understands disability as a social relationship rather than a specific set of characteristics shared by individuals with impairments. Such a perspective allows a variety of bodies and minds to be included in the analytic dynamics of social, political, and legal exclusion, and it accounts for a definition of disability that is inextricably linked to the meaning of blackness, both its ideological meaning and the ways in which it manifested materially as a "deficient" body.

The majority of voices in the colonial archives belong to free white men. Finding the voice of the disabled in the early modern period is difficult under the best circumstances, and even more so when that disabled individual was enslaved in the Caribbean. For this reason, the majority of my sources were written by English or Creole whites. The pre-nineteenth-century Caribbean does not offer the kinds of sources available to historians of the United States (WPA interviews, for example). Whenever possible, I draw on works written by former captives during the abolitionist period, all the while recognizing that even these sources bear the imprint of white abolitionists. I use sources that are not from Barbados or Jamaica, such as Mary Prince's narrative, when such sources seem to offer a form of expression that is less mediated than those of the enslaved and disabled themselves. Such sources are rare and precious and should be incorporated as often as possible. This book retrieves a history of disability in the colonial Caribbean from the archives and analyzes how concepts of monstrosity, race, disability, and enslaveability intersected in the development of modern understandings of blackness and disability in the Anglo-Afro Atlantic world.

While *Between Fitness and Death* takes on the complicated task of understanding the damaging material effects of disablement, it also explores the possibility that disability represented a refusal of the dominant normative order of the British Atlantic world. In certain contexts, for instance, disability came to be revalued among bondspeople as a form of resistance to the institution of slavery. The disabled body of the enslaved can potentially be seen as a site of resistance to the commodification of human beings and as a form of protest against one's status as a commercial object. The study of disability in the context of Atlantic slavery therefore gives us the chance to read disability among the enslaved in multiple ways—not only as a sign of victimization and "lack," but also as a sign of power and possibility. Although *Between Fitness and Death* focuses on the violent conditions of enslavement and presents an intellectual history of racism and ableism, it leaves space for a social history of disability among the enslaved.

Indeed, the discursive and material go hand in hand. The experiences of the enslaved depended both on how their bodies responded to the material conditions of slavery and the ideas enslavers imposed on their bodies. This book examines disability in slave societies as a form of both discursive violence and real-world violence. Discursive and material disability suspended enslaved Africans and their descendants in multiple liminal spaces within the world of Atlantic slavery: in the cultural and legal perception of blacks as monstrous, the enslaved were suspended between the human and the animal; as forced laborers on the open market, the enslaved were suspended between fitness and death; and as runaways and revolutionaries, the enslaved were suspended between the figure of the self-emancipatory rebel and the figure of the broken, disabled, bondsperson. At every level, Atlantic slavery inserted black bodies into the emerging racialized world of transnational and imperial relationships as disabled bodies—supposedly unfit for anything other than the most brutal forms of labor.

When we place the unfree laborer at the center of our discussion of disability in the Atlantic World, we come to understand two things: first, that the histories of disability and slavery overlap in significant ways; and second, that Caribbean bondspeople form an integral part of wider disability history. As the first industrial workers, Caribbean bondspeople labored in a factorylike setting where one's physical health was important but was also at risk of serious decline due to long hours and dangerous work conditions. But as forced laborers, the experience of disability among the enslaved differed significantly from their free, white counterparts. Impairment did not exempt enslaved individuals from work. Because their bodies were the property of slaveowners, they were put to use under the constant threat of violence until they were of no value to the estate. Disabled bondspeople who were rejected by colonists—either on the coasts of Africa, the auction blocks of the Caribbean, or the sugar plantations—were at greater risk of violence. Scholars of slavery have written a great deal about the disposability of enslaved bodies; however, through violent methods slavery exploited but did not dispose of enslaved bodies until such bodies were utterly useless to plantation production.[19] Thus, within the economy of slavery was a calculated effort not to dispose of bondspeople but to keep them alive but "in a state of injury," suspended between fitness and death.[20]

CHAPTER 1

Imagining Africa, Inheriting Monstrosity

Gender, Blackness, and Capitalism in the Early Atlantic World

English racism was born of greed.

—Peter Fryer, *Staying Power: The History of Black People in Britain*

This is some monster of the isle, with four legs, who hath got, as I take it, an ague. Where the devil should he learn our language? I will give him some relief, if it be but for that. If I can recover him, and keep him tame, and get to Naples with him, he's a present for any emperor that ever trod on neat's leather.

—William Shakespeare, *The Tempest*

The place of monstrosity in the emergence of slavery and antiblack racism is key to understanding the historically entwined construction of racism and ableism in the Atlantic World. Even before the rise of the Atlantic slave trade, European writing often equated Africans and their descendants with animality and monstrosity. In the early modern period, the most popular theories on the origin of blackness all posited an original whiteness for all humans from which blackness was a collective aberration.[1] While these ideas did not by themselves lead to African enslavement, the incipient idea of a particularly African form of monstrosity served in the seventeenth century to naturalize and defuse moral doubts about the enslavement and dispossession of Africans in the English Atlantic world. European racism was not enough, in and of itself, to justify African enslavement. The seventeenth-century transformation of these ideas from vague notions of difference into an ideology of systematized, racist, and violent subjugation required a new institutional, economic, and political set of relationships and interests: black monstrosity.[2]

This chapter traces the intellectual, legal, and anthropological processes by which the English transformed the concept of blackness into a collective, inheritable, and racial monstrosity, a category of being that made Africans, and in particular African women, supposedly fit for servitude. In the early modern European imagination, deformity and monstrosity raised concerns about what it meant to be human.[3] The English notion that Africans were monstrous beings suspended Africans in the liminal space between the human and the animal, enabling colonists to exploit Africans' humanity by enforcing forms of disablement onto the enslaved. Early modern conceptions of monstrosity, deformity, and the corporeal as physical signs of an inner goodness or sin greatly influenced colonial understandings of Africa and the New World. Africans thus entered the English imagination as deformed and monstrous beings in need of containment and control at a cultural moment coinciding with colonization and expansion of the slave trade.

No clear boundary between deformity and monstrosity was recognized in the early modern period: monstrosity was simply an element of deformity. Deformity referred to both perceived ugliness and those physical anomalies that were deemed "unnatural," as well as functional impairments like a crooked spine, clubfoot, or amputation.[4] Monstrosity did not apply to one particular physical abnormality; rather, English people used it to describe a variety of phenomena, all of which were strange or striking enough to evoke an offense against God.[5] It was widely believed in early modern Europe that the birth of a deformed child might be interpreted as a sign that something calamitous was likely to happen. The monster's ambiguous status in medieval and early modern Europe provoked widespread and long-lasting fear among Europeans because they transgressed against the natural order.[6] Sixteenth-century English writer Thomas Raynalde claimed that "imperfection is when any particular creature doth lack any property, instrument, or quality which commonly by nature is in all other, or the more part of that kind, comparing it to other of the same kind and not of another kind."[7] "All that is imperfect is ugly" argued Martin Weinrich in 1596, "and monsters are full of imperfections." Regardless of the various meanings ascribed to them, both deformity and monstrosity reflected the connection—widely assumed at the time—between bodily deformation and moral depravity.[8]

By the mid-sixteenth century, the determining factor in monster identification was no longer physical deformity alone, but rather deviant inner characteristics and behaviors.[9] In post-Reformation England, the popular belief that monsters were judgments of God was still prevalent, however, new medical texts, written by Englishmen, began to blame monstrosity on women's imaginations and wombs.[10] Monstrosity now signified the inner deviance and sin of women and the uterus as a threatening and dangerous force.[11] Monsters became not just a "confusion of categories," but the very embodiment of moral ambiguity and paradox.[12]

Sixteenth-century English accounts of African monstrosity facilitated the transition toward the more concrete violence of the supposedly known African of later seventeenth-century accounts. Beginning in the seventeenth century, English travelers who went to Africa seeking economic gain placed a new emphasis on ethnographic detail, claiming to portray bodies, land, flora, and fauna in the Caribbean and Africa in geographically and anthropologically accurate ways. As England's role in African trade grew, so too did its presence in the Americas. While at the outset early colonies like Virginia (1607), Saint Christopher (1625; now Saint Kitts), and Barbados (1627) received very little material support from James I or Charles I, the application of English colonial power in the West Indies—including the 1655 colonization of Jamaica—increased dramatically over the course of the seventeenth century. The writings of elite metropolitan political figures of English colonization bolstered the institution of slavery and made blackness a hereditary and legally codified form of disablement.[13]

By the end of the seventeenth century, English thinkers understood the link between blackness and monstrosity in explicitly gendered terms. They explained the origin of black skin using the medieval and early modern concept of maternal imagination. This held that a pregnant woman's thoughts and imaginations could imprint on her fetus and determine the infant's physical appearance.[14] English conceptualizations of black skin color as a monstrosity inherited from mothers was inextricably intertwined with the legal notion of maternal inheritance. In the English Caribbean colonies as well as regions such as Virginia, the freedom or servitude of a child of mixed ancestry was conditional on the mother's status.[15] The maternal inheritance principle was never documented in any of the Anglo-Caribbean's slave codes yet it was universally adopted in the English Atlantic world. The ideological claims of maternal imagination and maternal inheritance overlap, suggesting an intergenerational link between monstrosity and enslaveability. The English notion that blackness was a heritable and racial form of monstrosity remained a feature of seventeenth-century English conceptualizations of Africans and their descendants, as a timely and advantageous justification for Africans' subjection in the transatlantic economy.

Marveling at Monsters

By the time English voyagers landed on African shores, in the 1550s, their imaginations were already full of monstrous African beings belonging more to the realm of the fantastic than the human. Sixteenth-century Spanish and Portuguese travel writings and English translations of ancient texts circulated among the English elite and influenced English perceptions of Africans and their descendants. These texts told fanciful tales of races whose body parts were organized differently than those of "normal" human beings: some lacked necessary organs, whereas others were half-man, half-animal. Sixteenth-century English writers, including Thomas Hackett, Richard Eden, and Sir Walter Raleigh told such tales and drew on concepts of monstrosity to determine what made them different from and supposedly better than Africans.

In the early modern period, the line between human and animal, though fluid, was also heavily policed. It was for precisely this reason that monstrous births, viewed above all as evidence of the transgression of the animal-human boundary, were so threatening.[16] Monstrous births caused such fear and horror among the English because they threatened the divide between human and animal.[17] Early modern English folk believed, for instance, that bestiality resulted in "a monster, partly having the members of the body according to the man, and partly according to the beast."[18] English geographer and staunch supporter of Elizabethan overseas expansion Richard Hakluyt published in 1589 a collection of voyages written by numerous travelers to Africa and the Americas titled *The Principal Navigations, Voyages and Discoveries of the English Nation*. *Principal Navigations* reproduced the marvelous depictions of Africans found in ancient texts but on a much larger scale. Drawing on Pliny, he described the Blemines as being "without heads . . . having their eyes and mouth in their breast," whereas, other parts of the continent were said to have "Satyrs . . . which have nothing of men but onely shape."[19] A visible physical deformity, or "mark" of a different species, was therefore a determining factor in the identification of monstrosity. Humans "possessing features or appendages which were either of unknown origin, were rightfully the marks of another species, or were simply too large" also fit this criterion.[20] The belief that mixed conceptions resulted in monstrous offspring gave proof to the notion that humankind was not so distinct a species that it could not procreate with animal-kind. The uncertain distinction between man and beast meant that the boundary between the two needed to be carefully protected.[21]

And yet Europeans distinguished between the births of monstrous individuals, which were often seen as accidental, and the existence of monstrous races. Monstrous races were often understood as the descendants of the divinely cursed, most notably Canaan, whose mark of punishment was interpreted as a deformity inherited by his descendants.[22] Medieval and early modern European writers understood racial deformity or monstrous races as evidence of the animality of those peoples who inhabited the outermost edges of the known world.[23] Englishman John Pory's 1600 translation of Joannes Leo Africanus's famous work on Africa linked the supposed animality of Africans to intellectual deficiency: "The Negroes likewise lead a beastly kind of life, being utterly destitute of the use of reason, of dexterity of wit, and of all arts. Yea they so behave themselves, as if they had continually lived in a forest among wild beasts."[24] To early modern English people, clothing was a distinctly human attribute and, therefore, cultures that wore little to no clothing were considered bestial.[25] Men with long hair were also considered bestial, for "beasts are more hairy than man, and savage men more than civil."[26]

For Europeans, nakedness symbolized savagery; travelers often commented on the nakedness of various African societies and linked their lack of dress to the most egregious forms of heathenism and immorality.[27] Africans, wrote one English writer, "are Man-eaters . . . the children make no scruple of devouring their parents, or the parents their children. They all go naked from the waste up, and every man has as many wives as he pleases, never taking care for the children, which sometimes the mothers are inhuman enough to devour."[28] Europeans' belief in African monstrosity relegated Africans to the outer limits of humanity and testified to their supposed moral deficiency. Early European knowledge production about Africa created boundaries that made English expansion a moral and profitable undertaking.[29]

Although Europeans did include positive descriptions of indigenous and African people in their writings, the majority were negative.[30] Columbus's early accounts of the indigenous people of the Caribbean juxtaposed the supposed monstrosity and savagery of the Caribs with the beauty and innocence of the Tainos.[31] And Bartolomé de las Casas famously condemned the Spanish treatment of the indigenous people of the Greater Antilles, who he claimed were not an enslaveable people.[32] On occasion, Renaissance painters depicted enslaved Africans in Europe wearing gold and expensive jewelry, but such images reflected the status of the slaveowner, not the individual African. As Kate Lowe points out, Europeans, especially Italians, sometimes gave Africans of high-ranking or noble status "greatly superior treatment to non-royals, even if not always treatment equal to European royalty, and not always the same treatment as earlier princely ambassadors."[33] But these early depictions of indigenous and black bodies were rare and were not to last in European discourses.

For the most part, European portrayals of Africans in the sixteenth century were full of contradiction.[34] Richard Eden's 1553 English translation of Sebastian Münster's *A Treatise of the Newe India* described indigenous women as both attractive and repulsive: "Theyr bodies are very smothe and clene by reason of theyr often washinge," he wrote, but "they are in other things filthy and without shame." Eden looked to the supposed sexual deviance of indigenous women to separate them from Europeans: "Thei use no lawful coniunccion of marriage, and byt every one hath as many women as him liketh, and leaveth them again at his pleasure." And yet, according to Eden, indigenous women's monstrous and savage sexual practices are put to good use for "the women are very fruiteful . . . they travayle in maner without payne, so that the nexte day they are cheerfull and able to walke. Neyther have they theyr bellies wrimpleled or loose, and hanging pappes, by reason of bearinge many chyldren."[35] Eden's portrayal of indigenous women is, on the one hand, an admittance of indigenous beauty and strength and, on the other hand, an insinuation of how such unnatural bodies can be put to new purposes. African and indigenous men were not spared from European contradictions. Pieter de Marees, whose writings about Ghana were translated into English in 1625, described African men as being of "very good proportion, with fair members, strong legs, and well-shaped bodies" but that they "are very lecherous, and much addicted to uncleanness . . . are great drunkards . . . [and] in their feeding, they are very greedy."[36] Marees's passage portrays African men's bodies as strong and well made, but it also suggests that such abilities were wasted on their inner deviance and savagery.

As a monstrous race, Africans differed from individual monsters—a distinction that was crucial to the consolidation of antiblack thought and the justification of African enslavement. Pliny the Elder's *The Historie of the World* (ca. 77 CE), which was translated from Latin into English by Thomas Hackett in 1566 and remained influential well into the seventeenth century, described hybrid races and monsters—men and women with missing body parts and beast-like characteristics. Ethiopians, for example, had no noses or nostrils and they spoke in sign with no upper lips or tongues "but a little hole to take their breath at." In the west were "a people called Arimaspi, that hath but one eye in their foreheads."[37] Pliny's depictions of Africans were repeated in several other works, including the most widely read travel narrative of the medieval and early modern world, *The Voyages and travailes of Sir John Mandevile knight* (ca. 1366), which was translated into English in 1496. The text was written in spoken languages and regional dialects and was, therefore, accessible to those hearing it read aloud, which meant that it both influenced and reflected common values and assumptions among many Europeans.[38] Drawing on Pliny's texts, Mandeville described the Blemmye and the Anthropophagi as missing essential body parts. "And in one of the Iles," he wrote, "are men that have but one eye, and that is in the middest of their front. . . . And in another Ile dwell men that have no heads, and their eyes are in their shoulder, and their mouth is on their breast." The author repeated the visual spectacle of monstrous races with missing or misplaced facial features and claimed that some "have no head no eyes, & their mouth is in their shoulders." Eyes, mouths, and noses were frequently described as being located in strange parts of the body. "In another Ile" he wrote "are men that have flat faces without nose, and without eyes, but they have two small round holes in stead of eyes, and they have a flat mouth without lips. And in that Ile are men also that have their faces all flat without eyes, without mouth, and without nose, but they have their eyes & their mouth behind on their shoulders."[39]

Although Mandeville's descriptions inspired a plethora of fantastic adventure tales, even more reputable explorers like Christopher Columbus and Martin Frobisher relied on them for the "practical geographic information" they supposedly contained.[40] Mandeville's work influenced these explorers' sense of both Africa and the indigenous Caribbean. For example, prior to having encountered the Caribs of the Lesser Antilles, Columbus drew heavily from Mandeville's portrayal of the Anthropophagi to create a dichotomy between the gentle Tainos and the monstrous Caribs, "men with one eye, and others with dogs' noses" who he described as "strong, swift, [and] healthy." In a clear echo of Mandeville, Sir Walter Raleigh spoke, during his travels to Guiana, of "a nation of people whose heads appear not above their shoulders . . . called Ewaipanoma; they are reported to have their eyes in their shoulders, and their mouths in the middle of their breasts, and that a long train of hair growth between their shoulders."[41] The popularity of Mandeville's account demonstrates how swiftly proto-ethnography about Africans could be transformed into an ostensibly fact-based discourse.[42]

Race prejudice against Africans was especially prominent in England. Unlike other European countries—particularly the southern states of Portugal, Spain, and Italy—England did not enjoy a reciprocal trade relationship with northern Africa during the fifteenth and sixteenth centuries.[43] Long before they came into sustained contact with people who had black skin, the English associated blackness with evil, death, baseness, and danger, while they associated whiteness with purity, virginity, beauty, and good magic.[44] This specific national context abetted an English understanding of Africa and Africans as geographical and corporeal transgressions. These views also served as a foil for the development of an English national identity, one that included the ability to dominate the threat posed by Africa's so-called monstrous races.

Spanish, French, Portuguese, and Dutch portrayals of Caribbean indigenous monstrosity also received considerable attention in England.[45] Compared to their European counterparts, the English had very limited contact with other indigenous peoples of the Caribbean beyond those of Saint Christopher. The macabre, to say nothing of impressionistic, secondhand image of the Caribs as flesh-eating monsters therefore prevailed in the minds of some English readers. This fact reinforces Stephen Greenblatt's argument that the "marvelous" was a meaningful device through which medieval and Renaissance people "apprehended and thence possessed or discarded, the unfamiliar, the alien, the terrible, the desirable, and the hateful."[46]

A growing number of Spanish and Portuguese accounts of the New World and Africa, translated into English during the latter half of the sixteenth century, helped to foster a new kind of cosmopolitan and incipiently imperial consciousness in England. Peter Martyr's *The decades of the newe world of West India* (translated into English by Richard Eden in 1555) collected the writings of European travelers to the New World, including Columbus, Balboa, Cortés, and Magellan. Eden's translation also criticized the English for failing to emulate Spain's colonization of the Americas.[47] Such censure reflected an increased desire among some English elites to become involved in colonization in the Americas as well as the trade in African slaves. The translation of Bartolomé de Las Casas's *The Spanish colonie, or Briefe chronicle of the acts and gestes of the Spaniards in the West Indies, called the new world* (1583) had a similar impact, in that Las Casas's accusations of Spanish cruelty toward the indigenous people of Hispaniola helped create "the Black Legend"—a view of Spanish colonialism as an unrivaled evil, based on translations of Las Casas's descriptions of horrific acts of violence against the Tainos. Protestants, in particular, used such propaganda to argue in favor of their own, supposedly more humanitarian form of colonialism.[48] Individual Englishmen in the employ of the Spanish and Portuguese were involved in these early colonial efforts. Their experience, together with the translation of European travel accounts, increased elite Englishmen's interest and confidence in their own potential to explore and trade in Africa and the Americas.

After the 1550s there was a small but significant increase in English exploration and trade with Africa. This pursuit of wealth drove John Lok, son of a prominent London merchant and alderman, to bring five Africans to England from what is now Ghana. These individuals, whom Lok described as "people of beastly living," were to be instructed in English so they could return to Africa as interpreters for English traders interested in gold, ivory, and spices.[49] The first Englishman to trade in African slaves was John Hawkyns. On his first voyage (1562–63), Hawkyns acquired at least three hundred Africans and sold them to the Spaniards on Hispaniola for £10,000 worth of hides, pearls, sugar, and ginger. Queen Elizabeth I supported his second voyage (1564–65), lending him a 600-ton vessel and three hundred men to help in his trading pursuits. From the 1570s onward, Hawkyns brought Africans to England as servants, prostitutes, and court entertainers. Though she supported this venture, in 1601 Elizabeth renewed the 1596 Caspar van Senden license to expel "negroes and blackamoors" from the English realm; she did so on the spurious grounds that the growing population of enslaved Africans in England was contributing to the country's food shortage.[50] England's black population nonetheless remained, and in fact increased, starting in the 1650s with the expansion of the slave trade and the growing demand for sugar, which brought black people to England as household servants for wealthy English families.[51] These larger economic and political changes that brought Africans and their descendants to various places within the British Empire led to an increase in discourses about blacks and their place in the emerging racialized world.

A small number of works published in the latter half of the sixteenth century foreshadowed an interest in ethnographically detailed depictions of Africans that would come to be the norm a century later. Johannes ab Indagine's text, translated from Latin to English by John Daye in 1558, offered physiognomic justifications for surmising individual character from outward appearance. According to Indagine, "the nose tending or stretching to the mouth, declareth honesty, strength, and apte to learning," whereas "a nose like an ape, betoketch a libidinouse and riotous person." The sign of "very ill men" was "crooked & hollow inward" legs, and "soft and swelling legges" signaled "evil mannered men." Black skin, he argued "doth also show the evil affections of the mind, as envy, anger, rancor, machinations & privy hatreds."[52] Indagine's widely influential work went through seven editions in England before the end of the seventeenth century; it influenced Edward Topsell's comparison of men and primates, for example, thus preparing the ground for the study of comparative anatomy and racial craniometry in the nineteenth century.[53]

But serious, proto-scientific works on African corporeality were rare in the sixteenth century. Fanciful, mythologically derived descriptions still dominated European tales of African monstrosity and animality in Africa and the New World. Along with Sir Walter Raleigh, sixteenth-century writers like Thomas Hacket (1566) and George Abbot (1599) continued to reproduce fanciful tales of indigenous and African monstrosity, animality, and deformity. George Abbot claimed that in the "South part of *Africke* . . . [are] supposed to be men of strange shapes, as some with Dog heads, some without heads, and some with one foot alone, which was very huge."[54] Although European knowledge of Africans was increasing during this period, European writers continued to utilize ethnocentric generalizations about Africans and myths of monstrous races.

Other English writers contributed to the development of this supposedly more evidence-based discourse about Africans and human variety, with texts focusing on the link between geography, gender, and the origin of black skin color. The presence of Africans in late sixteenth-century England had called into question dominant theories that tied skin color to climate, and the birth of dark-complexioned children born to white fathers unsettled gendered discourses of inheritance that viewed the female body as merely a passive recipient in the process of generation. And yet, in spite of these uncertainties, English writers were nonetheless reluctant to accept that mothers might have a role in their children's skin color. George Best's *A True Discourse of the late voyages of discoverie, for the finding of a passage to Cathaya by the Northweast* . . . (1578) argued that blackness "proceedeth of some naturall infection of the first inhabitants of that Countrey, and so all the whole progenie of them descended, are still polluted with some blot of infection, by a lineall discent they have hitherto continued thus blacke."[55] In his explanation of the continuation of black skin color, Best linked blackness to moral depravity, sin, and pollution. Best then told of an Ethiopian "as blacke as cole" who with "a faire English woman" had a son who was "in all respects as blacke as the father was, although England were his native countrey, and an English woman his mother."[56] He then related the biblical story of Noah's disobedient son, Ham. After Ham sees his father naked, Noah curses Ham's own son, Canaan, as "a servant of servants."[57] In the eighth-century Tanhuma version of the story, Ham's body is left black and deformed: his "lips became crooked and . . . the hair of his head and his beard became singed and . . . his pepuce became stretched."[58] The physical deformity that was Ham's curse—deformed lips, crinkled hair, and enlarged penis—were stereotypes that Europeans later associated with enslaved Africans.[59] In Best's theory of the origins of black skin color, disability becomes a negative trope used to denigrate blackness while reinforcing the stability of white supremacy.

According to sixteenth-century European interpretations of the story, Canaan "was together with his whole *Family* and Race, *cursed* by his *Father*," marked with blackness and held in perpetual slavery.[60] As Lynda E. Boose argues, Best's adherence to this view demonstrated his reluctance to acknowledge that a black son could be fathered by a white man—a reluctance shared by many European race theorists at the time. (Of course, European men fathered black children in Africa and the New World, but in those instances they could ascribe the child's dark skin to the climate, since, as Boose points out, "the black child was not on hand to betray the secret.")[61] The notion that blackness resulted from the curse of Ham was also a belief in the Noahic descent of Africans. Such belief, however, did not promise European sympathy toward Africans.[62]

Shakespeare's *The Tempest* can be seen as a bridge between the fantastic literature of the sixteenth century and what Europeans perceived as the more empirically accurate texts of the seventeenth century. Indeed, the play's portrayal of Caliban reflects the development of an imperial discourse that sought to create, through existing notions of deformity and monstrosity, a gradation of men based on physical appearance. Yet, in its emphasis on the poisoned inheritance Caliban receives from his mother, Sycorax, *The Tempest* heralded a world in which freedom and enslavement were passed down from mother to child as a way to perpetuate slavery and safeguard white planters' access to the bodies of enslaved women. Caliban is called many things in *The Tempest*—"strange fish," "devil," "monster," "strange beast," "mooncalf," "abhorred slave"—each of which raises doubts about his humanity and casts him as both an ethnic "other" and a deformed or disabled individual.[63] Indeed, before we even meet Caliban, we are told he is a "savage and deformed slave."[64] Caliban is therefore affiliated with the animal kingdom, and he is defined in relation to his masters—Sycorax, Prospero, or Stephano. When Trinculo, Stephano's companion, first sees Caliban, he considers the profit he could make from displaying Caliban's aberrant body in English cabinets of curiosity: "Were I in England now, as once I was, and had this fish painted, not a holiday-fool there but would give a piece of silver. There would this monster make a man. Any strange beast there makes a man."[65] Trinculo thus suspects that by displaying Caliban as an aberration he can be made a "man." Prospero and Stephano are temporarily masterless men, who in their apprehensions of the marketplaces of their homelands and the unleashing of their own monstrous desire to elevate themselves through Caliban, further compound the disarray and disorder unleashed by the tempest. In this way, deviance and deformity proliferate on multiple fronts in Shakespeare's Atlantic World and the monstrousness of the black body helps to discursively manage the (never-ending) disarray and consolidate authority under changing conditions of early modern and then modern capitalism.

In the colonial period, not all deformities were imagined along the same conceptual lines, nor treated the same as Caliban's condemnation to slavery and hard labor reflects. *The Tempest*, for example, treats slavery and forced physical labor as punishments fitting only certain kinds of deformities and monstrosities. Caliban declares that, had Prospero not prevented him, he would have "peopled else This isle with Calibans." With these words he gives voice to his greatest crime: threatening the Europeans of the play with an inheritable and reproductive monstrosity—a collective racial and national *difference*. It is this racial monstrosity that renders Caliban a threat, thus activating his enslavement. As punishment, Caliban is made to carry logs for Prospero. Caliban's geographic location on an "uninhabited" island sets his monstrosity apart from individual monsters in Europe who do not pose a similar racial threat. Geography, the inheritance of racial difference, and the ability to *reproduce* that difference (to "people else this isle with Calibans") are essential to understanding why forced labor and the loss of freedom was an effective management strategy for some deformed and monstrous bodies but not for others.

Shakespeare's portrayal of Caliban reflects several of the components that made up English ideas of Africanness in the precolonial and early colonial eras. Difficult to classify, Caliban is placed in a category where the distinctions between human and animal are blurred and where the physical descriptions of his body serve as indications of his moral character. Yet, despite his perceived deformity—perhaps even because of it—Caliban is *made* to labor. Shakespeare's depiction thus encapsulates how the preoccupation with monstrosity, supernatural creatures, and foreign lands in precolonial England intersected with emerging conceptions of race in the English Atlantic world. *The Tempest* reflects the growing sense among some English people that strange, foreign bodies representing a "race of monsters" from a distant place needed to be put to use, lest they get out of control.

In the context of England's imperial and economic expansion in the seventeenth century, Africans' supposed monstrosity became part of the logic of English capitalism. The new opportunities for the English to accumulate capital in the industries associated with the slave trade created a novel context in which generations of sailors, captains, investors, planters, and writers, from the 1640s to the turn of the eighteenth century, were implicated in slavery. It was in this specific historical context that English elites began using the language of monstrosity to express racist sentiments of a distinctly modern cast that increasingly placed black skin at the center of arguments for the supposed inferiority of Africans and their descendants. Implicit in such notions was a utilitarian argument claiming that Africans' supposed monstrosity made them better suited than other humans to enslavement and hard labor. English writers' consistent emphasis on the supposed monstrosity of Africans mirrored evolving legal justifications of enslavement as an inheritable status in the English Atlantic world. In seeking to emphasize their own intellectual, cultural, spiritual, and physical superiority over Africans, mid-seventeenth-century English writers came to articulate an increasingly coherent antiblack racism. It was during this period, after all—from roughly the 1620s to the 1660s—that English discussions of black bodies began to shift from fanciful to real.

'Twixt Human and Beast

As the English were increasingly imbricated in trade and exploration in Africa, the enslavement of Africans, and colonization in the Caribbean, literary conventions that shaped writing about Africans began to change. Though seventeenth-century writers continued to draw on medieval and Renaissance texts for information about Africa, the more extravagant depictions of African bodies began to disappear from their writings. The reason for this shift in European discourse about Africa was twofold. For one, there was increasing European presence in Africa as the Dutch, Danes, Swedes, English, and French established trading posts. Though the English had limited engagement with sub-Saharan Africa during the early seventeenth century, the diffusion of knowledge production about Africa and Africans among the English people was widespread. English elites were reading a number of new European travel narratives related to Africa, while the illiterate classes in port cities like Liverpool heard tales of the continent firsthand from the mouths of sailors and merchants. Second, wider intellectual trends among European elites that included a growing interest in natural philosophy and history shaped a more rational or real view of Africa and Africans.[66] The new interest in natural history and ethnography meant that English writers were also more inclined to describe the phenotypic characteristics of Africans instead of merely reproducing the fanciful creatures portrayed in previous accounts. New standards of truth were emerging in English travel writing about Africans: "eyewitnesses" had to provide anatomical details about, and expose parts of, the African body that, by convention in England, were not normally displayed in public. Monstrosity remained a key characterization of Africans and their descendants, but the concept was ever more intertwined with emerging scientific debates about blackness, heredity, and especially maternal imagination, which was increasingly associated in English racial discourse with notions of blackness and the laws regulating enslaveability.

The establishment of England's American colonies and the introduction of sugar to the European economy, as well as the subsequent expansion of the slave trade, expedited the shift in European discussions about black bodies. An influential and socially diverse group of English people—shipbuilders, sailors, planters, lawmakers, intellectuals—encountered Africans more frequently because of the slave trade and became interested in blackness and its origins. This new generation of seventeenth-century writers that included Richard Jobson and Thomas Herbert drew on earlier notions of monstrosity and deformity to make such arguments for the supposedly inherent monstrosity of Africans and their apparent kinship to animals. These writers did not represent a "popular consciousness," but their views dominated English writing about how bodies should be organized in the world.

African bodies underwent a conceptual shift from the fantastical into the realm of the "known," the classifiable, and, crucially, the potentially controllable. Drawing on the new rational view of natural phenomenon and anticipating the work of Philip Thicknesse, Oliver Goldsmith, and Edward Long by almost two centuries, seventeenth-century English writers suggested a correlation between Africans and animals. Perhaps one of the most influential texts in this regard was Edward Topsell's The historie of foure-footed beastes (1607), the first major English-language zoological work printed in England.[67] Topsell linked Africans to animals by suggesting that the Pygmys written about by ancient and medieval European writers were "a kind of Apes, and not men" because "they have no perfect use of Reason, no modesty, no honesty, nor justice of government, and although they speak, yet is their language imperfect; and above all they cannot be men, because they have no Religion." Topsell continued his comparison and claimed that "Men that have low and flat Nostrils are Libidinous as Apes that attempt women, and having thick lips, the upper hanging over the neather, they are deemed fools, like the lips of Asses and Apes."[68] By comparing African primates' physical and sexual characteristics to black people, Topsell's work exemplified an emerging intellectual climate in which Africans, though not fully human, were no longer seen as distant, mythical monsters.[69]

At the same time, the language used to describe Africans became more graphically sexual, blending the fantastic, the fanciful, and the downright false with obscene eyewitness details that emphasized Africans' supposedly monstrous sexual organs and abnormal reproductive practices. Gendered descriptions of monstrous sexual and reproductive organs showed Africans as a monstrous race whose reproductive activities, and whose tendency to inherit monstrosity from their mothers, confounded and violated distinctions between human and animal. Richard Jobson's The Golden Trade (1622), which chronicled his 1620–21 trading ventures along the Gambia River, epitomized the crucial ways in which English slave traders deployed sex, gender, and monstrosity in order to place Africans on an animal–human continuum. Jobson's narrative focused much attention on the reproductive organs of Africans, both female and male. For example, he described African women's breasts as monstrous, and seized on black men's supposedly distended sexual organs, as evidence that Africans had collectively inherited the curse of Ham. According to Jobson, Ham's discovery of Noah's "secrets" led to the curse such that, "in laying hold upon the same place where the original curse began, whereof these people are witnesse, who are furnisht with such members as are after a sort burthensome unto them, whereby their women being once conceived with child . . . accompanies the man no longer, because he shall not destroy what is conceived."[70] On the one hand, the claim that black men's abhorrently large penises caused fatal consequences to black women's reproductive bodies affiliated black men with the savagery of the animal kingdom and cast them as absent and deficient fathers. On the other hand, Jobson's claim also implied that black men's abnormal genitals hindered their sexual activities and expressions of masculinity. Conveniently, this accusation insinuated that white men were in a unique position of potentially privileged access and authority over black women's bodies and reproductive abilities. And, as Jennifer Morgan argues, Jobson's description of African men's penises corresponds with his contemporaries' depictions of African women's breasts—"both sexual organs were seen as pendulous and distended, somehow disembodied from their owner, and physically burthensome."[71]

Locating deformity and monstrosity in the female body had a long tradition in England, which impacted the English perception of African women. Based on ancient texts, medieval and early modern discussions of the sexes situated monstrosity and deformity in the female body and established the male as the yardstick against which all other individuals were measured. The construction of the female as monstrous perhaps has biblical roots, in Eve's formation from Adam's "crooked" rib. Throughout the early modern period, Eve exemplified the monstrosity and deceit that all women possessed due to the fall from grace and innocence as is shown in a misogynist satire titled *The Female Monster* (1705):

> This Venom spreads thro' all the Female-kind;
> Shew me a Woman, I'll a Monster a find,
> They're false by Nature, and by Nature taught,
> The Treachery that *Eve* so dearly brought.[72]

The displacement of tropes of monstrosity onto African women as a means of marking out the collective monstrosity of Africans went hand in hand with efforts to racialize the difference between white and black women. As racial slavery became a more significant component of English imperialism, contrasts between the fair white female body and the darker black female body became more frequent in English writings.[73] A sexualized racial opposition emerged in which women of English descent embodied the privileges and virtues of womanhood while women of African descent shouldered the burden of women's inherent evil and sexual lust.

Common among these Atlantic World travel narratives was the tendency of English writers to comment on the breasts and breastfeeding practices of African women. The long-breasted wild woman is part of a tradition that dates back to classical accounts of monstrous races and was used by Europeans to describe Irish, African, and indigenous American women during the early modern period.[74] Yet, English travelers and enslavers put graphic and demeaning depictions of black women's monstrously deformed organs, both in Africa and in the Caribbean, to a new purpose. As early as 1555, Englishman William Towrson claimed that "one cannot know a [African] man from a [African] woman but by their breastes, which in the most part be very foule and long, hanging downe like the udder of a goate." Some African women's breasts were so monstrously long, he maintained "that some of them wil lay the same upon the ground and lie downe by them."[75] Like many other writers of his generation, Thomas Herbert, who had powerful connections to the slave trade, frequently commented on black women's bodies, and in particular their role in child bearing and rearing.[76] In 1634, Herbert described women from the Cape of Good Hope as monstrous, "giv[ing] their Infants sucke as they hang on their backes, the uberous dugge stretched over her shoulder."[77] Herbert wrote extensively of the supposed similarities between Africans and nonhuman animals. He argued that those in the Cape of Good Hope resembled baboons, which "kept frequent company with the [African] women." This "unnatural mixture" resulted in a language "'twixt humane and beast."[78] Herbert's mention of language as a defining feature of humanity foreshadowed what would become a major focus of debate in eighteenth-century discussions about the human-animal boundary.[79] But in the seventeenth century, English fears over the human-animal boundary were most commonly expressed through the notion of monstrosity, as evidenced by Herbert's assertion that the "copulation or conjecture" of Africans and baboons produced a language that was not quite human but not fully animal either. Their "savage life, diet, and exercise" was evidence that Africans descended from Satyrs, the mythological human-animal hybrid.[80] Herbert concluded his discussion of "this wild race of men" by connecting the so-called monstrosity of Africans with an inner deviance: within virtually all Africans there are all evils.

They are inhumane, unwholesome, drunken, most dishonest, most deceptive, most lustful, most treacherous, most impure in the obscenities of every lewd act, and most addicted to blasphemies."[81]

Richard Ligon, who likewise had personal investments in Caribbean slavery, oscillated between flattery and racial prejudice in his descriptions of Africans, in particular African women. After backing the losing side in the English Civil War, Ligon went to the Caribbean in the hopes of escaping his marginalization and restoring his finances. His *True and Exact History of the Island of Barbadoes* (1657) reflected the crude materialism of the time by frequently emphasizing the potential wealth generated through investments in slavery and the slave trade and "explicitly prompt[ing] its readers to consider how they could benefit from the plantation economy."[82] Ligon traveled to Barbados with Thomas Modyford, a fellow royalist who received a commission as colonel under Charles I and later served as governor of both Barbados and Jamaica. Modyford and Ligon landed in Barbados near the beginning of the sugar revolution of the 1640s, when the island was transitioning to a highly racialized labor force. Unlike the translations of more fanciful Spanish, French, and Portuguese accounts of the Caribbean, English elites seized on Ligon's *History* as an authoritative firsthand account of Barbados and its black inhabitants.

For both indentured servants and enslaved Africans, the physical ability to perform labor was the source of both their worth on the market and their commodification and exploitation. Ligon compared the purchasing of both English servants and enslaved Africans in Barbados with the purchasing of livestock, which suggests that in these early years of sugar production and coerced labor the English had yet to isolate blacks as particularly akin to animals.[83] According to Ligon, a Barbados planter wanted to purchase a female servant and so approached his neighbor to make an exchange of "hoggs flesh" for "womans flesh." Ligon explained that "the man brought a great fat sow, and put it on one scale," and the servant named Honor, who "was extreame fat, lassie, and good for nothing . . . was put in the other." When the man "saw how much the Maid outwayed his Sow: he broke off the bargaine, and would not go on." Ligon's description indicates that the value of a female servant was measured in the same manner as a piece of livestock. Her body was depicted as abnormally large and animal-like. Ligon finished his retelling of the story claiming that "'tis an ordinary thing . . . to sell their servants to one another for the time they have to serve; and in exchange, receive any commodities that are in the Island."[84]

Ligon's description of the slave market similarly draws comparison between the purchasing of livestock and the purchasing of black bondspeople. The physical health and ability of the captive was of utmost importance to planters and so

Africans were inspected by purchasers "stark naked" so as not to "be deceived in any outward infirmity." According to Ligon, planters "choose them [enslaved Africans] as they do Horses in a Market; the strongest, youthfullest, and most beautifull, yield the greatest prices." The animalization of Africans on the open market was somewhat justified in Ligon's mind, for "most of them [Africans] are as neer beasts as may be, setting their souls aside." Like cattle and horses, Africans were bred, according to Ligon.[85]

Both explicitly and implicitly, he repeated African racial stereotypes that had existed long before the English came to the Caribbean. He described enslaved Africans as a simple people who responded better to violence than reason and whose bodies "have none of the sweetest savours."[86] And yet, in his first encounter with an African woman, Ligon described her as "a Negro of the greatest beautie and majestie together; that ever I saw in one woman. Her stature large, and excellently shap't, well-favour'd, full eye'd, & admirably grac't."[87] Such complimentary language was, however, confined to this particular woman, and throughout his *History* the author made distinctions between individual Africans and Africans as a collective. Ligon's unquestioned assumption about the group inferiority of all Africans abetted the sexual exploitation of individual bondswomen. Later in his work, Ligon depicted a very different image of African women's physical appearances, one that summoned sixteenth-century travel writers' tendency to describe black bodies as deformed and monstrous. He prefaced his description by claiming that the black male body adhered to Albrecht Dürer's rules of proportion.[88] Men of African descent, he argued, were "well timber'd," "full breasted, well filleted and clean leg'd." Black women, on the other hand, did not meet such standards:

> But the women not; for the same great Master of Proportions, allowes to each woman, twice the length of the face to the breadth of the shoulders, and twice the length of her own head to the breadth of the hipps. And in that, these women are faulty; for I have seen very few of them, whose hipps have been broader than their shoulders, unlesse they have been very fat. The young Maides have ordinarily very large breasts, which stand strutting out so hard and firm, as no leaping, jumping, or stirring will cause them to shake any more, then the brawnes of their arms. But when they come to be old, and have had five or six Children, their breasts hang down below their navells, so that when they stoop at their common work of weeding, they hang almost down to the ground, that at a distance, you would think they had six legs.[89]

For Ligon, African women's bodies were monstrous but interchangeable oddities: extremities of disproportionate length and shape, unwomanly hips, and hypersexualized, to say nothing of animalized, breasts. In this we see the seemingly contradictory English perception of African women's bodies as deformed and misshapen, yet somehow ideally suited to the performance of hard labor.

The writings of men like Jobson, Thomas Herbert, and Richard Ligon are chilling reminders of the fact that, in the context of Atlantic slavery, the discursively violent depictions of black women were inseparable from *actual* violence against real-world Africans. Deploying images of African racial monstrosity allowed English writers and lawmakers to recognize the humanity of Africans and their descendants when it suited their purpose.[90] At the same time, enslaved Africans, like animals, could be treated as the private, chattel property of their owner, with no agency over their own bodies or those of their offspring. For instance, the recognition of female slaves as humans enabled planters to strategically exploit their reproductive freedom, whereas the denial of their full humanity allowed planters and lawmakers to exercise rules of animal husbandry over the enslaved population.[91] One of the hallmarks of slaveholding sovereignty was the power of lawmakers and slaveholders to move legally between the categories of human and animal in their treatment of the enslaved. This enabled colonial authorities to take advantage of Africans' humanity by disabling them from the privileges associated with being human.

This perception of African women served to align them with a beastly licentiousness in order to justify the matrilineal inheritance of enslaved status. As Camille A. Nelson argues, in both property law and slave law, the owner possesses both the animal/slave and the offspring. "Therefore, the conception of slaves as personal property," she writes, "created a legal bridge by which techniques of animal husbandry could gain a foothold [in slave societies], given the complete agency exercised by the master/owner over his slave property."[92] The enslaved, thus, existed in an uncertain space: recognized as human, yet being monstrous, and therefore somehow deserving of treatment as animals. In the English Atlantic world, the enslaved were forced to occupy this space of potentially limitless violence and disablement. The repeated portrayal and treatment of Africans as beasts helped legitimize and naturalize their enslaved status in the Atlantic World. The emphasis on the sexual organs of people of African descent thus served a legal end as well, in that it aligned Africans and their descendants with monstrosity and animality and, in so doing, justified slavery as a condition that African children inherited from their mothers. At the same time, it served constantly to reinscribe how *close* Africans were to whites, how *human* they were. This proximity was both the source of their usefulness and the source of the danger they supposedly posed to the English people.

During the second half of the seventeenth century the institutions govern-ing England's growing empire marked the limits of subjecthood, enslavement, and abjection in the English Atlantic world. As abject, the enslaved occupied a state in between subject and object ("the in-between, the ambiguous, the composite," as Kristeva puts it in another context).[93] As we see, the Navigation Acts (1660 and 1663), the Elizabeth Keys case of 1662, and the passage of the first comprehensive slave laws of the Anglo-Atlantic worked together to define enslaveability and freedom in the English colonial world. Within this wider context of imperial law and the exertion of power over black bodies, English discussions of Africans moved from a discourse that was merely derogatory to one that was disabling.

Monstrous Mothers:
Bodies, Blackness, and Inheritance

In the context of the Restoration, the Glorious Revolution, and the rapid ex-pansion of the English slave trade, blackness and its origins entered public discussion in England as a matter of debate. During the second half of the sev-enteenth century, a variety of English writers insisted that black women passed on their supposed monstrosity—and therefore their enslaveability—to their children. After 1660, at which time the legal principle of maternal inheritance was applied to the American colonies, a related concept—that of maternal imagination—was emerging as a leading explanation for the origins of black monstrosity. Simply put, monstrous races were black—and vice versa—*because* they inherited their characteristics from women rather than men.

In the early years of English settlement in the Caribbean, racialized catego-ries of fitness were defined, whereby black people were increasingly viewed as particularly able to perform hard and physically disabling labor, while simul-taneously seen as unable to live in freedom. In the first few decades, enslaved Africans worked alongside white indentured laborers from England to clear Barbadian rainforests to make room for plantations, in turn producing timber, one of the island's first commercial crops.[94] The rise of sugar cultivation required larger work forces than the supply of free and indentured servants could fulfill, and, although African captives were more expensive to purchase than inden-tured servants, planters quickly realized that a predominately enslaved labor force provided them with the best chance of gaining considerable profit.[95] In the early years of sugar production, white and black laborers continued to work alongside one another. Both groups were poorly treated, with white *and* black laborers being severely beaten, mutilated, and branded, in addition to receiving very minimal care for diseases and illnesses like yellow fever.[96] (Indeed, so brutal were the conditions that in the seventeenth century the term "to Barbados someone" was used to describe the act of kidnapping an individual to send to a West Indian plantation where they then died.)[97] Black and white inhabitants of the English Caribbean commonly repeated that "the Devel was in the English-man, that he makes everything work; he makes the Negro work, the Horse work, the Ass work, the Wood work, the Water work, and the Winde work."[98]

Despite the supposed equality of treatment among enslaved Africans and indentured Europeans, English conceptions of blacks began to shift so that categories of political fitness and fitness for freedom became racialized. Caribbean racialized categories of fitness increasingly defined black people as particularly able to perform hard and physically disabling labor, but simultaneously unable to live in freedom. Colonists found a legitimate defense of the person-as-private-property in Sir Edward Coke's *Institutes of the Laws of England* (1628), which greatly reflected the *jus gentium* of Roman law.[99] Coke invoked theories of servitude and "race" in his observation that "bondage or servitude was first inflicted for dishonouring of parents: for Ham the father of Canaan (of whom issued the Canaanites) seeing the nakedness of his father Noah, and shewing it in derision to his Brethren, was therefore punished in his son Canaan with bondage."[100] Nation, lineage, and inheritance were key components of the racist ideology Coke expressed with the curse of Ham theory. The Canaanites suffered perpetually heritable enslavement for the sin of their nation's founding father. Skin color and phenotype were not the components that made Coke's theory racial; it was, rather, the biblical sanction for the enslavement of a race/nation of people, defined as such by their descent from a common, disinherited, and dishonored ancestor. But even so, Coke's justification for the enslavement of an entire "race" of people was still missing one of the key components of Atlantic slavery. In his defense of property in persons, as in the biblical story, enslavement is passed through the paternal line—a significant difference from the principle of maternal inheritance that would come to define slavery in the Atlantic World. By the mid-1660s, European indentured servants were given only skilled positions, whereas black enslaved people were kept in the fields and, by the end of the century, English indentured labor had more or less stopped. Along with changing conceptions of race and labor capacity, the servant conspiracies and rebellion in Barbados in 1649 and 1657 expedited the shift from planters' reliance on indentured servants and African slaves to a solely enslaved African labor force.[101]

By the mid-seventeenth century, the English Americas, including Barbados and Jamaica, adopted the principle of maternal inheritance.[102] The law's purpose was to expand and sustain slavery by making all children born of bondswomen the property of the mother's owner. The status of the mother would henceforth determine the status of the child.[103] Never codified in the English Caribbean slave codes, maternal inheritance served as a silent, if salient, justification for African dispossession in the seventeenth-century English Atlantic world. Black female bodies were used as a means of accumulating wealth and property, which made enslaved women particularly vulnerable to white men's coercion and manipulation of their sexual and reproductive agency. This gendered form of legal disablement robbed enslaved women of their reproductive liberties.[104] The intersection of race, gender, reproduction, and disability that was inscribed onto black bodies in the name of legally protected property interests led to what Orlando Patterson terms "natal alienation"—the denial of socially acknowledged kin, a past and future, and membership in the legitimate social order.[105]

Seventeenth-century English writers saw black skin as the most prominent signifier of Africans' monstrosity, a sign of their inner difference, and the basis of their dispossession in the Atlantic World.[106] In his 1684 antislavery piece, Thomas Tryon wove a fictional conversation between an English slaveowner and an enslaved African in which the slaveowner addresses the bondsman: "your very *Hue*, that sooty *Skin* of yours, serve[s] for an Emblem of the darkness of your Minds. . . . In a Word, you are in most particulars the very next Door to *Beasts*, and therefore we hardly so much care and esteem for you, as we have for our *Horses*, and other Cattel." In rebuttal, the bondsman utilizes the climatological theory to explain the origin of black skin color. "Can we help it," he asks the slaveowner, "if the Sun by too close and fervent Kisses, and the nature of the Climate and Soil where we were Born, hath tinctur'd us with a dark Complexion?" The bondsman undermines the idea that blackness was inherently connected to deviance in his rebuke: "In a word, in our *Hue* be the only difference, since *White* is as contrary to *Black*, as *Black* is to *White*, there is as much reason that *you* should be our *Slaves*, as we yours."[107] Although fictitious, Tryon's conversation between a slaveowner and an enslaved person reflected seventeenth-century English understandings of blackness as a symbol of the supposed inner deviance and animality of Africans and their descendants.

Morgan Godwyn, an early critic of slavery, recognized the connections between deformity-monstrosity, race, and inheritance and justifications for slavery. In the 1660s, Godwyn traveled to Virginia and Barbados, where he tried to Christianize the enslaved but was met with hostility from planters.

He eventually returned to England and penned two condemnations of slavery, particularly planters' refusal to baptize the enslaved. According to Godwyn, planters refused to baptize the enslaved because of the notion that Africans and their descendants were not fully human. Godwyn looked to the African body to refute such claims: "The consideration of the shape and figure of our *Negro's* Bodies, their Limbs and Members; their Voice and Countenance, in all things according with other Mens; together with their Risibility and Discourse should be sufficient Conviction" that Africans are indeed human. Godwyn understood that the liminal space of humanity in which Africans inhabited in the English imagination was a primary justification for African dispossession. He challenged the notion that Africans were animals by mocking planters for the "comical frenzie" of employing "Cattle about Business, and to constitute them [enslaved Africans] as *Lieutenants, Overseers, and Governours*." If Africans were naturally beasts, asked Godwyn, "what will become of those *Debauches,* that so frequently do make use of them for their *unnatural* Pleasures and Lusts? ... Sure they would be loth to be endited of *Sodomy,* as for lying with a Beast."[108]

A good many English writers and thinkers also viewed the heritability of blackness as a permanent defect. The curse of Ham theory, as well as the notion that black skin was a form of monstrosity or deformity, allowed English elites to adhere to theories of monogenesis—the belief that humanity descended from a single source—while maintaining that "blacks had degenerated from their common ancestor, Adam, while the whites had stayed constant or even improved."[109] A potential cosmological inconsistency was therefore avoided: the English could maintain the belief that the same God created Africans while also recognizing a hierarchy of man organized through skin color.

In one of the earliest detailed writings on race and the origin of the human species, *Pseudodoxia Epidemica* (1646, with six editions by 1672), Sir Thomas Browne dedicated three chapters to "Of the Blacknesse of Negroes." He described blackness as a "Riddle" as he considered the false origins and possible causes of black skin color. Like other writers of the time, Browne couched such thoughts in religious terminology and attempted to explain the origin of black skin in biological and biblical terms. In so doing he argued against popular theories of the time—namely, that black skin was either the result of the sun or of God's curse on the descendants of Ham. Browne challenged the climatological theory by asking why, if the sun caused the blackness of Africans, did Africans when "transplanted, although in cold and flegmatick habitations, continue their hue both in themselves, and also their generations." He argued against writers such as George Best and stated that the notion of blackness as a curse from God is "a perpetuall promotion of Ignorance." For his part Browne, at least at first glance, seemed to argue that blackness was not a deformity and that it did not offend the classical canons of beauty set out by Aristotle and Galen. But closer reading reveals that, despite his seeming cultural relativism, Browne speculated that blackness was a "mutation" and "defect," a deviation from the norm caused by either hereditary disease, something in the air, water, or land, a compound in the blood, or even cannibalism. He first speculated that blackness derived from "the water of *Siberis*, which make Oxen black, and the like effect it had also upon men, dying not only the skin, but making their hairs black and curled." In his mention of hair, Browne suggested that blackness as well as other African phenotypic characteristics were procured and, therefore, not original. Browne also suggested that maternal imagination caused blackness and cited the story in Hippocrates of a white woman "from an intent view of a Picture conceived a Negroe." From this, Browne went on to argue, in seeming contradiction, that blackness "is evidently maintained by generation, and by the tincture of the skin as a spermaticall part traduced from father unto son." He argued that the sperm of "Negroes [is] first and in its naturals white, but upon separation of parts, accidents before invisible become apparent; there arising a shadow or dark efflorescence in the outside, whereby not onely their legitimate and timely births, but their abortions are also duskie, before they have felt the scorch or fervor of the Sun."[110] Blackness, therefore, was an aberration from the original whiteness and was caused not by outside influence such as the sun but increasingly internal, even biological, peculiarities. Browne's rejection of the idea that environment affected skin color increasingly fit with the trend to maternal imagination and maternal inheritance and the notion that the origins of blackness resided *within* the body.

By contrast, other writers of the time suggested that African phenotypic characteristics were caused by the maternal practices of working-class African women. According to the English bookseller and writer Nathaniel Crouch (pseudonym Robert Burton or Richard Burton), Africans' black phenotypic features were deformities caused by deviant mothering. Though Crouch is not known to have traveled to Africa or the East Indies, in 1686 he nonetheless published *A View of the English Acquisitions in Guinea, and the East-Indies, with An Account of the Religion, Government, Wars, Strange Customs, Beasts, Serpents, Monsters, and other Observables in those Countries*. The work, a great success, deployed many of the prejudiced depictions of deformed African women then circulating in late seventeenth-century England.[111] Of black women's labor practices, for example, Crouch speculated that "this may be the reason of the flatness of their noses by their knocking continually against the back and shoulders of the mother while she is walking or at work." According to Crouch, the maternal practices of the upper classes proved this to be the case, for "the children of their gentry whose mothers do not labour, nor carry their infants about them, have very comely noses."[112] Thus, Crouch's musings also contain a class statement about the enslaveability of "ordinary" Africans. According to Crouch, elite African children, whose mothers did not labor, were supposedly devoid of the physical deformities displayed by their more common counterparts. Physical appearance, then, was a visible demonstration of one's class status and, therefore, suitability or unsuitability for enslavement. Aphra Behn's *Oroonoko: Or, The Royal Slave*, published two years after Crouch's work, also yoked African phenotype to class status and disability. In her novella, Behn described the prince Oroonoko as possessing a noble variety of blackness that placed him close to European whiteness and allowed him to transcend his "uncivilized" African origins: "His nose was rising and Roman, instead of African and flat. His mouth the finest shaped that could be seen; far from those great lips which are so natural to the rest of the negroes. The whole proportion and air of his face was so nobly and exactly formed that, bating his color, there could do nothing in nature more beautiful, agreeable, and handsome."[113] Behn condemned Oroonoko's enslavement precisely because he was an aristocrat and a man of honor, while she endorsed the enslavement of the other Africans on the plantation, in part because of their implicit deformity when compared with the noble Oroonoko.

Other publications, like the *Athenian Mercury* discussed in the introduction, argued that blackness was a monstrosity that only the divine could "cure." Although the *Mercury* was not the first to link the so-called cure of deformity and blackness with divine intervention, it was unique in its explanation that slavery led to salvation and, therefore, the healing of blackness.[114] According to this logic, blackness was a deformity that reflected an inner deficiency that could only be healed through supernatural intervention. Here we see the moral model of disability at work, in the suggestion that one's physical appearance reflects one's inner morality. Such notions worked to justify African enslavement in the Atlantic World as both a form of punishment and, in seeming contradiction, a cure of a supposedly African form of inner and outer monstrosity.

English conceptualizations of blackness and the legal and social arguments for Atlantic slavery formed relationally in the colonial period. To the extent that blackness was perceived as a deformity, slavery became understood as its "cure"; to the extent that blackness was understood as a physical sign of moral depravity, slavery was framed as a punishment. Over the course of the sixteenth and seventeenth centuries, the English transformed the concept of blackness into an inheritable monstrosity, a category of being that suspended Africans and their descendants somewhere between human and beast. The development of English ideas of African monstrosity occurred precisely during the period of England's growing involvement in the slave trade and the expansion of its overseas empire.

The African woman was key to such formulations. Drawing on medieval and early modern ideas of maternal imagination, English thinkers increasingly explained the origin of black skin as a monstrosity that mothers passed onto their children. The notion that black skin color was an inheritable monstrosity coincided with the Anglo-Caribbean's adoption of the legal principle of maternal inheritance in the mid-seventeenth century. The English figured the black female body, in its heritability and "monstrosity" or "deformity," as excessive and a threat in need of containment and discipline. The business of controlling bodies (as opposed to eliminating or completely "curing" them) worked to the advantage of the colonial economic system that was dependent on the perpetuation of slave labor.

The linking of deformity and monstrosity with African peoples over the course of the seventeenth century allowed those invested in slavery and the slave trade to assign different values to human life; thereby legitimizing enslavement and the wealth it generated. Monstrosity is, therefore, key to understanding the historical intersections between English racism, capitalism, and slavery during the seventeenth century. England was now a nationally organized mercantilist enterprise, and its ability to accumulate capital came at the expense of black bodies. This wealth, as well as the support granted to its acquisition by the monarchy and Parliament, helped ease any moral doubts about the legitimacy of the institution and its devastating consequences for Africans and their descendants.

And given the bodily violence inherent in such a project, it is a fair guess that certain moral doubts obtained. The legal principle of maternal inheritance exposed enslaved women to sexual violence and removed any protection over their bodies or those of their children. It was a form of legal disablement that denied enslaved persons unfettered access to both their pasts and their futures through ancestors and children and that seriously threatened their lives in both an ontological and a very practical sense. The legal disablement of the enslaved, coupled with the legally sanctioned disfiguring and disabling of enslaved bodies, made slavery a preeminent site of disability. For the enslaved, disability therefore became the ultimate expression of English racism. Emerging notions of race in the seventeenth century fostered and validated such violence against African bodies as the limits of "worthy" humanity were set against or defined by the backdrop of English capitalism.

CHAPTER 2

Between Human and Animal

The Disabling Power of Slave Law

> Because the slave's life is like a "thing," possessed
> by another person, the slave existence appears a
> perfect figure of a shadow.
>
> —Achille Mbembe, "Necropolitics"

On 27 September 1661, the Barbados Assembly passed into law an act that recognized a legal, moral, and anthropological theory of enslaveable humanity. This was reflected in the opening lines of the Barbados slave code (a near replica of which made its way into the Jamaica code three years later):

> Negroes [are] an heathenish brutish & an unsertaine dangerous kinde of
> people to whom if surely in any thing wee may extend the legislative power
> given us of punishinary Lawes for the benefit and good of this plantacon
> not being contradictory to the Lawes of England there being in all the body
> of that Lawe noe tract to guide us where to walk nor any rule sett as how
> to governe such slaves yett wee well know by the right rule of reason and
> order wee are not to leave them to the Arbitrary cruell and outragious wills
> of every evil disposed person but soe far to protect them as wee doo many
> other goods and chattles and alsoe so somewhat farther as being treated Men
> though without the knowledge of God in the world.[1]

As an *uncertain* kind of human, the enslaved needed the protection of their masters from "evil disposed" people. According to this line of reasoning, enslavement was the conduit through which Africans were "protected" from the errors that resulted from their undetermined humanity. Lawmakers agreed that they "may extend the legislative power given to us of punishary Lawes for the benefit and good of the platacon not being contradictory to the Lawes of England." However, they admitted that "in all the body of [English] lawe [there is] noe tract to guide us where to walk nor any rule sett as how to governe such slaves."[2] In acknowledging that they had no English laws from which to draw inspiration, Barbados lawmakers created a legal category of African humanity that had no precedent in metropolitan law. From the outset, English Caribbean slave law recognized Africans' humanity while seeking to reduce its legal significance in order to exploit it more effectively. To this end, the Barbados and Jamaica laws joined together two fundamental facts of the period: slavery as the just punishment for a monstrous race, and the use of monstrous races as enslaved labor in the interest of capital.

From the mid-seventeenth century to the abolition of slavery in 1834, the lives of enslaved individuals in the British Caribbean, from birth to death, were regulated by a vast array of laws that functioned to disable the enslaved both discursively and physically. This chapter maps out a dialectic of disablement by exploring the relationship between the *disabling* force of these laws and the law as an *enabling* force that brutalized and marked the bodies of the enslaved from the comprehensive codes of the seventeenth century to the ameliorative laws of the late eighteenth century. Antiblack racism and support for slavery and the slave trade created a space of abjection that suspended captive Africans and their descendants between the categories of human and animal. The animalization of enslaved Africans was not an ontological or an a priori assumption on which slave law was based; it was, rather, a form of punishment, a means to force Africans and their descendants into a perpetual labor justified as a way both to contain and to profit from racial monstrosity. Thus, the slave laws of Barbados and Jamaica recognized the humanity of the enslaved but treated it as a suspect and exploitable form of humanity and a foil for the monstrous link between human and animal. The English legal category of the monster is, therefore, key to understanding English lawmakers' construction of Africans as human *and* animal.

This chapter draws on legal scholar Robert Cover's argument that "legal interpretation takes place in a field of pain and death" to show how the founding laws of the English Caribbean established a culture that sanctioned the owner's right to govern and punish her or his property to the point of causing lasting impairment. According to Cover, "judges deal pain and death." English Caribbean slave law granted slaveowners the power of judges to interpret the law and, therefore, "restrain, hurt, render helpless, even kill" the enslaved individual.[3] And yet, in slave law there was essentially no room for interpretation.

The first comprehensive slave laws of Barbados and Jamaica entrusted slave-owners with almost unlimited power to punish the enslaved on plantations and at their own discretion. In this sense the slave laws themselves were a "field of pain and death." For instance, several laws ordered bondspeople to "suffer such punishment as the court shall think proper to inflict, not exceeding life or limb."[4] Slave law, thus, allowed for any kind of violence inflicted onto the enslaved including any that dismembered or killed them, for it operated in a field of assumption that the laws holding whites accountable for "exceeding life or limb" would not be enforced. Legal interpretation, thus, was a violent act, and this act of interpretative violence produced physical violence in the world.

Drawing on Julia Kristeva, I argue that the slave laws governing Barbados and Jamaica, to the extent that they viewed the enslaved as human, recognized only an abject form of humanity, one whose monstrous nature rendered it "unassimilable."[5] This abject space of debased and exploitable humanity was a fixed form of disablement, not in the process of *becoming* something else (e.g., as in childhood). The enslaved inhabited this space of disablement, or "state of exception," as "bare life," a term that Giorgio Agamben uses to describe a wounded, expendable, and endangered life: "a zone of indistinction and continuous transition between man and beast."[6] Though Agamben does not articulate his concept in relation to race and gender, "bare life" nonetheless opens new opportunities to rethink the linkages between gender, race, and disability in the context of Atlantic slavery.[7]

African humanity was the fundamental *problem* of slave law as well as what made slavery possible and profitable. Through a close examination of British Caribbean slave laws, focusing particularly on Barbados and Jamaica, this chapter argues that British Caribbean slave law always recognized the humanity of the slave, and its power derived from its ability to see Africans' humanity and effectively disable it, to take the slave apart as a whole legal being. It begins with a discussion of the development of law in the English Caribbean colonies and how such laws linked and diverged from English common law and Roman law. Following this introduction to legal development is a discussion of the law's deliberate construction of the enslaved as neither fully human nor animal in the early comprehensive slave codes of the seventeenth century. By examining the laws over time, we can better understand how the law suspended Africans and their descendants between the human and the animal through disability-inducing laws.[8] Next is an exploration of the principle of maternal inheritance as a legal notion that positioned enslaved women as legally equivalent to animals.[9] The chapter concludes with a discussion of the kinds of disability caused by legally sanctioned slave punishment and the ways in which slave law's criminalization

FIGURE 1. The 1661 Barbados Slave Code at the University of West Indies–Cave Hill Law Library. Photo courtesy the National Archives (UK).

of Africans and their descendants testified to the legal ambiguity of African humanity in slave law. On the one hand, the slave codes of Barbados and Jamaica disabled enslaved Africans by limiting their mobility, freedom, and autonomy, and divesting them of political status. On the other hand, they encouraged the physical impairment and disfigurement of captives by sanctioning punishments that disabled and disfigured—for example flogging, amputation, and branding—as well as by establishing a culture in which masters, mistresses, and overseers could punish captives however they desired and with impunity. In this way, disability functioned in slave society not only as an individual physical condition but also as a social, political, and economic process of oppression. Slave law and racial ideology *created* a distinct legal category of disablement that was applied to enslaved Africans in order to exploit them and to enable slaveowners to destroy them through disabling punishments.

The Development of a Disabled Legal Category

In order to understand slave law's construction of Africans and their descendants as inhabiting the space between human and animal, it is important first to understand the development of slave law in the English Caribbean colonies. When the English arrived in the Caribbean in 1627, the island of Barbados was unpopulated, the Caribs having migrated or been enslaved during Spanish colonization in the sixteenth century. This made Barbados a settler colony, which the eighteenth-century English jurist William Blackstone defined as a colony claimed by "right of occupancy only, by finding them desart and uncultivated, and peopleing them from the mother country."[10] This principle mattered a great deal because the type of colonization directly impacted the manner in which law was received, implemented and, perhaps most importantly, interpreted by English colonists and metropolitan authorities.

Although colonial lawmakers drew on English law, this was of no assistance in defining the social relations between captive and master or the race relations between black and white.[11] English settlers had a considerable degree of autonomy from the English Parliament in creating colonial law and retained only those aspects of English law they found useful to the Caribbean. In 1651, prior to the 1661 comprehensive slave code, the proprietary governor of Barbados, Francis Willoughby, and the Commissioners of the Commonwealth of England signed the charter of Barbados and together both parties agreed that "all Laws made heretofore by general Assemblies, that are not repugnant to the Law of *England*, shall be good; except such as concern the present difference."[12] The exception was legislation that "was specifically framed for [colonial authorities] by Parliament on special occasion, by the crown before a local assembly had convened, or by their own assembly."[13] The early slave codes of Barbados and Jamaica, like other laws governing the islands, were formed piecemeal in local legislatures and not in England, so they reflected the immediate concerns of the plantocracy.[14] They did not, moreover, mirror everyday practices but were often adhered to in the breach and implemented in ways that diverged from the written statute.[15] In England during this same period, no extant law defined the status of slaves, and neither was there a custom of using Roman law for legal development. Colonists could not, therefore, easily take Roman slave law and apply it to the colonies. This accounted for one of the fundamental differences between the Portuguese and Spanish colonies, on the one hand, and the English on the other.[16] The lack of legal precedent for the English permitted lawmakers great laxity in formulating laws that served the emergent needs of casting blacks as occupying liminal space between the human and the animal.

In the early decades of sugar production, lawmakers differentiated, in both a social and a legal sense, between servants and slaves, offering the former protections against violence while defining the latter as absolute private property subject to her or his owner's will.[17] Unlike British North America, Barbados functioned as a slave society before a comprehensive slave code had been written.[18] Between 1641, when the Barbados Assembly began to initiate legislation and the 1661 comprehensive slave code, at least 204 laws were passed in Barbados, of which several mentioned "Negro's" but none dealt solely with slaves or "Negroes."[19] According to the earliest extant laws of the island, passed in 1652, both indentured servants and enslaved Africans were restricted in their freedom of movement. However, unlike servants, enslaved Africans were not allowed to petition the courts for grievances or sue for their freedom. The enslaved were private property and served their masters for life, whereas servants entered into contracts and were legally free after they had fulfilled their contracts. As private property, the enslaved were subject to the absolute power and authority of slaveowners.[20] For instance, according to the 1673 Jamaica law, an indentured servant who killed an enslaved individual was only accountable to the slaveowner's penalty and not the law.[21] Such acts were intended to protect masters from having their servants incarcerated and, therefore, kept from their masters' service; meanwhile, they served to reinforce white supremacy within the Anglo-Caribbean by exonerating whites, regardless of class standing, from violence against enslaved Africans. As is discussed in further detail, servants were also freed from their service if they informed on a runaway bondsperson, unlike enslaved people, who remained in perpetual slavery but received a small monetary reward for the same.[22] It was these legal restrictions imposed on the enslaved that most obviously distinguished servants from slaves.

As the enslaved population of Barbados grew to outnumber the white population, slaveowners found it necessary to devise a special set of laws to deal specifically with the enslaved.[23] In September 1661, the Barbados Assembly passed a series of laws dealing specifically with the island's underclasses. These included, along with the slave code, two other acts: a servant act and a militia act.[24] We know from the 1661 slave code that previous laws existed though "imperfect and not fully comprehending the true constitution of this government."[25] Issued during the period of expansion of the slave trade, the 1661 code sharply distinguished servants from the enslaved.[26] For instance, in English law, masters took no part in the criminal proceedings against servants because the law recognized servants as individuals who were responsible for their own actions. In contrast, in Barbados masters were legally obliged to pay for the minor offenses of their bondspeople. As Susan Amussen explains, "this provision not only required masters to control their slaves but also recognized the vested interest of all slaveowners in each master's maintaining control."[27] The 1661 law was reenacted with minor changes in 1676, 1682, and 1688. This founding law subsequently influenced slave laws in several other colonies, including South Carolina, Jamaica, Saint Christopher, Tobago, Saint Lucia, Saint Vincent, and Antigua.[28]

Although these early comprehensive slave laws did not refer explicitly to skin color as the basis for slavery, they nevertheless reflected a nascent antiblack racism. The laws described Africans as "heathenish, brutish, and uncertain dangerous kind of people," who were consequently unfit to be governed by the laws of England. Of particular relevance here is that, already by 1661 and 1664, Africans were being constructed in law as the only enslaveable people, even though indigenous people were enslaved in Barbados and Jamaica in this period as well.[29] References to "Indian" enslavement resurfaced in later seventeenth- and eighteenth-century laws. Yet these lawmakers' primary concern was not Indian enslavement, but rather an Indian slave *trade* that was unsettling commerce with indigenous nations on the American mainland.[30] What is more, by 1661 and 1664, the racial and legal distinction between servants and slaves was made explicit as the titles of the Barbados and Jamaica codes make clear. "An Act for the Better Ordering & Governing of Negroes" (1661) and "An Act for the better ordering & Governing of Negro Slaves" (1664) institutionalized English notions of African depravity, and consolidated Atlantic slavery's main principles—racial hierarchy, tyrannical social control, and the incorporation of slavery into England's political economy. The words "negro" or "negroes" were relatively new to the English language, used in the mid-sixteenth century to refer to peoples originally native to sub-Saharan Africa. By the seventeenth century, the term took on an additional meaning, as it was applied specifically to enslaved Africans.[31] Morgan Godwyn observed that in Barbados and Virginia the words "Negro and Slave" had become synonymous, whereas the pairing of "Negro and Christian" and "Englishman and Heathen" had been made opposites, which implied "that the one could not be Christians, nor the other Infidels."[32]

The 1661 Barbados Slave Code and the 1664 Jamaica Slave Code created an entirely new judicial system that disabled the enslaved and completely separated them from whites on the islands. This new system eradicated trial by jury, which had long been part of English judicial proceedings. Lawmakers argued that

African bondspeople were unfit for English law and instead had to be tried by a system of slave courts tailored to the management and punishment of black bodies. These courts consisted of two magistrates—almost always major planters—and three freeholders; there was no jury and no opportunity for appeal for the enslaved.[33] Evidence given by enslaved people was not permitted for or against free persons; individual courts determined whether or not enslaved persons could be witnesses for or against enslaved individuals. Because the enslaved could not be fined, the new system of slave law mandated that they be physically punished instead.[34] Such laws placed the enslaved in a distinctly different legal category, while ensuring that the bodies of bondspeople would be marked with their enslaved status by way of physical punishment.

"An Uncertaine Kinde of People"

The early laws of Barbados and Jamaica set a precedent for laws that followed in their construction of enslaved Africans as possessing an anthropologically uncertain kind of humanity. In these seventeenth-century codes, captives were most commonly regarded as chattel and treated like animals.[35] In 1668, the Barbados Assembly changed the classification of Africans from chattel to real estate in "An Act declaring the Negro Slaves of this Island to be Real Estate."[36] The 1668 definition of enslaved status had more to do with free people than it did bondspeople. This special piece of legislation defined the enslaved as real estate solely for the purpose of probating estates of people who died intestate. Defining enslaved persons as real estate prevented slaveholders from rapaciously exploiting one another, especially widows and daughters, at moments of vulnerability. The enslaved were not defined as real estate in other circumstances. Like land and other goods, slaves were considered commodities and merchandise that could be sold and bought and made private property—considered in part as a chattel, in part as real property. This shift in legal terminology changed enslaved status from moveable to immoveable property and, in theory, placed more emphasis on the enslaved as *persona* instead of *res*. In practice, however, it only protected planters as property owners; the enslaved enjoyed no new freedoms.[37] The Barbados slave laws (and repeated in the seventeenth-century laws of Jamaica) constructed a slave whose humanity was recognized in order to facilitate its legal disablement. Whether chattel or real property, enslaved legal status affirmed the disabling anthropological uncertainty of "Negroes" as a basic condition of existence.

Although slave law clearly established the slave as "mere" property, the actual regulation of enslaved Africans on Caribbean plantations proved more difficult.

Owners recognized, at least in part, that the enslaved were persons possessing volition and an ability for resistance and agency. Thus slaves, as people, raised issues of public order and therefore required treatment beyond the paper slaves of legal codes in order to regulate them under this aspect of their activity. For instance, in Barbados the enslaved were prohibited from selling and bartering stock without permission from owners. The law clarified that enslaved individuals who were employed and, therefore, given permission to sell stock "have at all such times that he, she, or they are selling the same, a metaled Collar locked about his, her or their Neck or Necks, Leg or Legs, with the name of his or her Master or Mistress engraven thereon, and the name of the Parish wherein they live, and also the name of the person who made such Collar."[38] Such laws recognized the humanity of the enslaved but insisted on reducing that humanity to the status of animal by mandating that enslaved people wear collars as though they were animals. Such measures served as a visual and physical reminder of the enslaved individual's status as property.

In contrast to the 1661 slave code, the 1688 Barbados slave act focused less on protecting Africans' uncertain humanity and more on punishing them for the crime of racial monstrosity. In 1676, following a discovered enslaved rebellion plot, Barbados lawmakers made several amendments to the 1661 slave code in a law titled "A Supplemental Act to a former Act Entitled an Act for the Better Ordering and Governing of Negroes."[39] The Barbados Assembly repealed and replaced the 1661 slave code and the 1676 amendments in 1688, and the new law remained in effect, with minor revisions, until 1826 when, under pressure from the metropole, Barbados lawmakers implemented the Consolidated Slave Act as part of the policy on ameliorative reforms. The 1688 law's preamble claimed that Africans' "barbarous, wild and savage nature . . . renders them wholly unqualified to be governed by the Laws, Customs, and Practices of our nation." As such, lawmakers concluded "it is therefore becoming absolutely necessary that such other Constitutions, Laws and Orders, should be in this Island framed and enacted for the good regulating or ordering of them as may both restrain the disorders, rapines and inhumanities to which they are naturally prone and inclined."[40] The figure of the monster haunted both the 1661 and 1688 laws in ways that reflected the rapid shifts in English-Atlantic thought and policy. In the 1661 law statute, the "fantastic" African whose monstrous difference was accepted as a fact beyond the control of ordinary Englishmen, was giving way to the "knowable," controllable, and improvable African. Africans transitioned from "heathenish brutish & an unsertaine dangerous kinde of people" to people of a "barbarous, wild and savage nature." Slavery was the means for the human to triumph over the monster. By contrast, the slave act of 1688 emphasized slavery as the rightful punishment for Africans' monstrous nature, and legally sanctioned forced labor and extreme violence became the only means of exploiting Africans' otherwise useless reserves of humanity.

The legal uncertainty surrounding African humanity in the 1688 slave code meant that enslaved Africans were not deserving of certain "protections" originally granted to them in the 1661 slave code. For instance, in the 1661 law, Africans were protected from "the Arbitrary cruell and outragious wills of every evill disposed person."[41] In contrast, the 1688 law claimed to protect the enslaved from the "cruelties and insolences of themselves" as well as "ill-tempered" people or owners.[42] According to the 1688 slave code, the supposedly "barbarous, wild and savage" natures of Africans made them prone to "disorders, rapines and inhumanities," which caused whites to lose their tempers and commit murder. The enslaved were, therefore, responsible for whites' murder of them.

The 1688 slave code contained new disability-producing acts. In the 1661 slave code, capital-offense crimes included murder, burglary, highway robbery, and arson. In both the 1676 and 1688 codes enslaved individuals were sentenced to death even if they *attempted* to commit a capital offense. In 1676 and again in 1688, lawmakers included rape among the "grievous and heinous crimes" worthy of capital punishment.[43] Like the 1661 code, the 1688 law continued to apprehend and try bondspeople by the same process for "heinous and grievous crimes, as Murders, Burglaries, Robbing in the High-ways, Rapes, Burning of Houses or Canes," but for the first time the law stipulated why summary trial was used. "Being brutish," it explained, the enslaved "deserve not, for the Baseness of their condition, to be tried by the Legal Tryal of Twelve Men of their Peers or Neighbourhood, which neither truly can be rightly done as the Subjects of *England* are, nor is Execution to be delayed towards them, in case of such horrid Crimes committed." The law advised judges to use "violent circumstances" to gather incriminating testimonies from bondspeople, and it compensated owners of executed captives a maximum of £25 sterling.[44] Also new to 1688 was a clause prohibiting captives from meeting in groups, beating drums, blowing horns, or using any other loud instruments.[45] The prohibition of loud instruments and the addition of rape and the widening of capital offense crimes was likely a direct reaction by slaveowners to fears of enslaved rebellion. The myth of the black man as a sexual predator and the white woman as the symbol of white "purity" emerged in the first decades of plantation slavery and reflected English fears of Africans enacting their humanity, particularly through resistance. With regard to the 1675 enslaved rebellion plot, the author of *Great Newes from Barbadoes* claimed that some of the rebels "intended to spare the lives of the Fairest and Handsomest Women (their Mistressess and their Daughters) to be Converted to their own use." Reports of the 1688 conspiracy made similar claims, the rebels having conspired "to make themselves masters of the country, by murdering all the male inhabitants, or reducing them to slavery, and reserving the women for the gratification of their brutal appetites."[46] The corresponding language in these reports testifies to whites' widespread anxiety about black male sexuality.

The laws of Barbados and Jamaica suspended the humanity of the enslaved, but in the daily transactions of slavery, slaveholders relied on slave humanity. Seventeenth-century slave law expressed no delusions over the actual biology of Africans—it viewed them as people—and its power derived from imagining the enslaved as inhabiting a disabled form of humanity. Enslaved Africans were a special kind of property—human property—and, as such, colonial lawmakers dealt directly with African humanity. "Property in persons" possessed volition, after all—it could steal goods, run away, and plot and rebel against its owners.[47] For instance, in Barbados and Jamaica, laws that dealt with the death of a bondsperson conferred on slaveowners the power to reduce bonds*people* to the status and material existence of *animals*. Both the 1661 and 1664 laws distinguished between what it deemed to be acceptable and unacceptable killing; the 1664 legislation, for example, ordered whites to pay a fine for the latter. Lawmakers agreed that "if any slaves under punishment by his Master or his order for running away or any other crime or misdemeanor towards his said Master shall suffer in life or in member noe person whatsoever shall bee accountable to any Law." However, "if any Man shall of wantonness or only bloody minded & cruell intencon wilfully kill a slave of his owne hee shall pay unto the King his heires & successors thirty pounds sterl." If a white man killed another planter's slave, "hee shall soe pay to the owner of the slave double the vallue & unto our Sovereigne Lord the King his heires & successors fifty pounds sterl." If he "kills another mans slave by accydent" he will not "bee lyable to any other penalty by the owners account at Law." Thus, the killing of an enslaved person was admonished if by punishment or accident. All whites, including the poor and small freeholders, were justified should they "kill a slave by night out of the road or comon path or stealing his . . . swine or other goods" and "not bee accountable for it."[48] By blurring the boundaries between the subject's dying by "accydent" and being "wantonly" killed, the laws demonstrate that lawmakers did not view the enslaved as animals but, rather, bestowed power onto slaveowners to recognize the humanity of the enslaved and disable it.

Barbados received some backlash from the metropole with regard to the capital punishment of the enslaved. Governor Atkins thought the initial amendments made in 1675 "may seem to shock" the Plantation Office and so sent the law back to the assembly for review. By the 1680s, the Lords of Trade were not satisfied with this law; they felt that those convicted of "wantonly" killing an unfree person should face more than a fine. Just five years prior to the 1688 Barbados Slave Code, the Crown refused to ratify the Jamaica laws, noting that the provision of a fine for any man who would "willfully and wantonly kill a negro" seemed "to encourage the willful shedding of blood."[49] To this end, in 1696 the Jamaica Assembly declared that "if any Person shall willingly, wantonly or bloody mindedly kill a Negro or Slave, he, she or they so offending . . . shall be adjudged guilty of Felony for the first Offence, and have the Benefit of the Clergy." But lawmakers agreed that the second offense "shall be deemed Murder, and the Offender suffer for the said Crime according to the Laws of *England*."[50] Barbados, in contrast, continued merely to fine such criminals, arguing that the fines served both the owner and the king.[51]

Despite the charges against "wantonly" killing captives, the law's loose definition of slave "misdemeanors" in fact empowered masters to kill without penalty and diminished the value of African life, reducing theirs to the status of beasts. A master could physically harm an enslaved person's body for any "misdemeanor;" proof of the infraction, however manipulated, was the only evidence needed for a master to escape culpability for the death of her or his captive. Without the legal or social protection of the law, bondspeople were reduced to a mere naked, or bare life, thereby subjecting them to forms of disablement to which free whites were protected. The bondsperson of the English Caribbean was thereby excommunicated from the social body, and denied the safeguards offered to white members, so that her or his life could be taken by anyone with impunity. This system of slave courts was specific to the English Atlantic colonies. In the Spanish, French, and Portuguese colonies, enslaved individuals were tried by the same courts as free people.[52] In contrast, in the English Atlantic world, the enslaved individual was juridically separated from free people, exposed to the power of slaveowners and white society, and denied virtually all legal protection.

Even the protective legislation found in slave codes showed lawmakers' ability to deliberately, and out of self-interest, position African humanity as a legal ambiguity. In both Barbados and Jamaica, these laws obligated owners to provide bondspeople with clothing "to cover their nakedness once every yeare." Men were to be given drawers and caps, and women petticoats.[53] According to slave law, planters needed to supply bondspeople with food, even when incarcerated. For instance, in the 1661 Barbados slave law, the provost marshal was responsible for providing detained runaways "with sufficient food and drink" (a provision retained in both Barbados and Jamaica law well into the eighteenth century). If any runaways should die under the care of the marshal "for want of foode or dry or convenient lodgeing the provost Marshal shall bee responsible for them to the owners."[54] Of course, such protective legislation was not based on the well-being of the enslaved but rather on the self-interest of slaveowners and the state, whose economy depended on enslaved labor.[55]

Laws of manumission provide another avenue through which we can examine how the laws disabled blacks by creating a liminal space between the human and animal. In the English colonies, there were three means by which manumission could occur: legislative and court action, deed conveyances, and wills.[56] In 1692, after the discovery of a slave plot in Barbados, an act was passed manumitting bondspeople who informed on fellow captives planning to "commit or abet any insurrection or rebellion." Lawmakers recognized Africans as possessing human qualities such as political consciousness and reason when they admitted that "the Negroes and Slaves of this Island" had "been long preparing, contriving, conspiring and designing a most horrid, bloody, damnable and detestable Rebellion, Massacre, Assassination and Destruction . . . to be committed, done and perpetrated upon and against all the white Inhabitants hereof."[57] This law was not used until after the Barbados slave rebellion of 1816, at which time four enslaved individuals were manumitted.[58] Indeed, manumission in the English Caribbean was very rare, and the majority of the enslaved had little chance of gaining their freedom. In 1707, the Barbados Assembly passed an act to free enslaved individuals "who in time of Invasion by Her Majesty's Enemies, or other attempt to be made on this Island, shall engage and couragiously behave himself in time of battle, so as to kill any one of the Enemy."[59] Once again, lawmakers recognized the humanity of Africans when it suited their purposes, in this instance safeguarding the island from internal threat, but compensated slaveowners whose slaves were freed by such act, thereby validating property in persons as a legitimate form of property.

Jamaica's tumultuous history with Maroon communities, slave rebellion, and fugitivity made manumissions more common in Jamaica but still rare compared with other Atlantic empires. After seizing Jamaica from Spain, English colonists spent several years in conflict with African Maroons who had been Spanish captives, which shaped to a significant degree the creation of the 1664, 1673, 1678, and 1696 Jamaica slave acts. These laws reflected the island's most pressing problems: slave rebellion and Maroon resistance.[60] In 1706–7 the Jamaica Assembly freed "a Negro Man nam'd Hilas" for fighting against "the Rebellious Negroes, and more particularly against the *French* . . . where he receiv'd Two dangerous Shots, One thro' each Thigh." Lawmakers argued that "for Recompence . . . and for the Encouragement of all other Slaves to engage cheerfully in Opposing any Enemy" the said Hilas "shall be freed immediately from Slavery, perfectly set at Liberty, and for every hereafter shall have and enjoy all the Benefits and Privileges that all other free Negroes have or enjoy in this Island."[61] Following the slave rebellion known as Tacky's War in 1760, several enslaved people were manumitted. According to the law's preamble, "sundry horrid and detestable rebellions and conspiracies have been lately formed by several slaves . . . to destroy the settlements and plantations, and to murder their masters, mistresses, and overseers, and many white people have been destroyed in such rebellions." Lawmakers manumitted thirteen enslaved men and women for having "been instrumental in discovering . . . and active in suppressing the said rebellions."[62] Lawmakers in the English Caribbean relied on seeing the enslaved as humans who could provide information about potential plots against slavery.

Of course, even when free, Africans and their descendants were denied legal protection and remained fully exposed to actual impairment or even death. Indeed, multiple pieces of legislation were required to *legally* disable both free and unfree Africans and their descendants. In 1721, Barbados issued a law denying free people of color the right to benefit from their subjecthood. Unlike previous laws, it stipulated that, to testify in court or participate in other legal proceedings involving whites, the freeperson could not have African ancestry.[63] Nonwhites, including the enslaved, could testify in court only when an enslaved individual was on trial. Over time, the 1721 law came to be interpreted as preventing free people of color from testifying in courts, even against one another.[64] By preventing free people of color from participating in the judicial system, the statutes show that it was not legal status alone that confirmed black non-subjecthood.

The cost of caring for disabled enslaved people was a driving force behind manumission laws in both Barbados and Jamaica. As early as 1739, Barbados lawmakers claimed that freed people of color had become idle and a menace to white society. According to the law's preamble, "several Negroes and other Slaves" had been set free by their masters but were not given "proper provision for their maintenance and support," which caused the manumitted slaves to "continu[e] their baseness" and "instead of supporting themselves by honest labour and industry, through idleness and other vices been greatly injurious to the Inhabitants, in enticing and corrupting other Slaves to steal and rob their Owners."[65] In 1774 the Jamaica Assembly claimed that manumitted slaves had become public nuisance on the island: "the frequent manumission of negro, mulatto, and other slaves, by persons not making a provision for them, is a great nuisance to the community, and promotes frequent thefts." Lawmakers declared that "no person or persons whatsoever, save and except the legislative body of this island, shall have power or authority to manumise, enfranchise, or set free, either by deed, will, or otherwise, any negro, mulatto, sambo, or other slave whatsoever" until they "have first given good and sufficient security, to the churchwarden ... for the payment, to such negro, mulatto, or sambo, (*of*) an annual sum of five pounds, for and during the natural life of such negro, mulatto, or sambo, that shall be so manumised and set free."[66] By the late eighteenth century, as part of amelioration, laws were put in force to ensure that owners, and not the state, provided for their disabled laborers in an attempt to keep them from "wandering" the island. To this end, Jamaica's Consolidated Act of 1788 declared that "no master ... shall discard or turn away any such slave or slaves, on account or by reason of such slave or slaves being rendered incapable of labour or service ... by means of sickness, age, or infirmity." Rather, slaveowners were legally obliged "to keep all such slave or slaves upon his, her, or their properties, and to find and provide them with wholesome necessaries of life." This was a perverse form of social welfare, made not in the interest of the enslaved but to ensure that disabled bondspeople do not "become burdensome to others for sustenance."[67]

The 1788 law further mandated that "wandering sick, aged, and infirm" bondspeople be held "in the nearest workhouse, there to be fed, but not worked, at the expence of the master, owner, or possessor" until the end of the court trial. Above all, whites considered disabled and ill bondspeople a threat to the social order of plantation society and a burden on poor relief.[68] Indeed, the emphasis on slaveowners' responsibility toward their disabled bondspeople did not favor the enslaved individual since it led to life sentences of hard labor for impoverished bondspeople and discouraged legislatures from manumitting even able-bodied bondspeople unless the public was compensated beforehand against the possibility that the freed individual might become destitute.[69] In 1801, the Barbados Assembly raised manumission fees from £50 to £300 for women and £200 for men. Manumission numbers had increased in the last decades of the eighteenth century. In particular, more women were being manumitted than men, and slaveholders were manumitting old and disabled bondspeople to avoid taking care of them.[70]

In other contemporary slave systems—those of the Iberian Atlantic and the Mediterranean, for example—manumission was a more realistic prospect. The Iberian Atlantic practice of gradual manumission, or *coartación* was based on the medieval legal notion that enslavement was an "unnatural" condition, used to transition outsiders into society.[71] In the Mediterranean, bondspeople labored in brutal conditions and were subjected to harsh physical punishments and sexual abuse before, as was often the case, being set free.[72] This differed markedly from slavery in the Atlantic, and in particular in the English Atlantic world, where, as Robin Blackburn writes, "slavery was a curse that even the grandchildren of the grandchildren of the original African captive found it exceedingly difficult to escape."[73]

From manumission laws that recognized African humanity only to defend against potential rebellions, to regulatory laws that consistently blurred the boundaries of African humanity, the founding laws of Barbados and Jamaica show how the disabling power of slave law suspended the enslaved in the space between human and animal. Kristeva defines abjection as something that "disturbs identities, systems and orders. Something that does not respect limits, positions, rules. The in-between, the ambiguous, the mixed up."[74] For Judith Butler, the abject signifies "those 'unlivable' and 'uninhabitable' zones of social life which are nevertheless densely populated by those who do not enjoy the status of the subject, but whose living under the sign of the 'unlivable' is required to circumscribe the domain of the subject."[75] The founding laws of Barbados and Jamaica assigned the enslaved to just such a world of abjection. Neither object nor subject—neither fully human nor merely chattel—the bondsperson was rejected, expelled, and disposed of. The enslaved were a part of the English legal system but were unfit to be protected as human agents under common law. As abject, the enslaved African "lies there, quite close, but cannot be assimilated" into the political economy of plantation slavery.[76]

Enforced Kinlessness and Sexual Violence

The root of the enslaved's abjection was the principle of maternal inheritance, a principle that sustained slavery by extending the status of the mother to the status of the child, irrespective of the status of the father. Unlike the mainland colonies, the Anglo-Caribbean slave codes never articulated the maternal inheritance principle.[77] However, by the end of the seventeenth century, the principle that the status of the child was determined by the status of the mother was adopted throughout English America, including Barbados and Jamaica. In fact, the principle of maternal inheritance was applied in the Spanish Caribbean as well, where it became a prevailing legal practice so widespread that it was taken for granted (indeed, Spanish colonists never codified it in a written statute).[78] It could be that the principle of maternal inheritance was not given legal authority because it was so widespread as a customary practice that lawmakers felt it unnecessary to include it in the laws. Another way to look at this is to suggest that the rape of black women by white men and the enslavement of the offspring was so widespread that lawmakers felt it unnecessary to acknowledge it in legislation. The mere threat that enslaved black men posed to white male anxiety over white supremacy and notions of masculinity was enough to give legal authority to the crime of rape—but only when the perpetrator was black. This principle "confirmed humanity" for children born of free women and "reduced the children of enslaved mothers to the status of cows and horses."[79] Maternal inheritance positioned the enslaved woman's womb as a site of abjection's reproduction by enslaving it as property and producer.

Through the notion of maternal inheritance, black women were conceived as breeders and white women, subsequently, as key to the continuation of white supremacy.[80] The principle of maternal inheritance differed from the laws that regulated the sexuality and reproductive abilities of white servant women in Barbados. As early as 1652, the Barbados Assembly attempted to discourage men from having sexual relations with servant women by making them serve the woman's master for three years or provide the master with a servant for three year's service should the woman servant become pregnant. Such laws attempted to prohibit nonpropertied men access to female servant's bodies by placing a price on sexual relations with women servants that only men of property could afford.[81] In contrast to the principle of maternal inheritance, which exposed enslaved women to all forms of sexual coercion and violence, the 1652 law made it so that only propertied men could access the bodies of servant women.

Maternal inheritance rested on the anthropological assumption that black women suffered from an inherent monstrosity. For English colonists, black women's physical monstrosity symbolized their sole purpose as producers of crops and slaves.[82] In slave law, therefore, the enslaved were disinherited from everything save their monstrosity, their blackness, and their enslaveability.[83] In the English Caribbean, lawmakers adopted the principle of maternal inheritance to ensure that monstrosity and enslaveability were perpetually inherited among the enslaved populations. Slavery's purpose was not to destroy the monster, but to perpetually reveal and exploit the only use deemed fit for the racial monster, which was as a unit of labor and profit for others. Reducing African humanity to the legal status of a domestic animal made it possible to exploit the monster's human potential and contain the danger posed by monstrosity. Colonial rule turned a world of potentially infinite monstrosity into a world of potentially limitless capitalist gain.

English common law distinguished between deformity and monstrosity, defining the former as human and the latter as an animal-human hybrid. Such legal definitions are useful in understanding links between the principle of maternal inheritance and the notion of black skin color as a monstrosity caused by maternal imagination. Henry of Bracton's *On the Laws and Customs of England* (c. 1235) stipulated that a child born with "larger number of members, as one who has six fingers, or if he has but four [or only one], will be included among children," and so too if she or he is "crooked or humpbacked or has twisted limbs or otherwise has its members useless."[84] Unlike later laws, the thirteenth-century law concerning monsters did not describe these creatures' physical appearance, though by suggesting that monsters were a product of bestiality, the authors implied that monsters resembled both human and animal. The category of the monster disappeared from English law until 1590, when the first English translation of canon law was published.[85] In *A Brief Treatise of Testaments and Last Wills*, lawyer and part-time judge Henry Swinburne defined the legal "monster, or misshapen creature" as an individual with animal qualities: "having peradventure a head like unto a dogs head, or to the head of an ass, or of a raven, or duck, or of some other beast, or bird." Such creature should not be "accounted amongst the testators children, for the law doth not presume that creature to have the soul of man, which hath a form and shape so strange and different from the shape of a man." Swinburne distinguished between a monster (as an animal-human hybrid) and deformed person (a person with abnormal physicality but of human origin). But if an individual was born with deformities but have no mark of an animal species, such individual should be legally granted its inheritances. "If the creature brought forth," he declared, "do not vary in shape from a man or woman, but have somewhat more than God by the ordinary course of nature alloweth, as having six fingers on either hand, or one foot, such creature is not excluded, but is to be accounted for the testator's child."[86] By the late sixteenth century, then, monstrosity was being defined by resemblance to an animal-human hybrid. In the eighteenth century, William Blackstone (whose own definition of monstrosity would last well into the following century) reinforced this emphasis on monsters' bodies when he described the human-animal hybrid as "the exclusive locus of legal monstrosity" and "a more absolute form of difference from humanness."[87]

In his attempt to provide the humanity of the enslaved, antislavery critic Morgan Godwyn argued that, like deformed beings, Africans should also be entitled to the inheritances associated with humans, not animals. According to Godwyn, "A Crooked Person, Dwarf, or Hermaphrodite" was "as truly of the *Species of Man*" and, therefore, was permitted "to succeed to an Inheritance" in both Common and Civil law. Indeed, "even Monstrous Births partaking of Mankind, having the benefit and help of Reason, may very well . . . be admitted to succeed to their Parents *dying Intestate*."[88] Godwyn told a story of a man who had sex with his wife while wearing a devil costume and the woman gave birth to a monster. The couple went on to have other children and, on the death of their parents, the children "endeavor[ed] to exclude this Monster, not only from the birth-right of being Heir and Eldest Son, but even from the total *Succession* of any thing that he should claim." The matter went to court, where the judge ruled that the monster should have what was owed to him as eldest son, arguing that even monsters "*who are born of Mankind, and are capable of Reason, and of the future Resurrection*" should be afforded inheritance. For Godwyn, if monsters were entitled to the benefits of humanity, so too should Africans for, "Why should Colours do more than Deformity?" "Negros," according to Godwyn, like "crooked person, dwarfs, and hermaphrodites" are "born of Man" and not beast and should, therefore, reap the benefits of human inheritance.[89] Africans and their descendants should not, therefore, suffer the inheritance of perpetual slavery as though they were beasts, but the inheritance of property and wealth as though human. The legal notion of human-animal hybridity developed between the sixteenth and eighteenth centuries paralleled English travelers' and lawmakers' belief that Africans' monstrosity and enslaveability was inherited from enslaved mothers.

The principle of maternal inheritance positioned enslaved women as legally equivalent to animals, and it implied that Africans somehow lacked the ability to form and maintain kinship ties. Again, this accorded with the larger imperatives of English slave law, which did not recognize marriage between captives because such familial ties would have undermined the institution of slavery by providing bondspeople with some protection over their families and children. As Saidiya Hartman puts it, maternal inheritance "made your mother into a myth, banished your father's name, and exiled your siblings to the far corners of the earth."[90] For Orlando Patterson, this was "natal alienation," a term mentioned in chapter 1 but whose pervasive effects are worth considering in more detail here. "A genealogical isolate," the enslaved person was denied all claims and obligations to ancestors, descendants, and social heritage. Slavery worked to prevent the enslaved from integrating their ancestors and heritage into their lives and worldviews.[91] The female body, and specifically the womb, was the primary corporeal location for this form of dispossession in the British Atlantic world.

Perhaps the most infamous example of the dreadful license granted to European colonists comes from the diaries of the Jamaican overseer and planter Thomas Thistlewood, which are best known for detailing his sexual exploits with 138 enslaved women. Over thirty-seven years, Thistlewood engaged in nearly four thousand acts of sexual abuse, the large majority of which were perpetrated on his own or his neighbors' bondswomen. Only the very young and the very old were exempt from Thistlewood's sexual terrorism. He continued to rape his female captives even when they were heavily pregnant. He twice sexually assaulted his female captive Abba when she was over eight months pregnant—once a month before she gave birth and yet again two days before she gave birth. When Abba gave birth on 17 October 1771, Thistlewood suspected the child to be his, describing the infant as "very yellow, it seems." The infant died one week later. From 1771 to 1774, Abba had a sexual relationship with an enslaved man named Jimmy. Thistlewood viewed Jimmy as a sexual rival and increased his sexual assault of Abba during these years, all the while punishing Jimmy for various forms of "impudent" behavior. In 1774, Jimmy took up a relationship with Phoebe, another of Thistlewood's slaves, and once again, Thistlewood exercised his sexual prowess over both individuals by asserting his sexual rights over Phoebe, including raping Phoebe while she was heavily pregnant with Jimmy's child.[92] As Thistlewood's diary shows, the principle of maternal inheritance functioned to disable the enslaved, like Phoebe, by denying them forms of protection over their bodies, the bodies of their partners, and the bodies of their offspring, which undoubtedly led to high rates of physical, emotional, and psychological impairments.

The deliberate and violent form of enforced "kinlessness" created by maternal inheritance was a form of institutionalized disablement that targeted an entire group of people: African women and their descendants. As a result, enslaved kinlessness was different from other forms of kinlessness—orphanhood, for example—that could befall free people. Slave law had the ability to *deny* the enslaved their family relations, to violate those ties, and to make it so that enslaved individuals could have parents, children, and other kin and yet *not* have them at the same time. The principle of maternal inheritance made the reproduction of "Negroes" a sort of technology of power, one that excluded the enslaved from the benefits of being human.

Slave law also served to disable bondsmen from reproductive agency. The castration of bondsmen was one common punishment ordered by planters; by doing so they demonstrated "the ease with which white men slipped over into treating their [captives] like their bulls and stallions whose 'spirit' could be subdued by emasculation."[93] Unlike animals, however, the enslaved were castrated as *punishment*.[94] Although opaque, the early slave codes of Barbados and Jamaica can be interpreted as sanctioning the castration of enslaved men.[95] The 1661 and 1664 slave codes of Barbados and Jamaica sanctioned "corporall paines or punishments not injurious to life, limb, *or member*."[96] In these laws, the term *member* is used separate from *limb*. In contrast, in the late seventeenth- and early eighteenth-century laws of both islands, *member* is used as a synonym for *limb*. The 1688 Barbados Slave Code referred to punishments that "suffer in life or member," and the 1702 Jamaica law referred to "any member cut off."[97] There are many possible explanations for why in the early slave codes lawmakers were so vague in their use of the word *member*. The laws were written to apply both to men and women, and it may be that the insertion of *member* obliquely sanctioned male castration without having to rewrite the law in gender-specific ways. The inclusion of *member* would have targeted men for punishment, while leaving enslaved women still capable, through rape by white men, of reproducing and thereby of increasing the owner's property. That the law is not clear, however, like so much about slave law, speaks to more than just a desire for economical language. The language of these early laws was deliberately unclear, leaving room for plausible deniability about this practice and about the outright application of practices used for horses and bulls to human beings.[98]

Regardless of the ambiguous language in slave law, castration was in fact practiced on English Caribbean plantations. A physician by trade, Hans Sloane traveled to Barbados in 1687 as the personal doctor to the governor, the Duke of Albermarle.[99] In his travel account, he described the seventeenth-century punishment for enslaved people who participated in violent rebellions. Planters began with "burning them, by nailing them down on the ground with crooked Sticks on every Limb, and then applying the Fire by degrees from the Feet and Hands, burning them gradually up to the Head, whereby their pains are extravagant." According to Sloane, "Gelding, or chopping off half of the Foot with an Ax" were used as punishments "for crimes of a lesser nature."[100] Sloane's use of the term "gelding"—an act reserved for horses—further demonstrates the animalization of the enslaved in England's Caribbean colonies. According to Sloane, the castration of male slaves was a punishment equal to the dismemberment of one's foot, reserved for crimes "of a lesser nature" than rebellion.

Castration was a method of bestializing bondsmen and preventing them from having sex—the "privileged domain of ability"—and biologically fathering children.[101] In the aftermath of a slave conspiracy in 1692, the Barbados Assembly paid one Alice Mills ten guineas for the castration of forty-three rebels.[102] This suggests that there were people—in this case a white woman—who were skilled in castrating men without killing them. Such a technology of violence testifies to disability's function as a penal tool in English Caribbean slave societies. In Jamaica, too, unfree men were castrated following slave uprisings, while in Montserrat, Equiano saw an enslaved man "staked to the ground, and cut most shockingly [i.e., castrated], and then his ears cut off bit by bit, because he had been connected with a white woman who was a common prostitute."[103] In Aphra Behn's novella, Oroonoko is tied to a whipping post, flogged, castrated, and dismembered.[104] Morgan Godwyn, who traveled to Barbados as a missionary in the 1670s, described with distaste the treatment of bondspeople at the hands of their captives, although he offered no opposition to slavery. Godwyn wrote that planters practiced "emasculating and beheading them [the enslaved] ... cropping off their Ears (which they usually cause the Wretches to broil, and then compel to eat them themselves) [and] amputations of legs, and even Dissecting them alive."[105] The emphasis on dismemberment showed that the black male body became a repository for white male anxiety about black men as potential heteropatriarchal rivals. As we see below, for enslaved Africans and their descendants, legally sanctioned corporal punishment was the most distinctive form of disablement.

"That the Mark Thereof May Remain"

The wounds inflicted on enslaved bodies contributed to the creation of a visual world in which bodily mutilation, dark skin, and African phenotypic features were the outward marks of enslaved status.[106] Through physical punishment, lawmakers and slaveholders defined individual captives through signs on her or his body. Scars, amputations, and brands acted as a means of identification, a permanent sign of enslaved status and a visible testament to the bearer's transgressions against the rules of servitude. Brands that scarred slaveowners' and traders' initials into the flesh of the enslaved visibly communicated these individuals' commercial status. Brands that served as punishments—for running away, for instance—made visible the individuals' inner "flaws." The Barbados slave code of 1661 and the Jamaica slave code of 1664 essentially placed slaveowners on par with judges in terms of their ability to interpret the law. Slaveowners were given the power to mete out draconian punishments however they saw fit. Although subsequent laws did not explicitly delegate such sovereignty, neither did they have to, since they were based on an established slave-owning culture that enabled and empowered slaveowners to violently map physical mutilations onto enslaved bodies and in doing so reestablished the notion that Africans' supposed inner degeneracy was manifested onto their skin.

Although spectacle was a key element of penal practice in both England and the Caribbean, its purpose and effect differed according to geographic and sociopolitical locale. In seventeenth- and eighteenth-century England, public forms of punishment were meant to shame the individual criminal and her or his family, and to deter others from criminal activity. They were also, at least partly, a form of entertainment: crowds of men, women, and children joined the spectacle and together shamed the individual while watching the torture.[107] Branding, whipping, nostril slitting, and execution were administered in both the metropole and the colonies.[108] But while English punishments were usually of limited duration, colonial punishments were neither carried out at a fixed place nor performed over a specific span of time, allowing the slaveowner to prolong the event for as long as she or he wished. In the Caribbean, the spectacle of public punishment was not about community, solidarity, and shame but, rather, about *power* and *difference*.[109] In cases of slave uprisings or group crimes, lawmakers in seventeenth-century Jamaica, facing a shortage of bondspeople, ordered the execution of only one criminal as an example to others.[110] This decision was based, of course, on the slaveowners' desire to increase profits and not on the well-being of the enslaved. Likewise, in an attempt to secure future laborers, the Jamaica Assembly forbade the execution of pregnant bondswomen.[111] Even so, if a pregnant woman died during or shortly after punishment, no one was held accountable. Of Jamaica, Charles Leslie wrote: "No country excels them in a barbarous Treatment of Slaves, or in the cruel Methods they put them to Death."[112] Diana Paton's study of court trials in eighteenth-century Jamaica reveals that convicts were frequently sentenced to such punishment (in addition to having their nostrils slit or their ears cut off close to their heads) for crimes such as theft and running away.[113] According to British abolitionists, "by splitting the offence, and inflicting the punishment at intervals," slaveowners were able to "evade" the law.[114] Thus, despite the tension between law and practice, a custom had been established in Jamaica that empowered slaveowners to dismember and punish the enslaved in spite of the law.

The slave laws served to mark captive bodies with signs of criminality, creating a visually striking divide between free and unfree society. Deliberate facial disfiguration was a physical sign of recidivism, one that rendered the enslaved individual's criminal past immediately visible. Although indentured servants were whipped in the seventeenth century, with the replacement of indentured labor with enslaved labor, Caribbean slave societies were sharply divided between white/free and black/enslaved and the punishments sanctioned by law reinforced these legal differences by allocating physical punishment to blacks only. The meaning of disfigurement was heightened by the fact that, as a form of punishment on living bodies, it was an unfamiliar practice in most African societies.[115] In the English Caribbean, though, lawmakers devoted a great deal of attention to the challenge of making disfigurement an enduring mark of slavery's disabling effect. Barbados's 1688 slave code ordered that captives convicted twice of "petty larcenies" should have their nose slit and be "branded in the Forehead with a hot Iron, that the *Mark thereof may remain*."¹¹⁶ Lawmakers italicized the words "mark thereof may remain" to ensure that the punishment inflicted sear the flesh enough to make the brand an indelible defacement on the enslaved body. In Jamaica, it was a felony to deface a brand. The law declared that "whosoever shall steal a slave, or deface his, her or their mark, shall be guilty of felony, and shall be excluded the benefit of clergy."¹¹⁷ In later Barbados law, branding served as the punishment for one's third attempt at running away. The 1731 law ordered that the individual receive thirty-nine lashes on her or his bare back and "be branded in the right cheek with a hot Iron, marked with the letter R."¹¹⁸ Thus was ensured easy identification and the regulation of the bondsperson's mobility, since the captive wore indelible proof of her criminal past on her face and therefore embodied the crime herself.¹¹⁹ Branding also had the power to identify as "disobedient" those captives who had repeatedly committed crimes against their owners, no matter how slight. After years of dealing with Jimmy's defiant behavior, Thomas Thistlewood had Jimmy "flogged, given a new bill and a new hoe, and sent him, by Lincoln, to work with the rest of my negroes." In addition to banishing Jimmy to the fields and whipping him, Thistlewood rebranded Jimmy with Thistlewood's initials on the left shoulder.¹²⁰ It made legible the already "hyper-visible" black body and served as a form of surveillance by publicizing the individual's relationship to slavery both on and off the plantation.

These penalties persisted until the amelioration period, at which point Jamaican authorities removed any direct reference to forms of torture that led to permanent disfigurement and disability, and replaced them with hard labor or death, which they somehow considered less brutal. In 1788, for instance, the Jamaica Assembly declared that for their first offense convicted captives would suffer death or life sentences of hard labor, "or otherwise, as the said justices and freeholders shall in their discretion think proper to inflict."¹²¹ However, the Barbados and Jamaica statutes clarified that bondspeople were excused of such criminal offense if they were found to have acted violently in defense of their owners.

In their 1661 and 1664 slave codes, Barbados and Jamaica, respectively, ruled against "offer[ing] any violence to any Christian as by strikeing or the like."¹²² But although the founding laws dealt specifically with violence against Christians, the centrality of skin color to Jamaica's sociopolitical and legal order was recognized quickly. Indeed, by 1674 the law's wording was changed to "any white Christian," thereby excluding converted blacks and Jews.¹²³ In 1678 the law was amended once more, this time along explicitly racial lines. The law declared that "if any Negro Slaves shall offer any violence by striking or the like to any white person" such bondsperson "shall for the first Offence be severely whipped . . . for the second Offence . . . be severely whipped [and] his or her nose slit, and face burnt in some place." For the third offense, the enslaved individual was to suffer "death or other inferior punishment."[124] By way of comparison, the laws governing the Leeward Islands specified that "if such White Person be any Way hurt, wounded, or disfigured by any Slave's Resistance, such offending Slave or Slaves shall have their Nose slit, or any Member cut off, or be punished with Death."[125] The physical wounding or disfiguring of whites, therefore, was a crime worthy of severe bodily mutilation or death. These kinds of bodily markings were called into being in runaway advertisements to describe and track fugitive bondspeople.

The criminalization of Africans and their descendants through slave law reflected the tensions in the various conceptions of bondspeople as human, as sentient and acting beings, and as property. Seventeenth-century English writer Morgan Godwyn understood the contradictions inherent in slavery's recognition of African humanity. He asked, if Africans were not truly human, "why should they be tormented and whipt almost (and sometimes quite) to death, upon any, whether *small* or great Miscarriages . . . were they (like Brutes) naturally destitute of *Capacities* equal to such undertakings?"[126] English Caribbean slave law was concerned primarily with defining on what grounds bondspeople were allowed to enact their humanity. In 1716 the Jamaica Assembly echoed English treason laws by stipulating the death sentence for any unfree individual who "imagine[s] the Death of any White Person."[127] Colonial treason laws thus equated whiteness with sovereignty. In 1352, King Edward III changed the definition of treason "from behavior to thought, from a physical to a mental action, and from an overt into a covert violation of royal prerogative, extending his control over even the 'imaginings' of subjects." This redefinition meant that any words spoken or written about the king, even without intent to bring about his death, could be interpreted as malicious and, therefore, treasonous.[128] Jamaica law raised all whites to sovereign status and, in doing so, contributed to the abjection of the enslaved. For the enslaved, all crimes could be defined by the state or individual slaveholders as treachery, and, thus, a premeditated criminal act against the order of slave society.[129] As such, slave law inherently criminalized the enslaved.[130] This was further emphasized by the fact that the majority of slave law dealt with offenses—the crime of running away, for example—that, by definition, only an enslaved person could commit. Slave law was intrinsically disabling for the enslaved, for the site of criminality was shifted from the *act* to the *person*.

Limb removal was a technology of violence used against enslaved individuals to disable them from emancipatory potential. The 1661 Barbados Slave Code and the 1664 Jamaica Slave Code specified that enslaved individuals convicted of crimes should suffer "coporall paines or punishments not injurious to life, limb, or member." Runaways were an exception, for if under punishment they "suffer in life or in member noe person whatsoever shall bee accountable to any Law."[131] By 1696, the laws of Jamaica had changed whereby dismemberment was being used as a punishment specifically for bondspeople who fomented rebellion or was suspected of such. The preamble to the 1696 law explained that the "often Insurrections and Rebellions of the Slaves within this Island hath proved the ruin and destruction of several Families" and, therefore, it was necessary that such rebellious bondspeople "be punished according to their Demerit, and their bloody and inhuman practices." An enslaved person found with "clubs, wooden swords, or other mischievous weapons" was to "suffer death, transportation, dismembering, or other punishment, at the discretion of two justices and three freeholders."[132] In 1717 the Jamaica Assembly made it illegal for masters to dismember captives on their own property, though little was done to limit slaveowners' power to damage, as opposed to outright kill, their human property.[133] The preamble to the law suggests that lawmakers were most concerned about planters executing bondspeople without having registered their value to the governor, council, and Jamaica Assembly than to the well-being or fair process of convicted bondspeople.

Some found more inventive ways to impair bondspeople. For instance, in 1780 the *Gentleman's Magazine* in London published an anonymous antislavery letter reporting on the physical disabling of the enslaved in the Caribbean. The author wrote that slaveowners had found "new and ingenious means of tormenting [enslaved Africans] without divesting them of life, which is held valuable, and worth preserving, by no other tenure than the interest of the oppressor who calls himself their master." According to the author, an owner on one of the French islands took his fugitive and tied "up the leg by a chain or rope to the back part of the neck, and fixing a wooden leg to the knee, as a surgeon would do to the stump of an amputated leg." In time, the letter went on, "the joint of the knee becomes contracted, and the negro cannot run away, though he can work with this artificial leg."[134] Disability was thus produced by slavery, not simply in a conceptual way, but through the actual ways in which the enslaved were treated.

These brutal punishments were performed at the cost of reducing the captive's ability to labor productively and at the risk of devaluing her or his worth on the open market, for punitive marks on the enslaved body testified to the supposedly "rebellious" nature of the individual. Plantation management guides and fellow slaveowners encouraged planters to punish bondspeople harshly and swiftly. Jamaican planter and slavery advocate Edward Long placed the onus on Africans' supposedly "intractable and ferocious tempers," which, according to him "naturally provoked their masters to rule them with a rod of iron."[135] Thistlewood described whipping a returned fugitive and then rubbing pepper, salt, and lime juice into the wounds.[136] One eighteenth-century plantation management manual directed planters to gather captives together to witness the punishment of their fellow bondspeople and "to proceed slowly—let the hand of correction be heavy when it falls."[137] In the world of English Caribbean slavery, very particular forms of violence were reserved for very particular kinds of people.

In the Barbados and Jamaica statutes, some of the most brutal corporeal punishments were reserved for runaway and "rebellious" bondspeople in an attempt to disable the spirit and emancipatory instinct of the enslaved. They stipulated that if, during punishment for running away, a captive lost either a limb or her life, the person meting out the punishment could not be held accountable—since whites were rarely held accountable for any damage they inflicted on the enslaved, this statute was more a warning to bondspeople that running away was likely to get them killed.[138] From the first comprehensive codes of Barbados (1661) and Jamaica (1664), lawmakers attempted to entice bondspeople to apprehend runaways with monetary rewards and "a badge of a red cross" to be worn "on his right arme whereby hee may bee knowne and cherished by all good people for the good service to the country."[139] In Jamaica, where marronage—running away as an act of strategic resistance or with the intention of self-emancipation—posed a serious threat to whites, captives who revealed the whereabouts of runaways were rewarded "forty shillings per Head for all Slaves taken and brought in alive, and Twenty shillings per Head for every Slave killed or driven Home." The same reward system applied to rebellious captives. Jamaica law specified that freemen or servants who "kill or take any rebellious slave or slaves . . . shall forthwith receive as a reward five pounds currant money."[140] If, however, a bondsperson captured or killed a "rebellious slave," she or he was awarded forty shillings and "a serge coat with a red cross on the right shoulder."[141]

This "red cross" identified the individual as a turncoat. At the same time, it offered the informant an opportunity to conceal her or his body under this garment—in stark contrast with the bodily exposure experienced by runaways. The coat also worked as a form of surveillance among the enslaved population, a policing measure that served constantly to remind bondspeople that their actions were on display. When a bondsperson committed an offense, her or his body was criminalized through violent inflictions that attempted to shame and identify the individual as a threat to white society; the same logic was at play when an enslaved individual captured or killed a rebellious captive. The black body, when it betrayed other black bodies, went unpunished; instead it was adorned with a coat of "honor" that visually identified the bondsperson's ostensible loyalty to whites. Such clothing, then, served as a mark of obedience that distinguished the informer from the disfigured, disabled, and exposed body of the rebel. At any moment, however, the ostensibly loyal bondsperson could find her or himself on the receiving end of a more permanent marking should her or his behavior change.

The visual world created by these types of punishments continued even in death, where black corpses were mutilated, disfigured, and dismembered. During and after execution the enslaved body's materiality was essential to its negative symbolic power. For "heinous" crimes such as robbery, murder, killing or maiming of cattle, and rape, bondspeople were sentenced to death in both Jamaica and Barbados. After the public executions, the prisoner's corpse was often displayed in significant places—under a cotton tree, at the scene of the crime, outside the slave's residence. Such a spectacle transcended time, making the past immediately present to those who remained in slavery.[142] Arriving in Savanna la Mar in Jamaica in 1750, Thistlewood described how his host, William Dorrill, ordered the corpse of a runaway dug up and beheaded, the head fixed on a pole, and the body reduced to ashes. In October 1751, Thistlewood emulated this practice when he took the head of a runaway, "put it upon a pole and stuck it up just at the angle of the road in the home pasture."[143] But the immediate effects of this practice were almost less important than the memories it imprinted on enslaved passersby. As Vincent Brown argues, "the recycling of these kinds of stories re-introduced past evidence of white power to the present and fastened it to particular places through the bodies of the dead."[144] The dismembered corpse, like the dismembered living body, held significant power in slave society. It served to create a visual grotesquerie out of the black body—a monster that haunted slave society.

The power to cause disability, and to link disability to the shifting boundary between humanity and enslavement, was a hallmark of slave-owning power. Slave law had a vital role in this dynamic by suspending the enslaved between human and animal, in a space of abjection, where lawmakers recognized the humanity of the enslaved but effectively disabled it by treating Africans and their descendants like animals. The principle of maternal inheritance positioned African women in a category equivalent to animals and only recognized their humanity when it suited slaveowner interests. Slave law took place within a "field of pain and death." Lawmakers, who were themselves slaveowners, punished the enslaved with impunity. Slave law disabled the enslaved both discursively and physically. This almost sovereign power resulted in legally sanctioned punishments that disabled the enslaved both physically and psychologically. In addition to the physical violence endured by the enslaved, slave law also served to limit bondspeople's mobility and freedom of movement.

The racial logic that upheld Atlantic slavery left little room to view the deliberate disabling of captives as problematic, for according to that logic the institution of slavery was merely disabling the "already disabled." Thus, black bodies were physically or intellectually impaired *by* certain types of legal discrimination. Excluded from subjecthood and citizenship and reduced to property, excommunicated from society and removed from the protections offered to its free members, the enslaved lived in a space of abjection. The slave laws worked to position bondspeople in naked exploitation, even if captives' acts of autonomy and volition continuously demonstrated the limits of the dehumanization of Africans by English Caribbean slave law.

Through legally sanctioned punishments, the black body became codified; it became a sort of text, a living reminder to both whites and blacks of slaveowners' arbitrary sovereignty over enslaved bodies, and of bondspeople's refusal to accept the terms of their enslavement. Disability functioned in slave society not only as an individual physical condition or impairment, but also as a social, political, and economic process of oppression. What is more, slave law and racial ideology *created* a distinct legal category of disablement, which was applied to enslaved Africans in order to exploit them and to enable slaveowners to destroy them through disabling punishments. Slavery relied on, and the enslaved lived in, a space between the endless violence of slave law and the complex possibilities of the corporeal.

CHAPTER 3

Unfree Labor
and Industrial Capital

Fitness, Disability, and Worth

Slavery thus is not an aberration of modernity, as
liberal humanists claim, but rather essential to its
paradigm.

—Hershini Bhana Young, *Haunting Capital: Memory,*
Text and the Black Diasporic Body

In 1796, Sampson Wood, manager of the Newton plantation in Christ Church,
Barbados, wrote his annual report. It was typical of plantation reports in the
British Caribbean in that it contained little information about the enslaved that
did not fit into certain identifying categories: the age, sex, employment, kin,
and physical and mental conditions of each enslaved individual on the estate.
In his conclusion, however, Wood displayed obvious pride in the fact that,
despite the physical toll that slavery exacted from its subjects, the majority of
the forced laborers on the Newton plantation had contributed to plantation
production. Of those who did not contribute, due to illness or impairment,
Wood expressed his disdain and his desire to have them leave the plantation:

> You will perceive by this list that all who can be of any service in the planta-
> tion are put to some occupation or other. All have something to do, except
> diseased people and cripples, or those who have a kind of right to be idle, as
> it were, by prescription & long (I must say bad) habit, for it is an ill example
> to the other people on the estate & indeed a hardship for whilst they are
> labouring, those are at their . . . leisure, & have the same daily food, cloath-

ing, and allowed them & more than the labourers. I wish they would take
themselves off to a distance, as Becky did, I am sure I should not hinder them.[1]

The presence of disabled individuals on the plantation, according to Wood,
created animosity among the "able-bodied" laborers because the disabled received the same provisions but did not produce an equal amount of work. Of
course, the "ill example" is from Wood's perspective and not from the enslaved
themselves. Although it is difficult to access the voice of the disabled bondsperson from the archives, ex-slave narratives provide some indication of how the
enslaved responded to those who became impaired in enslavement. While on
Grand Turk Island in the early nineteenth century, Mary Prince witnessed an
enslaved man named Daniel who was "lame in the hip, and could not keep up
with the rest of the slaves," a failure for which he was subjected to his master's
sadistic and incapacitating punishments. "He was an object of pity and terror
to the whole gang of slaves," Prince wrote, "and in his wretched case we saw,
each of us, our own lot, if we should live to be so old."[2] Prince suggested that
the enslaved viewed such physical conditions not as a personal tragedy, but
rather as a direct result of enslavement—a condition to which all forced laborers were susceptible. Wood's complaint, therefore, should likely be interpreted
as a projection of his own aversion to nonworking African bondspeople, and
not a transparent reflection of what enslaved people thought of the disabled
among them.

Wood desired that disabled individuals remove themselves "as Becky did."
The Newton inventories do not detail who Becky was or where she went, and
it is unknown under what circumstances she left. Did Becky leave on her own
volition, or was she driven off by the cruelty of an unsatisfied manager or slaveowner? Did her physical disability, clearly a liability as far as Wood was concerned, enable her to leave a life of enslavement? If so, how did Becky cope as
a disabled self-emancipated black woman off the plantation?

The answers to these questions may always elude us, of course. But we do
know that Becky's manager viewed her as a useless worker because of her physical condition. Wood's construction of disability as an impairment that nega-
tively affected the relationship between impaired and able-bodied bondspeople,
and therefore plantation life more broadly, shows that a modern understanding
of disability began to emerge in the capitalist world of Atlantic slavery, one
that distinguished between impairment as a physical reality and disability as a
socially and historically constructed category. According to disability scholars,
physical impairments and anomalies took on new significations with the onset
of industrialization in mid-nineteenth-century Europe and North America,

when "disability" in its modern sense emerged.[3] Advocates of this approach argue that the new definition emerged because industrialization changed the way impairment was understood. Although features of industrial capitalism existed in the early modern period, the intensification of economic logic that characterized nineteenth- and twentieth-century industrial capitalism changed the perception of physical impairment, whereby "the impaired body had become disabled—unable to be part of the productive economy, confined to institutions, shaped to contours defined by society at large."[4]

The colonial Caribbean confounds this chronology and the implicitly Eurocentric geography of disability history.[5] As a "synthesis of field and factory," sugar plantations were dependent on field labor and on workers' technical mastery and skilled artisanal knowledge.[6] Sugar production was a precociously industrial and modern undertaking. Nevertheless, the Caribbean and the enslaved continue to be "expunged from the figurative time-space of 'Western modernity.'"[7] When disability is placed at the center of an analysis of Atlantic slavery, it demands that we rethink timelines of disability history, not only in terms of temporality but also of material and conceptual borders between the metropole and the colony, and between free-white and enslaved-black working bodies.

Enslaved people lived in the space between fitness and death, a space of physical debilitation resulting not only from natural processes like aging but from enslavement itself. Scholars of slavery often treat mortality statistics as the ultimate indicators of the well-being of the enslaved population, and death as the exemplary image of slavery's brutality.[8] While premature, painful, and often violent death was an integral aspect of slavery, the space between fitness and death—comprised above all by a methodical disfiguring and disabling of the body—characterized the majority of one's life in enslavement. I define fitness as not merely being physically capable of performing hard labor, as many enslaved individuals were despite compromising illnesses, impairments, and malnutrition; rather, fitness was representative of the ideal enslaved body, one that was young and free from disease, impairment, deformity, and other corporeal challenges that planters and traders desired. The fit enslaved body was the ideal body and, as such, it was virtually unattainable once it entered the economy of Atlantic slavery due to the debilitating nature of enslavement. The state of slavery—the labor, punishment, and material neglect that characterized enslaved people's lives—worked at every level to undermine the state of fitness that planters and merchants demanded. Although merchants and slaveowners claimed to desire enslaved individuals whose bodies were strong and healthy and, therefore, fit to perform the physically taxing labor required of sugar production, they quite literally destroyed this ideal body in order to create a labor force that was still capable of plantation production but was physically, emotionally, and psychologically subdued.

The space between fitness and death was not static. The enslaved moved in and out of this liminality. For instance, in plantation records, white authorities often listed young children as "not fit to do anything," indicating that their bodies were not mature enough to constitute fit for sugar production.[9] Others acquired diseases like smallpox or the yaws and while quarantined were removed from the space between fitness and death. In tandem, the ideal enslaved laborer was not the same for everyone. Slave ship merchants, for instance, desired captives whose bodies could survive the traumas of the Middle Passage and then secure the highest bid on Caribbean auction blocks. This meant that merchants rejected captives who showed any signs of incurable disabilities and infirmities, such as lameness and old age. Caribbean planters, in contrast, had a different economic context in which they valued enslaved laborers. Once enslaved Africans entered the economic world of Atlantic slavery, they became commodities whose bodies were used for production until they were useless to plantation production. This meant that, unlike merchants, planters did not reject the ill and the disabled but found new ways to obtain profit from such bodies through any means necessary.

The physical destruction endured by African bondspeople was the result of a system based on the legal disablement, punishment, and enslavement of the so-called monster. "As an instrument of labour," writes Achille Mmembe, "the slave has a price. His or her labour is needed and used. The slave is therefore kept alive but in a *state of injury*, in a phantom-like world of horrors and intense cruelty and profanity."[10] In this chapter, I explore this "state of injury." In so doing I draw on Nirmala Erevelles's argument that "race and disability are imbricated in their collective formation of the black disabled body."[11] This chapter begins with a discussion of the Middle Passage as one of the first stages of slavery-induced disability. Although slaveowners and traders desired a bondsperson who was physically and psychologically healthy, slavery worked to systematically weaken and debilitate the enslaved from the very moment of their seizure in sub-Saharan Africa. By the time the slave ship reached the coasts of the Caribbean, the captive Africans' bodies bore the marks of slavery's violence. Those who survived the Middle Passage were placed on the open market, their worth calculated based on their physical ability to perform hard labor. Once on the plantation, the enslaved endured hostile living conditions, legally sanctioned punishments and the chance violence of masters, overseers, and drivers, and brutal forms of labor, all of which could result in disability. By exploring these three sites of slavery-induced disability—the Middle Passage, the market, and the plantation—this chapter demonstrates that the "state of injury" produced by Atlantic slavery is key to understanding these connections.

The Middle Passage: Producing Impairment

The seizure of Africans, which marked their initial transformation into commodities for the international market, also initiated their "state of injury."[12] The traumas of capture, forced marches, and incarceration required a particular kind of violence, one that created and kept the enslaved in a state of injury. This first phase of the disabling process broadens our understandings of the traumas of slavery by looking at the ways in which disability functioned as a crucial means of creating the space between fitness and death from the very beginning of capture. The coffle of captives traveled hundreds of miles before reaching coastal trading factories, and by the time they reached the coast, "bruises covered [captives'] arms and legs, which had been cut and pricked on branches and thorns in narrow forest paths that admitted only one person at a time."[13] Bondspeople disappeared along the way—those who could not keep up with the strenuous journey, including pregnant women, were left for dead or died en route; others were sold at inland markets. Only the lucky escaped and prevented their enslavement.[14] Iron abraded their wrists, ankles, and necks, causing open sores and contusions. They were given very little food or water on the journey, which caused "sunken cheeks and distended bellies." On reaching the coasts, they were imprisoned in the dungeons of trading factories while they awaited transportation to the Americas. On the same floor where they slept and ate, they also defecated, which facilitated the spread of diseases. Their diets were inadequate to provide calorie and nutritional needs: corn and a grain prepared following local custom called cankey.[15]

Each of these depravations was disfiguring in its way, and they served to emphasize individuals' captive status, thereby making it extremely difficult for them to escape without being recognized as escapees. Perhaps even more emblematic was the practice of branding, which served as one of the first physical manifestations of the newly commodified enslaved body and gave corporeal permanence to the belief that Africans could be treated like domestic animals.[16] As one of the key technologies of the transatlantic slave trade, branding thereby marked a "theft of the body—a willful and violent . . . severing of the captive body from its motive will, its active desire."[17] Traders and planters used hot irons to sear the flesh and mark the bondsperson with signs of sovereign ownership—either the trader's or the planter's initials. This mark of bondage made visible the body's relationship to its owner; as such, it served as a form of identification and surveillance. But it also stigmatized the bondsperson with disgrace.[18] Branding, in other words, along with myriad other marks of punishment, worked to shame the enslaved by permanently inscribing black bodies with criminality and chattel status. In particular, disfigurements caused by punishment and impairment carried a stigma that disabled the enslaved by decreasing an individual's "worth" on the open market.

Saidiya Hartman suggests that captives revalued their brands as a means to establish kinship ties. "The mark of property," she writes, "provides the emblem of kinship in the wake of defacement. It acquires the character of a personal trait, as though it were a birthmark."[19] Hartman uses Toni Morrison's *Beloved* to demonstrate this point. The mother of Sethe, the novel's protagonist, points to the brand mark on her rib and says to her daughter, "This is your ma'am.... If something happens to me and you can't tell me by my face, you can know me by this mark."[20] Hartman draws the harrowing connections between Sethe's mother's brand and the principle of maternal inheritance when she writes that "the stamp of the commodity haunts the maternal line and is transferred from one generation to the next. The daughter, Sethe, will carry the burden of her mother's dispossession and inherit her dishonored condition, and she will have her own mark soon enough, as will her daughter Beloved."[21] Hartman's analysis of Morrison's text explores how survivors of slavery might have revalued physical stigma. The brand's acquisition of value as a sign of kinship and love, however, could not displace its value as a sign of property. The brand, therefore, tied kinship inextricably to pain and loss.

The next stage in the transatlantic journey, the Middle Passage, constituted an important moment in the production of enslaved disability. Enslavement denied Africans' kinship ties and "robbed them of the markers of their social existence."[22] This "social death" produced disability—giving rise to psychological pain and trauma that disabled the enslaved by alienating them from the meanings associated with the human experience. Through violence and terror, the "ship-factory" served to produce the labor power on which plantations ran: the commodity called "slave" to be sold on the open market once reaching the Americas.[23] It was in this precise historical context that "black bodies became disabled and disabled bodies became black."[24] One of the contradictions of Atlantic slavery was that despite using disabling violence against captive Africans at every stage of their enslavement—keeping them alive but in a "state of injury"—slavery was premised on the desire for physically fit and healthy enslaved laborers who could make both merchants and slaveowners considerable profit. Ship doctors were responsible for helping ship captains weed out the sick, the physically and intellectually impaired, and the otherwise compromised—the elderly for instance—from the able-bodied to secure the very best captive bodies. Buyers in the Americas desired enslaved bodies capable of hard labor, while traders on the African coasts desired individuals who they estimated might survive the horrors of forced migration.[25] Alexander Falconbridge, a slave ship surgeon (1780–87) who became an abolitionist, explained that when the traders reached the African coast, the captain and surgeon inspected each individual captive to "inquire into the state of their health." According to Falconbridge, "if they [Africans] are afflicted with any infirmity, or are deformed, or have bad eyes or teeth; if they are lame, or weak in their joints, or distorted in the back, or of a slender make, or are narrow in the chest; in short, if they have been, or are afflicted in any manner, as to render them incapable of much labour; if any of the foregoing defects are discovered in them, they are rejected."[26] African women were inspected for two other qualities: beauty and reproductive potential.[27] For instance, slave ship captain John Newton routinely rejected female captives who were "long breasted," and "ill made"; in other words, past their reproductive years. On his first voyage to Africa in 1750, Newton purchased one captive female, "No. 46" but lamented that "she had a very bad mouth" and he "could have bought her cheaper . . . but the trade is at such a pass that they will very seldom bring a slave to a ship to sell." Newton also rejected four captives for being "all old." Impairment and old age among captives were therefore undesirable outcomes for slave traders, whose goal was to secure a good fortune through the sale of "fit" captives on reaching the Americas. The often devastating impact that capture, forced march, and imprisonment had on captive bodies did not prevent slave ship captains from purchasing them. John Newton noted that one of his female captives, "No. 47," died before the ship had set sail for the Caribbean, but he did not know what caused her death "for she ha[d] not been properly alive since she first came on board."[28]

Daily medical logs of slave-ship physicians such as the 1792 log of physician for the *Lord Stanley* Christopher Bowes, offer chilling evidence of the crippling conditions of the Middle Passage. The slave ship the *Lord Stanley* was moored on the West African coast as its captain gathered human cargo over two months. The ship set sail for Grenada on 27 June with 389 African captives in the hold.[29] The conditions on board a slave ship were so hostile that in the eighteenth century slave traders referred to slave ships as *tumbeiros*, translated variously as "floating tombs" or "undertakers." In the seventeenth and eighteenth centuries, more than three hundred captives were forced into the hold of the average ship bound for the Americas. Like the dungeons of the trading factories, overcrowding, poor hygiene, and contaminated food and water in the slave ship's lower decks made for a breeding ground of diseases such as smallpox, tuberculosis, bacillary, dysentery, and the yaws.[30] For the first month of Bowes's record, he referred to individual captives by their gender and age designation—"a girl," "a boy," "a woman," and "a man." By the end of the second month, by which point approximately 147 captives were on the ship, Bowes began to assign enslaved individuals a number. A typical entry from this period reads "the man No. 14 senseless in the morning at 11 A.M. died." This shift in practice, from referring to Africans by their age and gender to gender and number, offer evidence of slavery's recognition of African humanity ("the man;" "a girl") and its ability to disable that humanity by relegating it to a place of commodification ("No. 14").[31] And yet, the humanity of bondspeople consistently interrupted this process: put simply, Africans' need for basic medical care testified to Bowes's selective recognition of Africans' intrinsic, if exploitable, humanity.

The illnesses and diseases suffered by the enslaved during the Middle Passage were not always physically disabling, but they were essential to the production of impairment among bondspeople in the British Atlantic world. As on-board captives, enslaved individuals were not yet laboring bodies, as they would become on the plantation. And yet, the malnutrition and harsh living conditions that characterized the Middle Passage, which in the eighteenth century lasted an average of two to three months, and by which impairment was produced, were essential to the creation of the liminal space between fitness and death. Sickness and disease weakened the bodies and spirits of captives, and made them more vulnerable to other kinds of illnesses and impairments they would encounter on the plantation. What is more, many of the physically debilitating conditions experienced by the enslaved were in fact caused by illness and disease, which testifies to both the linkages and divergences between disease and chronic illness, on the one hand, and disability and physical debility on the other. On 12 April, just three weeks after the first captive African came aboard the *Lord Stanley*, and before the ship had even set sail, Bowes recorded his first treatment of a "sick slave," "a girl [who] complained of pain in the bowels with diarrhea." The most common "disorders" Bowes treated were "attacks of the stomach," "pains in the bowels with diarrhea," "difficulty breathing," and "pains in the breast."[32] The language used to describe captives' illnesses as "disorders" testifies to the ways in which such illnesses produced disability.

In Atlantic slavery, illness and disability often went hand and hand and reinforced each other. According to British abolitionist William Wilberforce, the "fixed dejection and melancholy" of the enslaved over "their concern for the loss of their relations and friends, and native country" caused them to become physically ill with the flux. Their "state of mind produced a general languor and debility, which were increased in many instances by an unconquerable abstinence from food, arising partly from sickness, partly, to use the language of Slave Captains, from 'sulkiness.'" Other severely ill captives refused medical treatment as an act of resistance and subsequently died. For instance, on 28 June: "A man No. 18 complained of pain in the right knee and left ancle with swelling of each." The following day he was "attacked with diarrhea." By 4 July he "would take no nourishment," and the next morning he died.[33] The psychological disability caused by capture and enslavement generated periods of physical debilitation and the physical illness brought on by the hostile conditions of captivity in turn caused psychological trauma that could lead to suicide.

Slave ship records indicate that a range of different bodies in varying degrees of health were transferred to the Caribbean slavers, and only those whom surgeons and captains deemed incurable were rejected from slave ships. While the *Lord Stanley* was moored on the African coast, three disabled captives were removed from the ship and returned to the shore.[34] The first, according to Bowes's 9 April 1792 entry, was a "man that was lame in his arm. . . . The boy received on the 10th was in place of the man sent ashore." It is likely that the man's impairment was acquired during his capture and enslavement, for a preexisting impairment would have dissuaded slave raiders, ship captains, and others from selling the individual in the first place.[35] Two months later, a "man boy affected with epilepsy" was "sent ashore."[36] In the world of Atlantic slavery, epilepsy was a feared disease that both traders and planters associated with insanity and uncontrollability. As a condition characterized by the uncontrolled body, epilepsy took on particular cultural relevance in slave societies, for in its disorder it threatened the very foundations of the institution of slavery—namely, whites' power and control over African bodies.[37] The third and final individual removed from the *Lord Stanley* was a man with dysentery. On 15 June, nine captives complained of symptoms of the "bloody flux," as the disease was known at the time. Brought on by overcrowding and contaminated food and water supplies, the bloody flux attacked the stomach and bowels and was the leading cause of death in slave trading factories and ships.[38] One of the nine captives, "a man No. 7 complained of pains in the bowels with diarrhea," and his condition worsened each day that Bowes inspected him. On 21 June, the man had not improved with the medical treatment prescribed and was therefore "sent ashore."[39] The man was not rejected because he had dysentery but because he was incurable. The flux was so common in the hold of slave ships that John Newton complained that after sending a girl captive ashore because she had the flux, he "had 5 slaves taken with the same disorder [flux] within these 2 days, but am unable to account for it or to remedy it."[40]

Disabled African captives who were rejected by slave ship captains were often met with violent and sometimes fatal treatment on the trading coasts of West Africa. Take for example the slave traders of New Calabar (modern-day Nigeria), who had a reputation for murdering rejected disabled captives. "Instances have happened at that place," wrote Falconbridge, "that the traders, when any of their negroes have been objected to, have dropped their canoes under the stern of the vessel, and instantly beheaded them, in the sight of the captain."[41] The violent abuse and murder of disabled captives whom captains deemed unfit for servitude reflected the capitalist and racist logic of Atlantic slavery. Thus, while disability may have prevented individuals from being enslaved and transported to the Americas, it did not protect them from the violence that often accompanies disability.

The ravages of the Atlantic voyage were such that the price fetched for those who survived often doubled, and yet, in a seeming contradiction of this process, these very conditions also diminished individual bondspeople's ability to perform labor. The healthiest-looking cargo was therefore sold immediately to eager planters, while the sick and disabled lingered, sometimes for months, eventually to be sold for the lowest prices. This economic reality places the purposeful disabling of captives on plantations in the realm of the paradoxical. But we would do well to remember that the production of disability within Atlantic slavery was not simply or fundamentally economic. Enslaved individuals whom planters deemed too "defective" to purchase due to physical or mental impairments (also called refuse slaves) were abandoned by traders in the Americas.[42] Atlantic slavery was a capitalistic system of power and exploitation whose resulting forms of value were measured in various ways. Slaveowners and merchants calculated that the debilitation of enslaved bodies might result in an immediate loss to their labor force, but such losses were temporary. The power and racial privilege they gained through the deliberate and systematic disabling of captives, on the other hand, lasted a lifetime.

The Slave Market:
Bodies, Value, and Disability

The slave market determined levels of fitness primarily by Africans' physical appearance, which was thought to indicate not just physical fitness, but moral and intellectual fitness as well.[43] While gender and age were important features in establishing prices within the slave market, disability played the most significant role in determining trading prices.[44] The health and condition of the enslaved were so crucial to the sale of the enslaved that on the auction blocks of Jamaica and in the port towns of Barbados, traders attempted to disguise the physical and psychological traumas of the Middle Passage in order to se-cure the highest offer. Because while gender was a factor in establishing prices within the slave market, the physical and psychological health and condition of the enslaved played the most significant role in determining trading prices. In his *Voyage to Jamaica*, Hans Sloane, a physician, slaveowner, and founder of the British Museum, wrote that "when a *Guinea* Ship corners near *Jamaica* with Blacks to sell, there is great care taken that the *Negros* should be shav'd, trim'd, and their Bodies and Hair anointed all over with Palm-Oil, which adds a great beauty to them."[45]

For planters, an impaired or severely ill bondsperson was worth less, both in terms of cost and labor efficiency, than an individual who appeared "healthy." For instance, runaway advertisements offer further evidence of the significance of visible and invisible afflictions in determining how slaveholding authorities calculated a bondsperson's worth. It was common for subscribers of runaway advertisements to offer rewards to individuals who apprehended fugitives. These rewards can be read as a reflection of this economy of worth and the way in which disability shaped one's worth as a forced laboring body. For instance, a 1780 advertisement in the Jamaican press recorded three bondsmen by the names of Jamaica, James, and Sambo. Jamaica was described as "of the Mungola country . . . about five feet three inches high, pretty stout made . . . about forty five years of age . . . and has been used to the brick making and fishing business." James was "of the Congo country . . . about 50 or 55 years of age, walks very lame, by trade a bricklayer," and Sambo as "a creole very old, his head quite white, pretends to be blind." The men's owner, Richard Latimer, offered a reward of £10 for Jamaica but only half a Joe (a Portuguese gold coin) each for James and Sambo.[46] Though all three bondsmen were skilled laborers, Jamaica's younger age and physical health and abilities likely drove his value higher than James and Sambo, two older men with various physical limitations. Unlike in some other capitalist contexts, such as industrialized Europe and North America, though, impairment did not exclude the enslaved from production, for enslaved bodies were property and as property it was their bodies and lives that were owned, not their time. Therefore, slaveowners could still profit from the labor of physically debilitated bondspeople and literally work them to death, until their bodies no longer had any economic use to them. The space between fitness and death served a purpose for slaveowners, for it suspended the enslaved in a liminal space where their bodies were too broken to rebel but were fit enough for forced labor. The physical toll exacted by the Middle Passage, then, was no accidental by-product, but rather an integral part of the enforced disablement, both physical and psychological, of the enslaved in the English Atlantic world.

As did manufacturers in industrial England, the profit-hungry Caribbean planter desired a labor force that was both physically and intellectually able to perform industrial labor. John Dovaston, a Jamaican plantation manager—and later a noted botanist in England—authored a plantation management guide in which he claimed that "the tokens of a sound and good negroe are let them be young and stoutly set in limbs, strait a full open eye, the tongue red, a broad large chest wide shoulders." Traders and planters, Dovaston continued, should strive to purchase bondspeople with "belly small, not large and watery, clean and strong bodys, large thighs and legs, and strain and of equal length." The detail with which Dovaston described the ideal enslaved laborer testifies to the importance of physical ability and well-being in constructing an efficient unfree labor force. Captives whose bodies bore the scars of smallpox and the yaws were marketed at a higher price because their bodies gave evidence of the individual's immunity to such illnesses. The hostile environment of slavery was a form of disablement that predisposed bondspeople to diseases, which caused temporary and permanent impairments and the marks left in the wake of such diseases increased an individual's economic value as property. Yet, because captives were "socially dead" people, the effects of disablement did not socially enable *them*, but rather worked to socially and economically enable *slaveowners*. Slaveowners financially benefitted from the sale of enslaved individuals who had survived and gained immunity to such disfiguring and sometimes debilitating diseases.

African bondspeople's minds were also key features of the enslaved labor force, whose ideal members were not only physically fit but intellectually pliable. Dovaston warned merchants and planters to "be careful that they are not foolish, which you may judge by their looks and attention on you." Those from the Congo, Dovaston claimed, were more "refined" in their senses, and "well featured, straight limb'd, and more tractable and easily taught to labour." Creoles, however, were the most sought-after laborers because "they understand the language you discourse in . . . and being born with you and his parents with him, he doth not think his labour slavery, and having never known any other goes with cheerfulness about it." Ibo and Gold Coast Africans were supposedly the best field laborers because "their disposition is dull and stupid and only fit for labour."[47] Of course, perceived intellectual disability has played a substantive role in justifying Africans' inferior status at different times in history.[48] But the twinning of intellectual disability and Africanness was taken further in the context of Atlantic slavery: it was inscribed in legislative acts, travel narratives, bills of sale, plantation accounts, and management guides. It served to make disability a more "real" and degrading "defect," and it worked as a powerful tool to deprive Africans and their descendants of political and social status, thereby positioning them in a subhuman status and transforming their bodies into commodities of exchange for the open market.

The slave market also assigned categories of monetary value to the various African ethnicities found in the British Caribbean in an attempt to create the "ideal" enslaved laborer as a tradeable commodity with a price. The trade in slaves was therefore governed by yet another logical contradiction. On the one hand it sought to forge a single, monolithic "race" from the many cultures, religions, physical appearances found in sub-Saharan Africa, while on the other it employed specific geographic and ancestral markers to better commodify captives. Indeed, planters were encouraged to make certain that their captives "come from a good part of that coast for the temper and dispositions, manners and complexions of negroes differ much according to the different parts of the coast of Africa where they are bought."[49] For planters, such qualities ensured efficient production and helped curb any threats to the social order of plantation society. In the second half of the eighteenth century, the British increasingly claimed that particular African ethnicities were either more or less "fit" for enslavement based on their supposed intellectual and physical capacities.[50] At the same time, however, they claimed that *all* Africans were suitable for slavery. The use of African ethnic stereotypes by the British served to reinforce the belief that the "race" of Africans were "defined according to its ability to serve."[51] Writing in the late eighteenth century, a formerly enslaved person turned abolitionist, Olaudah Equiano recalled planters' taste for "slaves of Benin or Eboe to those of any other part of Guinea, for their hardiness, intelligence, integrity, and zeal."[52] Equiano's description of these ethnicities must be analyzed in the context of abolition, and the role played by disability rhetoric in that struggle.[53] His comments rebutted proslavery claims that the physical and intellectual defects of Africans made them fit for servitude. For instance, he countered the European stereotype of the subservient Ibo by declaring that "deformity is indeed unknown amongst us, I mean that of shape." He continued refutation of proslavery arguments that slavery "saved" Africans from the brutalities of their homeland and testified to the psychological wounds of enslavement. "Our women" he wrote, "were . . . uncommonly graceful, alert, and modest to a degree of bashfulness. . . . They are also remarkably cheerful. Indeed, cheerfulness and affability are two of the leading characteristics of our nation."[54]

While acquiescent workers were central to the creation of an efficient labor force in both the Caribbean and metropolitan Britain, planters' fear of slave insurrections, coupled with the intense racial division of plantation society, meant that the desire for "non-rebellious" captives was acute. Marks of punishment—such as marks from the whip or missing ears—testified to the supposed rebellious nature of the individual and consequently averted potential buyers. In his description of sadistic slave punishments, Sloane mentioned that the scars from the whip "are on their Skins for ever after; and a Slave, the more he have of those, is the less valu'd."[55] He explained that "bad" slaves who "mutinour in plantations . . . are sold to very good profit," but "if they have many cicatrices, or scars on them, the marks of their severe corrections, they are not very saleable." Planters were to steer clear of the Coromantees—those from Akan in modern-day Ghana—"the most vicious and desperate slaves" who "if young," John Dovaston warned his fellow plantation managers, "their disposition is so ill suited to slavery and if old they will die before they will submit."[56] The ethnic labels assigned to Africans by the British did not necessarily reflect where African-born captives were actually from—they often referred to the location from which they left Africa—but the popular representation, in this case of "Coromantees," demonstrates the historical linkages between perceived disability and enslaveability. According to this logic, Coromantees' "vicious and desperate" natures made them more difficult to control than other Africans. Slave traders viewed this refusal to accept enslavement as a disability—an incapacity stemming from a desire for freedom. Europeans' application of African regional designations created a competitive market in which traders and planters vied and paid premium prices for the most desirable commodities. Traders' and planters' ability to pick and choose the "fittest" human commodities, which they then forced into a system of enslavement that routinely disabled human bodies, reconfirmed for whites their dominion over blacks and solidified Africans' abject condition in the economy of the Atlantic World.

Such instructions regarding the threat posed by Coromantees reflected the widespread fear among planters, and white society more broadly, of enslaved revolts and rebellions in the British Caribbean, especially in Jamaica. Although planters perceived Coromantees to be hardworking and loyal (if they could gain their loyalty), they also believed they had led the majority of revolts, conspiracies, and insurrections during the first century of British Caribbean slavery.[57] For instance, whites believed that Coromantees were responsible for plotting the uprising in Barbados in 1675 and had led Tacky's War, the 1760 slave rebellion, both of which resulted in new laws that sanctioned more draconian punishments against rebellious bondspeople and came down hard on the Afro-Creole spiritual practice Obeah.[58] Rebellions throughout the Atlantic World were often associated with the Afro-Creole religious practices of the enslaved. Obeah was believed to play an important role in organizing Tacky's War, which led colonial officials to pass anti-Obeah legislation in 1760. Similarly, many of the leaders of the Haitian Revolution (1791–1804) were vodou priests.

Obeah and other Afro-Creole religions like Vodou revalued disability among bondspeople as a spiritual gift, further illustrating that understandings of disability among Africans and their descendants in the New World could differ markedly from those of white colonists. The trust placed in an Obeah practitioner was often tied to her or him having a physical disability. A clubfoot, a deformed hand, or a blind eye, to name several common ailments, was interpreted as a sign that nature had compensated the Obeah man or woman with a higher degree of supernatural ability.[59] We see this in the case of Makandal, the leader of a Maroon community who plotted to poison the water supply in Le Cap decades before the Haitian Revolution: after losing his arm in the sugar mill, he became famous as a healer.[60] This visibility, in turn, enabled Makandal to organize such a large-scale plot. In this context, at least, disability functioned as a community-building tool and a marker of power and authority.

Plantation accounts provide important insights into slaveowners' views of the relationship between disability and forced labor. But while these records are an invaluable source for the study of the intersection of disability and slavery, many tend to mention disability only when such impairment threatened an individual's capacity as a laboring body. The language that managers used to describe these individuals generally fit three categories: superannuated, infirm, and invalid. Although their meaning overlapped, each category was used to describe a specific kind of disabling condition. For instance, "superannuated" described those "disqualified or incapacitated by age; old and infirm." Managers most often applied this to elderly people, older than sixty-five years of age, who could no longer work.[61] "Infirm" described individuals who were "not strong and healthy; physically weak and feeble, especially through age"; enslaved individuals categorized as such were usually over the age of thirty.[62] The term "invalid" is perhaps the closest equivalent to the modern term "disabled." Defined as "infirm from sickness or disease; enfeebled or diseased by illness or injury," managers used this to describe individuals of all ages, from the very young to the very old, who could not contribute to plantation production due to physical disability.[63] While some intellectually and psychologically disabled individuals were also placed in these categories, managers often simply designated these individuals as "mad."

The making of modern categories of labor was predicated on the valuation of impairments. The records of the Newton and Seawell estates, in Christ Church, Barbados, list large numbers of bondspeople categorized as diseased, infirm, superannuated, crippled, or otherwise physically or mentally "incapacitated." Among the sick or disabled, an individual's worth as a marketable commodity was determined by whether she or he was still a productive body able to contribute to plantation production. On the Newton plantation in 1803, fifteen individuals were listed under the category "infirm but useful," with an average market value of £23. Although old enslaved individuals were not given as high a market value as their younger counterparts, many of them were still valued as marketable commodities because they could still contribute to plantation production. For instance, compared to those listed as superannuated, who received no market value, those listed as old were given an average price of £23. By contrast, out of fourteen individuals listed in the same year under "old, useless, and diseased," nine were listed as having no monetary value, while the remaining five were worth £5 each. On both the Newton and Seawell plantations, severely disabled individuals were given no monetary value, whereas those with physical limitations retained some market value. In the Newton records of 1784, John Sayres, a "cripple," was valued at £0, in contrast to Bristol who, with a "lame hand," was valued at £25. Able-bodied and healthy workers were valued at between £42 and £165.[64] Physically and intellectually impaired slave laborers were systematically devalued on the open market. For both free and unfree workers, the labor was isolated, given a "value," and the majority of the profit from that labor accrued to someone else. In the case of the enslaved plantation worker, nothing accrued to the producer (i.e., the bondsperson), and their entire being was alienated, not just their labor and its produce.

Because enslaved individuals were forced to labor under the threat of violence, they often labored with injuries or disabilities, causing their bodies to deteriorate over time. In the records of the Seawell plantation, several first-gang laborers were described as "infirm," while the head boiler and watchman was "very old and weak with one eye." Whereas these individuals remained in their occupations, other impaired laborers were reassigned to less-disciplined tasks such as gardening and carrying water to the field laborers. In the 1796 Newton accounts, severely diseased individuals were categorized together, although their productive labor capacities varied. Those given no occupational description included four individuals afflicted with leprosy; Quaco Sam, who was listed as "dumb and has fits"; Glasgow, "a cripple, [who] walks on all fours"; and Mary Ann, who "does nothing, weak and sickly." However, Dublin, who had "lost a thumb," was said to work, while Esther Rose was listed as "diseased but does some work."[65] In her 1831 memoir, ex-slave Mary Prince recounted having to labor after being severely flogged by her owner. "The next morning," she wrote, "I was forced by my master to rise and go about my usual work, though my body and limbs were so stiff and sore, that I could not move without the greatest pain."[66] Because of their enslaved status, Africans and their descendants continued to labor despite the long-term disabling consequences of repeated episodic incapacitation, which increased and prolonged their "state of injury."

Unlike enslaved laborers, disabled workers in the industrialized metropole were increasingly excluded from modes of production and, subsequently, from wages. For these workers, "worth" was calculated in wages that tied them economically and ideologically to an expanding capitalist economy that both exploited and remunerated them. The industrial workspaces of nineteenth-century Britain were extremely dangerous; accidents that caused permanent injury, impairment, and death were common in the coal mines, textile mills, and on railroads. Unable to earn a wage—which in the modern capitalist economy had become a symbol of human worth—disabled workers were stigmatized for their so-called inability to contribute to society.[67] For the wage laborer, then, disability was an individual problem. By contrast, in the plantation economy, disability harmed not only the individual enslaved worker but also, economically speaking, the slaveowner. Simply put, enslaved laborers' "worth" did not correspond to wages—they were unpaid, of course—but rather to their resale value on the open market, as well as their individual output as workers. To be sure, disabled laborers fetched a lesser price on the slave market, but they demonstrated their "worth" as productive bodies on the plantation.

The Plantation: Disability, Disease, and Labor

Both commodified labor and disability became racialized in the English Caribbean as Africans replaced European servants as the primary laborers. Historians have noted that Europeans' fear of a miserable death and life of hard labor in the tropics, among several other reasons, led to the decline of indentureship.[68] The physically debilitating nature of plantation labor fed this fear. Although there were multiple factors driving the shift away from indentured servitude in the Caribbean, the replacement of white laborers for black ones implied that white bodies were somehow unfit for the frequency of impairment and disease involved in plantation labor—physical trials for which black bodies, as we have seen, were thought to be ideally suited. Edward Long argued that "the labour of one Negroe was thought equal to that of 4 Indians" and that Africans "were found to be more robust and handy slaves than the natives of America:

more capable of enduring fatigue; more patient under servitude." He continued his claims by arguing that Africans supposed fitness to hard labor made them uniquely suited to the violence that accompanied slavery: "the difference of temper between the Americans and the Negroes is so remarkable, that it is a . . . saying in the French islands, to thrash upon an Indian is to beat him; to beat is to kill him. But to thrash a negroe is to nourish him."[69] The "state of injury" endured by the enslaved would henceforth become a marker of blackness.

Disability shaped the workforce in the English Caribbean. In Barbados and Jamaica, for example, the average sugar plantation engaged anywhere from fifty to three hundred unfree laborers; these individuals were organized into gangs based on age, gender, and physical condition. The arduous process of sugar cultivation—land preparation, planting, weeding, and cutting—was followed by grinding cane, boiling the juice, curing and refining the sugar, and distilling the resulting molasses into rum. Because of the perishability of the crop, sugarcane had to be milled within twenty-four hours of harvesting.[70] Field work, the most labor-intensive aspect of sugar making, consisted of hoeing the soil, planting and cutting canes, and working in the mill.

This was the work of the "first gang" of laborers, which consisted of the strongest able-bodied male and female captives, between eighteen and forty-five years of age. The "second gang" weeded and trashed canes. The "third gang," or the "grass gang," was made up of small children who performed weeding and light gardening. Divisions of labor based on gangs were "affected by short or long-term illness or physical disability."[71] Accordingly, planters were advised "to examine individually the state and condition of every negro; and then to assort them in such manner, that they may never be employed upon any work to which their powers are not equal."[72] Despite the fact that the English increasingly exempted women, particularly those of the middle and upper classes, from their cultural understanding of work on the grounds that they were unsuited to hard labor, slaveowners put most enslaved women to work in the fields—the most physically demanding and disabling of labor positions—rather than in the great houses of Barbados and Jamaica.

The physical suffering faced by workers in industrial England followed on the suffering long endured by enslaved laborers on Caribbean plantations.[73] The boiling house—the architectural feature and work environment of the plantation that most resembled the factory—required the technical mastery of sugar boilers, who worked in extremely hot, loud, and dangerous conditions. So common was dismemberment among these individuals that plantation management guides gave advice to overseers on how to decrease the frequency of accidents. "Care must be had by your negroes in the feeding or supplying the rollers with canes," declared one plantation management guide, "that their hand does not get betwixt the rollers." If this happens, "it . . . will draw the whole arm in and tear it from the body, unless the limb be immediately chopped off: the water wheele be stopped; or the wind mill be put to the wing." According to the guide, these accidents often took place at night "when the negroes are drowsy, which often proves fatal." The writer concluded his advice on this matter by putting planters' minds at ease over the dangers of the sugar mill, claiming that "if it happens that the member is caught in the roller of a cattle mill, the cattle are immediately stopped, and the loss is no more a finger or two."[74] The trivializing of dismembered fingers here demonstrates that in the economy of violence that governed plantation life, disability made the bodies of the enslaved mere transposable units of labor.

Although field women did not occupy the same artisanal positions as sugar boilers and distillers, they performed a range of crucial roles in the process of sugar production, including supplying fuel for boilers, feeding canes to the mills, and of course, working in the cane fields.[75] In addition to this physically destructive work regime, bondswomen suffered from inadequate diet and numerous diseases, and faced debilitating punishments. Such hostile conditions had a physiological effect on female captives' ability to conceive and deliver children.[76] Enslaved women suffered from both emotional amenorrhea caused by psychological trauma and secondary amenorrhea caused by illness. Both forms were present during the Middle Passage and the seasoning process—a period of one to three years in which Africans faced a multitude of life-threatening dangers as they adapted to life in the Caribbean. The disorders contributed to low fertility rates among African-born bondswomen.[77] For women who did conceive, pregnancy and birth were extremely hazardous.

Despite it being a limiting physical condition, pregnancy did not exempt bondswomen from hard labor. Jamaican and Barbadian planters were generally unwilling to lose female laborers to pregnancy, and they complained about the costs of rearing enslaved children.[78] Enslaved women also exercised their own ways of avoiding pregnancy, including abortion and contraception.[79] Although babies carried to term had the potential to provide the owner with additional wealth as future unfree laborers, capitalist-minded planters nonetheless felt that pregnancy and childcare interfered with plantation production; the potential loss of productivity caused by congenital deformities and disabilities could also contribute to planters' hostility to natural reproduction. In the 1795 records of the Somerset Vale plantation, in Jamaica, eight of the forty-eight female field laborers were recorded as pregnant but still at work.[80] Not until after 1788, when the abolitionist movement threatened the Atlantic slave trade, were planters concerned with the reproductive capacities of enslaved women as a means of securing a viable labor force.[81] But planters' efforts to increase the slave labor force through birth rather than trade failed miserably during this period for the simple reason that the conditions of enslavement had a devastating impact on women's bodies and reproductive abilities. For those who did conceive, the intensive labor regime of sugar production, combined with the hostile living conditions and excessive physical punishments, often contributed to miscarriage and maternal and infant mortality.[82]

In her study of motherhood and disability in nineteenth-century America, Jenifer Barclay has found that disability among enslaved children "often enabled mothers and children to remain together when profit-driven slaveholders and traders otherwise would have separated them." Barclay has discovered that women with disabilities, whom southern planters viewed as "useless," were often assigned childcare roles.[83] In the Newton plantation records from 1776 to 1783, an enslaved woman named Esther Sayres is listed as the caregiver for her relation, John Sayres, "a cripple." Esther is not listed as having any other occupation but "to take care" of John. In the 1783 records, Esther and John's names are followed by "Sally a little girl a cripple."[84] Similarly, the 1791 Newton accounts list Phoebe and Nanny, who are described as "old and infirm," in the position of sick nurse in the dwelling house. Bondswomen were also often placed in charge of what were called "invalid gangs." The 1818 slave returns of Barbados, for instance, lists several plantations that were said to use women in this way.[85] These records alone do not offer evidence as to how enslaved women, like Pheobe and Nanny, perceived their roles as caregivers. From an economic standpoint, as caregivers they were forced to perform a labor that they were capable of, in the same way their able-bodied counterparts were compelled to perform whatever labor they were capable of.

Bondspeople endured infirmities that resulted from old age, and yet, like pregnant bondswomen and new mothers, they continued to labor on the sugar plantation. The majority of bondspeople listed as "old" in the 1776 Newton accounts are not given a specific labor description, but others, like Will, Chloe, Oggoe, and Miranda are described as "old but carries water for negroes."[86] Sambo, Cato, Peter, and Toley were said to be "in copper shop but old." Jacob Obina "beats corn but old"; and Doublin "in the garden but old." Watchmen (enslaved men who kept watch of plantation grounds at night for criminal or mischievous behavior) were often elderly and visually impaired. Elderly women were similarly put to use by plantation authorities. Fitah and Corribah were described as "in the kitchen, an old wench," whereas Occo Obina "beats corn but old." Even skilled positions were filled by bondsmen past prime labor age. The head carpenter on the Newton plantation was a man named Neddy, described as "old." Joe was a carpenter but "weak and infirm," and Simon who was "much afflicted with fever and ague" was the head carter. Although the majority of old bondspeople were listed among the useful, sometimes they were listed under the category "useless and diseased" and assigned no market value, indicating that age-related infirmities could eventually impair bondspeople and relegate them to the status of unmarketable commodities.

The legal ownership of human bodies caused repercussions for planters, whose property included bodies that had *once been* capable of laboring. In his 1774 plantation management guide, for example, John Dovaston encouraged his fellow Jamaican planters to care for old and sick bondspeople. "Let conscience and humanity," he wrote, "teach you to employ your old slaves, both men and women as watches or doctors, assistants . . . with the care of the sick." After planters "had their strength and youthful labour," they should "let them live in ease on the estate and be fed carefully, as long as nature will hold out." In suggesting the old bondspeople live out their lives in relative repose on the plantation, Dovaston was going against the common practice at the time, which was to "charge them with crimes they are innocent of and hang them for the sake of the reward; when they are old past labour, and of no value." For Dovaston, "such money received is the price of blood and will to a curse on the receiver of the same."[87] It is hard to imagine that many of Dovaston's fellow slaveowners took such advice, since in the world of Caribbean slavery physically impaired captives were clearly most economically useful in death, closing the space between "bare life" and death.

The enslaved lived in a hostile environment in which malnutrition, sickness, and disease were common. The enslaved were plagued by malnutrition, which led many to eat soil, a practice known as geophagy or pica, which during the era of slavery was called Africana Cachexia.[88] Like other physical illnesses, dirt eating was caused by the material conditions of slavery and the psychological distress that accompanied slavery. Whites did not understand dirt eating as a result of malnutrition but saw it as rebellious and self-destructive behaviour. According to a late eighteenth-century plantation management guide, providing forced laborers with rum "will lunge their labour foreward much better than strikes and blows," the negative repercussions of which—namely, a loss of productivity among injured workers—provides "convincing proof that *humanity works better than terror.*"[89] The author's pretense to "humanity" notwithstanding, the substitution of rum for food says much about the material reality of enslaved disablement in the plantation zone: it was not just the *labor* that destroyed African bodies; the cheap availability of sugar's nutrition-poor by-products also served to foster the "bare life" experience of the enslaved.

Unsanitary water and extremely tight living quarters were among the many factors that caused and helped spread a variety of illnesses and diseases on the plantation, including scabies, leprosy, yaws, parasites and worms, smallpox, diphtheria, whooping cough, measles, mumps, and influenza. Of course, whites were not immune to such afflictions, but the enslaved were more susceptible because of the hostile environment in which they were forced to live and work.[90] A common infection among bondspeople was transmitted by the chigger and caused festering sores and sometimes long-term impairment of the feet.[91] The yaws, which rarely affected whites, could lead to permanent physical disability, and was highly contagious among the enslaved due to congested living conditions.[92] John Dovaston cautioned his fellow planters about the kinds of illnesses to which the enslaved were prone. He described the yaws, for example, as "great ulcers that break out in various parts of the body, but chiefly on the arms, and hips." "The wounds," according to Dovaston, "yield very little matter, nor are they very painfull; but if not cured in time will spread in hard knots all over the body, and infect the whole mass of blood." As a result, "the muscles will be contracted and the features deformed; the face swell'd with large blotches, and death the consequence—unless skillfull application be had." Dovaston cautioned planters that "when any negroe is soon to have this disorder, he must be taken from amongst your other slaves, or he will infect the whole." Other illnesses included worms that caused an individual to appear "as tho he was mad, and run about with desperate and ghastly looks, at other times the slaves will be taken with shakes and fitts like those of an ague."[93] For the enslaved, these were what I call diseases of unfreedom: an everyday reality that constituted a silent but powerful and highly visible debilitation of the body.

Illness could temporarily impair an enslaved individual, but repeated sickness, like repeated punishment, could lead to long-term physical disability. Among unfree laborers in the English Caribbean, the distinction between chronic illness, impairment, and disability was not clearly demarcated.[94] As enslaved laborers, bondspeople's daily regime demanded physical and mental fitness; illness, disease, and physical impairment could prevent them from meeting the standards of plantation labor, standards that were normally achieved only by the able-bodied. But, like pregnancy, disease and severe illness did not necessarily exempt captives from labor. When Mary Prince became sick with rheumatism and Saint Anthony's fire, she "grew so very lame that [she] was forced to walk with a stick . . . and became quite a cripple."[95] After a short quarantine, Prince returned to work, still sick. Prince's disability demonstrates that enslaved people experienced degrees and gradations of disability and lived in a space between fitness and death. Such self-presentation suggests that in the specific context of the antislavery movement, it was politically expedient to present one's "defective" body in order to make claims about the violence of Atlantic slavery. But these abolitionist portrayals often stripped the enslaved of their political relevance in the Atlantic World and their ability to self-emancipate.

The inefficient labor of severely ill and impaired bondspeople was often met with cruel treatment from owners. Prince described a fellow bondswoman named Sarah as "nearly past work . . . who was subject to several bodily infirmities, and was not quite right in the head." Her overseer, Master Dickey, punished Sarah sadistically because she "did not wheel the barrow fast enough to please him." She died a few days after receiving her punishment. Prince herself was forced to labor despite boils and sores on her feet from working in the salt water; she described being chastised for not being able to move as swiftly as her master demanded.[96] In its description of such unremitting violence, Prince's narrative reinforces the fact that impaired individuals, whose bodies had become antithetical to the industrial work regime of plantation labor, suffered greater violence at the hands of overseers and owners than able-bodied and "compliant" laborers. Considered both "unproductive" and less immediately physically threatening to plantation authority, such people occupied a precarious place in the violence-fueled and profit-driven economy of slavery.

The treatment of disabled bondspeople in the British Caribbean connects and diverges with the treatment of the disabled poor in English poor law, illustrating that although disability produced distinct forms of dispossession that are historically specific, disability in the Atlantic World was also intimately interrelated. The history of the poor laws can be divided into the Old Poor Law—crystallized under Queen Elizabeth I in the 1601 Act for the Relief of the Poor—and the Poor Law Amendment Act of 1834. The Old Poor Law established a legal obligation for parishes to deal with two broad categories of applicants for poor relief: the "impotent" poor (the disabled, the sick, the elderly, orphans, and widows) and the "able-bodied" poor (those capable of work). The Old Poor Law was decentralized—local parishes were responsible to raise and administer relief directly to the "deserving poor" and to provide work for those who were able.[97] These parish-based poor laws were implemented irregularly and unevenly, with policy varying from locality to locality.[98]

For the disabled, who were classified under the "deserving" poor, the English poor laws were "enabling" in the sense that individuals whose impairments prevented them from working were provided with pensions and supports.[99] By the turn of the eighteenth century, however, parishes across the country began to set up workhouses to lodge and employ the poor. Most workhouse inmates were either very young, very old, or disabled.[100] Thus, like late eighteenth-century slave laws, English poor laws forbade the disabled from wandering and begging in the streets, though in the English Caribbean it was the owner's responsibility, and not the state's, to curb such "disorder." The housing of the disabled in workhouses during the seventeenth and eighteenth centuries seems to reflect a more generalized fear, common throughout the Atlantic World, of idleness and public destitution.

Some enslaved individuals exaggerated their ailments, or feigned disability altogether, in order to negotiate the terms of their bondage and, in so doing, revalued disability in the context of Atlantic slavery.[101] Indeed, runaway advertisements reveal that plantation authorities suspected enslaved individuals of feigning illness, injury, and impairment as a way to negotiate the terms of their enslavement. Masquerading a disability or severe injury provided bondspeople opportunities to move into less physically taxing labor positions. But fugitives could also use this to their advantage. The runaway Sambo was recorded as "a creole, very old, his head quite white, pretends to be blind." Another advertisement in 1780 recorded the following: "RUNAWAY, the following Negro Slaves . . . ABRAHAM, an old man of a yellow complexion, of the Eboe country, stout made; has a wife at Mr. Price's Estate at Luidas, named JUBA; a sawyer; sometimes pretends to be sick with the physick."[102] Of course, as fugitives, these individuals would likely have abandoned such feigned disabilities, since owners described these traits in hopes of identifying and apprehending them. But deftly employed, donning a mask of disability allowed fugitives to perpetually transform their bodies, thereby "generating identities beyond recognition."[103] This enabled captives to gain some amount of control over their bodies and resist to slaveholder authority. If an enslaved person could "pass" as disabled and be excused from work, she or he might become invisible to authorities when fleeing.

Simply put, masquerading disability could provide bondspeople some control over the kinds of labor they performed on the plantation and whether they would be sold to potential buyers.[104] Viewed this way, the body of the disabled bondsperson becomes a potential site of opposition to the commodification of human beings, and a form of protest against their status as commercial object and laboring machine; it also represents a form of resistance against the very things that made bondspeople modern—their physical abilities, their productivity, and their inextricable connection to an industrial capitalist economy.[105] The punished body was, on the one hand, a display and reproduction of its owner's mastery and power and, on the other, a living, breathing text that told of a captive's refusal to accept her or his enslavement. Thus, to study the disablement of black bodies in the context of Atlantic slavery is to ascribe to disability a multiplicity of meanings—to see it as a sign not just of victimization, but of protest and personhood as well.

Disability was pervasive among the enslaved populations of the Caribbean, and it shaped their daily lives and interactions with one another and with slaveowners. In Barbados and Jamaica, for example, enslavement occurred in a variety of environments, for example urban, domestic, and plantation. Bondspeople who worked in more urban or domestic spaces surely experienced disability, deformity, and disfigurement, but, as we have seen, sugar production was a particularly physically destructive enterprise.

The colonial Caribbean challenges traditional timelines of disability history and undoes teleological distinctions between the early modern and the modern. The industrial setting of Caribbean sugar making, coupled with the frequency of impairment among enslaved laborers, reveals that certain "modern" understandings of disability, which were thought to have emerged in nineteenth-century Europe, in fact existed even earlier in the Caribbean. For both the metropolitan worker and the enslaved laborer, physical ability was a measure of human worth, a value that in both cases was calculated in pounds sterling: this translated into wages for European factory workers, while for the enslaved it determined the price of one's body and soul on the slave market.

In spite of the many ways in which bondspeople revalued disability, when wielded *against* African captives, it nonetheless played a key role in their commodification. Enslaved individuals with impairments often faced unique conditions in their evaluation as property on English Caribbean plantations, and they posed challenges for slaveowners, who often viewed them as burdens to the estate that needed somehow to be incorporated into the existing labor scheme. But disability and commodification also intersected in the way Africans and their descendants were represented in the colonial press. Black people whose bodies bore the marks of servitude in the form of scars, burns, and impairments were displayed in colonial newspapers, which further bolstered the notion that black bodies could offer an outward reflection of the savage and depraved disposition contained within. Descriptions of enslaved bodies in runaway advertisements offer a window, albeit a highly distorted one, into the lives of individual runaways. But even more consequentially, they endowed the material world of English Caribbean slavery with meaning, thereby serving to structure, rather than simply reflect, reality for those inhabiting slave societies.

CHAPTER 4

Incorrigible Runaways

Disability and the Bodies of Fugitive Slaves

> It is precisely within the ordinary and everyday that racialization has been most effective, where it *makes* race.
>
> —Thomas C. Holt, "Marking: Race, Race-Making, and the Writing of History"

On 9 September 1788, Thomas Price ran the following advertisement in the *Savanna-la-Mar Gazette*: "*Ran away about four weeks since* FROM SMITH-FIELD, A Negro Man-Boy, ABOUT five feet high, has two scars on the back of his head, a hole in each ear, large features, walks lame from a hurt in one of his hips, several marks of a whip in his body, legs, and arms, and has the crab-yaws on one of his feet. Whoever will bring him to the Subscriber shall be handsomely rewarded. THOMAS PRICE."[1] The description of this name-less teenager poignantly demonstrates that disability among the enslaved was quite literally *produced* by slaveholding power.[2] Although it does not mention the cause of the two scars on the back of the boy's head, we can speculate that they were the result of capture or enslavement, and not "country marks"—the scarification practiced among some sub-Saharan African groups—which slave-owners usually specified in runaway notices.[3] The boy was "lame from a hurt in one of his hips," an injury that could have resulted from accident, disease, field labor, or chance violence, all of which were part of the daily experiences of the enslaved. His "body, legs, and arms" were permanently marked with signs of punishment—scars from the whip that told a conflicting story of enslaved resistance—referred to by whites as African rebelliousness—and the violence used by whites to deliberately subdue and disable the enslaved. His feet were infected with the yaws, a disease of unfreedom that rarely affected whites but was endemic among the enslaved because of the hostile conditions in which they were forced to live.

This chapter looks at the ways in which the bodies of enslaved people were portrayed in Jamaican and Barbadian runaway advertisements from 1718 to 1815 to demonstrate that slavery produced disability in multiple ways, and that runaway advertisements were themselves a disabling force in Caribbean slave societies.[4] I analyzed nearly a thousand runaway advertisements, which describe approximately 1,200 individual fugitives.[5] Careful attention to the advertisements reveal that enslaved people were debilitated in a variety of ways: discursively through law and legally sanctioned punishment, through work regimes and the material conditions of slavery, and psychologically through the trauma of enslavement.[6] The collection also reveals the particular kinds of physical injuries that were produced by slavery. Runaway advertisements demonstrate that dismemberment, branding, sensory impairments, and certain disabling diseases were common. Although some of these conditions do not necessarily constitute disability in the modern sense, disability must be understood in specific historical contexts. Scholars of disability emphasize that as a category of historical analysis, disability is not fixed, natural, nor stable, but rather socially constructed and particular to time and place.[7] In the context of Caribbean slavery, for instance, yaws—a highly contagious bacterial infection caused by poor sanitation and overcrowded living quarters—could cause chronic disfigurement and was potentially, though not universally, disabling.[8] Also, marks on the flesh, such as brands and scars from the whip, while not necessarily physically debilitating, could disable the enslaved by permanently marking their bodies with signs of criminality and so-called rebelliousness.

Degrees of severity among impairments are also difficult to assess because the lived experience of disability was shaped in large part by the specific condition of one's labor and relationship to slave driver or owner. While the data reveal certain patterns, we cannot be certain about subjective and embodied experience of any particular person; we must also consider specific contexts not always revealed in runaway advertisements. In short, it is impossible to measure the experience of a particular disability from the advertisement. Additionally, measuring the severity of impairments also assumes a universal experience of slavery and of disability, and it favors a medical approach to disability that relegates the construction and the embodiment of impairment to the margins of understanding. This medicalization also takes us away from the particular experience of the individual. For these reasons, I have chosen to resist measurement.

The opening discussion details chronological trends regarding distinguishing marks of violence described in runaway advertisements, before moving on to an introduction into runaway advertisements and the wider surveillance measures employed by Caribbean lawmakers and planters alike. The next three sections explore the various manifestations of slavery-induced disability that are described in runaway advertisements. An exploration of the corporeal punishments meted out onto fugitive enslaved bodies is followed by a discussion of the disabling material conditions of enslavement. The chapter ends with an analysis of the psychological traumas of slavery and the ways in which the enslaved used masquerade to disguise their bodily marks and disabilities to evade identification and apprehension.

Marks of Servitude

Runaway advertisements offer a window into bondspeople's physical, intellectual, and emotional impairments and suggest some possibilities about the changing reference to identifying marks over time. Over the ninety-seven years of advertisements examined, deformities, impairments, disfigurements, amputations, and marks of punishment all increased, whereas branding significantly declined over the final period (1796–1815). Such information may not map onto the wider enslaved population in this exact way; however, it suggests important changes with regard to identifying marks and the violence inflicted onto enslaved bodies. Many of the marks described in runaway advertisements imply violence; however, in notices in the first fifty years of this dataset, owners did not identify particular scars or wounds as being marks of punishment; by the late eighteenth and early nineteenth centuries, disfigurements, deformities, and impairments replaced branding as the most pervasive identifying mark. This did not necessarily mean that branding had fallen out of practice on Caribbean sugar plantations, but rather that slaveowners were more conscious of how runaway advertisements were being used by abolitionists as evidence of slavery's disabling and disfiguring violence.

The late eighteenth and early nineteenth centuries marked the first phase of amelioration (1788–1807), when, under pressure from the abolitionist movement, planters and lawmakers took legal measures to supposedly improve the conditions of slavery and encourage slave births. A critique of branding was a significant part of abolitionists' campaign. For instance, in his 1786 attack of slavery, British abolitionist Thomas Clarkson referred to branding and the slitting of ears (both mentioned in runaway advertisements) as "deliberate mutilation" and "shocking barbarity."[9] By 1824, Clarkson utilized runaway advertisements from the *Royal Gazette of Jamaica* to demonstrate the brutality of plantation slavery. "Numbers of [the enslaved]," he wrote, "appear to have been branded with the initials of their owner's names, and other marks, *on the naked flesh,* with a *heated iron,* in the same manner as young horses or cattle are branded when they are turned into our forests." Clarkson continued his attack and isolated branding as an emblem of slavery's tyrannical violence. "Some of these brand marks upon these slaves," he wrote, "consisting, as they often do, *of several letters,* must have tortured no inconsiderable portion of the flesh."[10] Runaway advertisements provided abolitionists evidence of slavery's violence straight from the pens of slaveowners, in particular, the ubiquity and inhumanity of branding, which had become a key feature of the antislavery polemic.[11] Slaveowners were not unaware that their runaway ads were being read and used in this way. Indeed, in the last period examined, 1770–95, which roughly coincides with the first phase of amelioration, the number of brandings mentioned in ads fell dramatically. The question remains whether slaveowners merely changed their rhetoric in advertisements or they replaced one form of disfiguring violence with another. Indeed, at the very moment when amelioration efforts to lessen the frequency of impairment and disfigurement among the enslaved came into effect, runaway advertisements indicate a sharp increase of deformities, disfigurements, impairments, amputations, and marks of punishment among fugitive bondspeople. The failures of amelioration and the power of slaveowners to damage the bodies of bondspeople with impunity were so deeply entrenched in Caribbean slave-owning culture that slavery remained an inherently violent institution despite amelioration efforts. I argue that, aware of abolitionist critiques, slaveowners shifted their public discourse to avoid those critiques.

Runaway advertisements reflect, enunciate, and catalog British antiblack racism and the damage it inflicted on the enslaved in the colonial Caribbean.[12] In publishing the details and images of the impaired, deformed, and disfigured black body in newspapers, slaveowners simultaneously highlighted and dismissed the danger posed by the figure of the fugitive, using an everyday medium of communication in order to reproduce, naturalize, and render quotidian the routinized violence of colonial slavery and the pretexts for its infliction. What is more, as reminders that they were under constant surveillance and subject to the threat of brutal violence by whites, the ubiquity of runaway ads was meant to keep black people in a state of terror. They drew together blackness and disability in a social "uniform" that functioned as a means of separating all blacks, including free people of color, from whites.[13] Slaveowners' control over the display of black bodies in runaway ads was in no way incidental: it was, rather, a key part of the logic of enslavement and of the emerging conceptions of racial difference and black disability in the early modern Atlantic World. Runaway advertisements were not simply impartial documents of slavery and

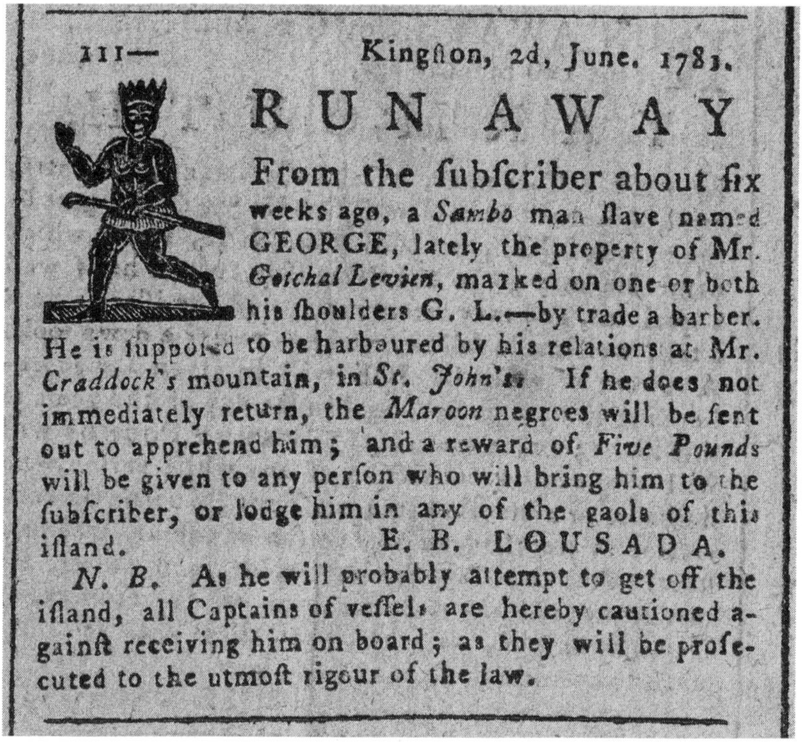

111— Kingſton, 2d, June. 1783.

RUNAWAY

From the ſubſcriber about ſix weeks ago, a *Sambo* man ſlave named GEORGE, lately the property of Mr. *Gotchal Levien*, marked on one or both his ſhoulders G. L.—by trade a barber. He is ſuppoſed to be harboured by his relations at Mr. *Craddock's* mountain, in *St. John's*. If he does not immediately return, the *Maroon* negroes will be ſent out to apprehend him; and a reward of *Five Pounds* will be given to any perſon who will bring him to the ſubſcriber, or lodge him in any of the gaols of this iſland. E. B. LOUSADA.

N. B. As he will probably attempt to get off the iſland, all Captains of veſſels are hereby cautioned againſt receiving him on board; as they will be proſecuted to the utmoſt rigour of the law.

FIGURE 2. Runaway advertisement for George, who was branded on his shoulders with his owner's initials, G.L. Note that the image depicts the fugitive wearing a head adornment or crown, suggesting that the individual was African born.

a disability analysis demands that we rethink prior assumptions about the neutrality of such primary documents.

Before considering the violent marks described in runaway ads, we should consider the contexts in which the bodies of runaways were marked by slavery's disabling violence. While colonial law is a consistent threat, we need to understand how running away functioned in that society, the history of the advertisements themselves, and how surveillance worked in Barbados and Jamaica.

Documenting the Bodies of Fugitive Bondspeople

In British Caribbean slave societies, running away from one's owner was the gravest nonviolent act an enslaved person could commit. Lawmakers claimed

FIGURE 3. An example of a typical newspaper page largely featuring runaway ads. Alongside runaway advertisements are "taken up" notices submitted by individuals who apprehended a fugitive bondsperson, advertisements for strayed livestock, and "for sale" notices advertising enslaved people. (*Supplement to the Royal Gazette* [Jamaica], 26 May–2 June 1781, American Antiquarian Society)

that Africans' "brutish and barbarous nature" caused them to run away and to "committ felonies and other enormities, not only to the terror and affrightment of the neighbourhood, but the danger of the Island in general."[14] Runaways explicitly challenged the institution of slavery by their unsanctioned absence from their owners, depriving owners of laborers, and potentially reducing plantation production. To the extent that they could entice other captives to run away as well, fugitive bondspeople also challenged owners' power over their remaining workforce.[15] As a mountainous, heavily forested, and comparatively large island, Jamaica offered captives more opportunities for concealment and permanent self-emancipation in the form of Maroon communities. Barbados, comparatively small, flat, and densely populated, was a more difficult place for runaways to evade discovery.[16] Still, enslaved individuals on the island took flight just as their Jamaican counterparts did. In both places this could represent either a temporary act of resistance or an effort to escape the system permanently.

In the British Caribbean, even the desire to escape enslavement by running away was cast as an incurable disability and was, therefore, criminal. Whites' labeling of certain runaways as "incorrigible"—meaning incurable or not able to be corrected—suggested that the desire to self-emancipate was considered a reflection of Africans' innate defectiveness. For example, in her study of slavery and disability in the antebellum United States, Jenifer Barclay argues that running away was seen as a vice just like drunkenness, one that "paralleled wider discussions of amorphous, ill-defined disabilities such as insanity, feeblemindedness, and epilepsy in American society." Similarly, in the colonies of the British Caribbean, plantation records illustrate that owners categorized perpetual runaways among the "infirm" and as "useless" to the estate. In the 1791 records from the Seawell plantation, in Christ Church, Barbados, two bondsmen, Tom and Jack, are listed among the "old" and "infirm," where they are given the description, "always absent except when confined." A similar description can be found in the 1772 plantation records of Melville Hall Estate in Dominica. Four enslaved individuals—Cudgo, Quaco, Wattie, and Blair—are described as being "useless upon the Estate, constantly running away, and returning when they're sickly and being recovered takes the same course again and use every method to destroy themselves."[17] These men's repeated flight led to their being categorized as "useless" and lumped with captives who did not contribute to plantation production due to physical impairments, debilitating disease, mental health issues, or old age. In short, planters and overseers viewed enslaved people's desire for freedom as an incurable disability. According to such logic, Africans were *by nature unfree.* This pathologizing of enslaved resistance served to reinforce the imagined connection between blackness and disability but also revealed whites' fear of runaways as dangerous individuals capable of inciting insurrection.

The documenting of fugitive bodies as a means of surveillance was legally inscribed in the earliest slave codes of Barbados and Jamaica. According to the 1661 Barbados Slave Code, captured runaways were to be taken to the prison where the "keeper of the prison" was to record all knowledge about the fugitive's apprehension—location and time—into a book and "insert the mark and description of the Negroe delivered."[18] In addition, within ten days of publication of the 1661 act, all owners were to provide the secretary a list of all their fugitive bondspeople.[19] By 1673, the marshal was obliged to "give a description of the said Negro's Marks as also as neare as hee can learne how long the said Negroes have been absent from their Master's plantacon with their names" and fix such description "upon the posts in ye most publique and open places att Port Royall and St. Catherines" so that "notice may been given to the Inhabitants of each parish of all such Negroes."[20] By 1678, Jamaica slave law mandated that descriptions of fugitive bodies be advertised in public spaces "in the Goales [Jails] of St. Jago de la Vega and Port Royall of the Penalty of one hundred pounds."[21] By the following century, authorities in prisons and workhouses were legally obliged to advertise runaways in the Jamaican press "the height, names, marks, sex, and country . . . of each runaway in their custody."[22] Through the invocation of these marks, the law disabled the enslaved by limiting their mobility, since through such identification enslaved people could be tracked by specific marks they bore on their bodies—scars, impairments, dismembered limbs and extremities, and other physical anomalies. These bodily marks—whether transient, permanent, natural, or inflicted—provide a narrative and testimony to their wearers' lives of suffering and survival.

By the mid-eighteenth century, runaway advertisements appeared daily in the British Caribbean press, and it was precisely their quotidian nature that gave these advertisements their power.[23] The disfigured, deformed, and disabled black body was made hyper-visible, though not as something spectacular, but rather as routine, ordinary, and unremarkable. As artifacts of the everyday, runaway advertisements suggest how the much more generalized, historically rooted, antiblack racism of the British Atlantic world was articulated in the everyday and the familiar.[24] Runaway notices served a practical purpose, which was to notify free society of fugitive bondspeople in order to apprehend them. And yet they also reflected a discourse used in the making of race and black disability in the British Atlantic world.[25]

Many of the physical afflictions emphasized in fugitive identification described marks common among the enslaved population because of their shared

 U N-away from Bull-Bay, in September 1763, a new Negro Man, named EDINBURGH, speaks little or no Englifh, is about Five feet Ten inches high, his Beard in tufts and has no mark. Whoever apprehends the faid Negro and will give Information to me at *Cherry-Garden* in Liguanea, fhall have a Reward of Four Piftoles, and all Charges paid, by

48u   DUNCAN M'FARLANE.

FIGURE 4. This runaway advertisement documents the sex, name, and height of the fugitive. (*Jamaica Gazette*, 3 January 1765)

experience of slavery. This resulted in a paradox: although runaway notices advertised for the return of individual fugitives, the marks of violence they described were so widespread as to be almost mundane, rendering the individual anonymous and implying the interchangeability of black people. Runaway advertisements published in the British Caribbean press read as catalogs of recognizable forms of abuse inflicted on the enslaved body and sanctioned by the institution of slavery. In colonial Barbados and Jamaica, black bodies were repeatedly and publicly displayed in newsprint in ways that white bodies were not.

As a genre, Jamaican and Barbadian runaway advertisements resemble other notices that were popular in the English press, most notably those for absented apprentices and fugitive bondspeople in England; however, disability as an identifying mark is largely absent from metropolitan advertisements. Like colonial runaway notices, metropolitan advertisements for enslaved runaways describe fugitives as having scars and other involuntary physical marks caused by disease. Runaway James Teernon was described in the English press as having "a scar on his forehead," while others were described as bearing the visible physical effects of disease.[26] For instance, on 20 December 1766, a runaway notice in the London newspaper the *Public Advertiser* described an enslaved fugitive as

a Negro Man slave, named Jack, and who calls himself John Dixon . . . aged about thirty two years, and is about 5 feet 7 inches high; he is rather wide between the knees, and his ankles bend inward; he is of a lusty form, very upright, has a very steady settled countenance and has had the small pox, his visage used to be roundish, but a certain disorder of three months continuance has reduced him, and made his cheeks look very hollow and changed his complexion to a yellow hue. He speaks English freely, in as good a manner as any English servant.

It was more common, however, for metropolitan advertisements to refer to the clothing of the enslaved as opposed to marks on their flesh. Indeed, as Gwenda Morgan and Peter Rushton point out, "comments on brands or whipping marks inflicted by judicial process or private discipline" were largely absent from English runaway advertisements.[27] One such ad, for a fugitive named Theodore, is typical in this regard; his owner described him as "about 5 feet 6 inches high, had on when he run away a blue jacket, and a green one under, wearing a hat and wig."[28] This practice speaks to the widespread presence of domestic bondspeople in the metropole, whose owners tended to dress them in expensive garments as a sign of their prestige and wealth.[29] By contrast, Barbadian and Jamaican runaway advertisements reflected the fact that British Caribbean slaveowners viewed bondspeople as expendable agricultural implements. The brutality of sugar production, coupled with the malnutrition and disease prevalent among the enslaved population, not to mention the heightened racist tension of slave societies, made slavery in the British Caribbean more physically destructive to the enslaved body than enslavement in England.

Metropolitan advertisements for absconded English apprentices differ most significantly from Caribbean runaway ads. Although apprentice advertisements describe the missing subject's appearance, it is again the clothing that serves as the key distinguishing factor, not the individual's body.[30] If peculiar scars or blemishes are mentioned, they almost always concern physical marks located on the individual's face or hands. Unlike those seeking enslaved fugitives in the colonies, metropolitan advertisements for both absconded apprentices and enslaved domestics excluded the mention of body parts that were typically concealed by clothing—breasts, stomach, back, thighs, and so on. For instance, William Cooper's 1755 advertisement in the *London Evening Post* described an absconded apprentice named John Shillitoe as "a tall thin Lad, nineteen years of age, pitted with the small-pox, two or three moles upon his face." According to Cooper, John was wearing "an Olive colour'd thicket Frock and Waistcoat, with silver vellum holes, and a pair of black leather breeches" when he fled. Like physical marks on the enslaved body, apprentices' clothing was described with considerable precision. A notice from the *Morning Post and Daily Advertiser*

(London) described a missing apprentice as having worn "a dark striped green coat, blue under coat with yellow buttons, striped waistcoat, black breeches, and new boots."[31] By contrast, enslaved individuals in the colonies were rarely recorded as having worn anything apart from "osnaburg" clothing, which by law owners were to provide to captives once per year.

Since they did not offer monetary rewards, the ads for runaway apprentices demonstrate that the individual's labor, not her or his person, was the locus of their commodification in the metropolitan economy. Because bondspeople were themselves physical commodities incorporated into a transnational economy, monetary rewards were always offered for runaway captives in both the metropole and the colonies. In the latter, these monetary rewards augmented the seemingly absolute power of slave law, which required all inhabitants to apprehend runaways and return them to their owners. It also served to criminalize the enslaved, since these runaway notices were more akin to "wanted" notices for criminals than to advertisements seeking information about "missing" persons.

The physical detail provided by colonial runaway advertisements reflected the degree to which the enslaved were watched, inspected, and violated by slaveholding authorities and then how such information was broadcast to limit their freedom of movement. In the Caribbean, owners, managers, and overseers subjected bondspeople to intimate physical inspection before purchasing them, whenever they claimed illness, or indeed at any time they saw fit. Drivers watched field laborers closely while they performed their duties and were, therefore, likely privy to individuals' injuries and illnesses. Moreover, the enslaved were often stripped naked for punishments, their bodies exposed to plantation authorities as well as to their fellow bondspeople.[32] Close physical scrutiny by owners, overseers, and managers afforded masters knowledge of those areas of enslaved people's bodies that would otherwise be concealed by clothing. The enslaved were property, and by detailing the marks inflicted on bondspeople's bodies, runaway advertisements confirmed this very fact.[33]

Discursive and Material Disability

The text in runaway advertisements produced a kind of discursive disability through the language subscribers used to make known their fugitive bondsperson. Under the headline "RUN AWAY" or "ABSCONDED," they contained a specific sequence of information conveyed in certain prescribed language: the location from which the captive fled, followed by the captive's name and description. This included details about the fugitive's physical and behavioral characteristics, her or his possible whereabouts and familial connections on neighboring plantations, and other instances in which the bondsperson had run away. Sometimes the subscribers speculated as to fugitives' destinations and fellow conspirators. For instance, John Agard advertised for his missing bondsman Primas in the *Barbados Mercury* in October 1784. Agard speculated that Primas was "harboured within the plantation of Maxwell Adams, esq. and in that neighbourhood where he was harboured and concealed months the last year." Agard also noted that Primus had "a connection with the negroes at the Bell Plantation, and may be employed in the Bay at the Watering Places" and that he had "been seen in the Roe buck," a popular area in historic Bridgetown.[34] Agard's list of possible whereabouts was custom in runaway advertisements in the British Caribbean. In advertising not only the individual and her or his bodily marks but the possible locations in which she or he may seek refuge, whites created a network of surveillance among other plantation authorities that greatly inhibited the runaway's ability to flee successfully. Indeed, the language used in runaway advertisements did more than just announce missing bondspeople. Runaway advertisements reflected disciplinary technologies of a particularly modern cast: unlike early modern European "wanted" advertisements, which targeted individuals, colonial runaway notices, while they too advertised for individuals, also reflected a much wider attempt to survey, control, and discipline the entire enslaved population. Indeed, to the extent that it gave the sense that owners and overseers maintained a shared vigilance with other concerned whites out of a mutual interest in preying on fugitive bondspeople, the language of runaway notices contained an element of Foucauldian omniscience. This sense of absolute power and surveillance, whether real or imagined, placed limits on the possibility of escape.

The text of runaway notices was often accompanied by one or two stock images of an able-bodied fugitive bondsperson. The circulation of this able-bodied image must be understood both in relation to, and separately from, the text it accompanied. On the one hand, the image of an able-bodied black man throwing off the burden of slavery embodied whites' greatest fears: black violence and retribution. On the other hand, these stock images contradicted the written descriptions of individual fugitives with which they were paired. The illustrations depict able-bodied individuals in flight; the written text more often than not described individuals beset with various physical infirmities—limps, amputations, scars, and other impairments. Walking sticks were often included in these illustrations to reflect that the runaway was suspected to have traveled a considerable distance, not that the runaway had a mobility problem.

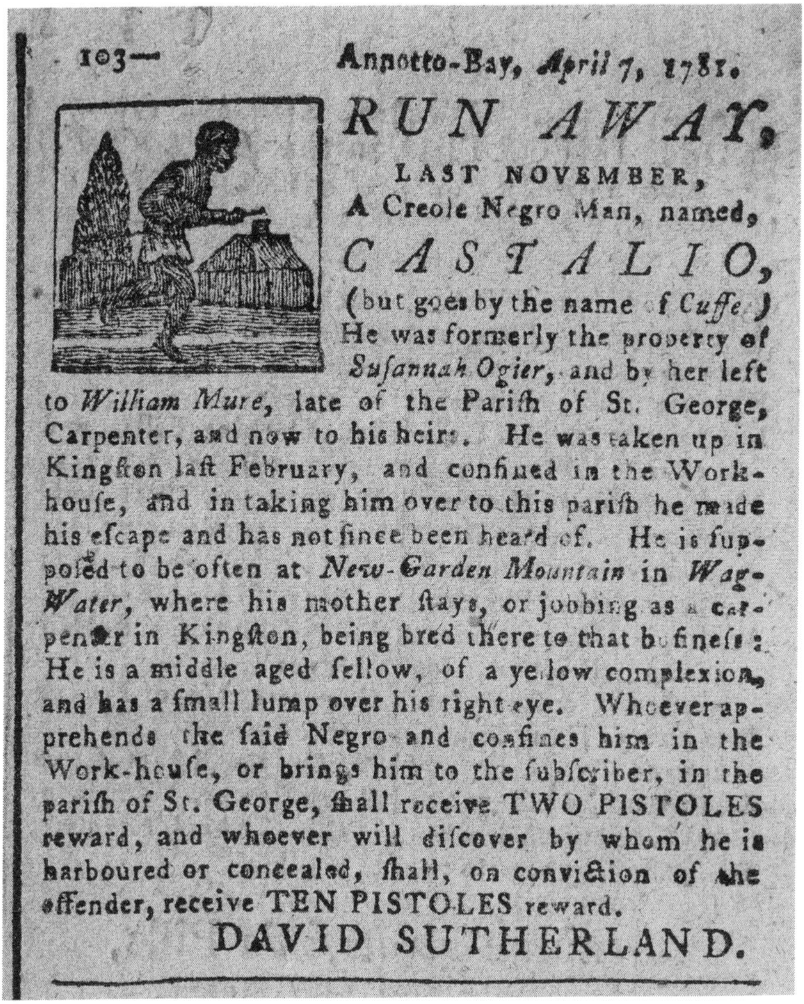

103—   Annotto-Bay, *April* 7, 1781.

RUN AWAY,

LAST NOVEMBER,

A Creole Negro Man, named,

CASTALIO,

(but goes by the name f *Cuffe*)
He was formerly the property of
Sufannah Ogier, and by her left
to *William Mure,* late of the Parifh of St. George,
Carpenter, and now to his heirs. He was taken up in
Kingfton laft February, and confined in the Work-
houfe, and in taking him over to this parifh he made
his efcape and has not fince been heard of. He is fup-
pofed to be often at *New-Garden Mountain* in *Wag-
Water,* where his mother ftays, or jobbing as a carpenter in Kingfton, being bred there to that bufinefs;
He is a middle aged fellow, of a yellow complexion,
and has a fmall lump over his right eye. Whoever ap-
prehends the faid Negro and confines him in the
Work-houfe, or brings him to the fubfcriber, in the
parifh of St. George, fhall receive TWO PISTOLES
reward, and whoever will difcover by whom he is
harboured or concealed, fhall, on conviction of the
offender, receive TEN PISTOLES reward.

DAVID SUTHERLAND.

FIGURE 5. Runaway figures, in contrast to for-sale advertisements, were often depicted in motion, with a mountainous or similar landscape behind them. This ad also portrays the runaway with a walking stick.

Thus, runaway advertisements demonstrate the tension between the hurt body and the representation of the hurt body. Advertisements for fugitive bondspeople indicate that slavery affected the black body—the black body was subject to slavery, but it also came to be known and cataloged through the slaveowner's gaze. Indeed, as one of the only detailed sources of written descriptions of bondspeople in the British Caribbean (some sale ads also provided detailed depictions), runaway advertisements reveal a great deal about the kinds of injuries suffered by the enslaved.[35] But these sources have their limits and therefore must be read against the grain.[36]

For instance, because runaway notices were written by plantation authorities, they are replete with whites' racist descriptions of African phenotypic characteristics and distinguishing blemishes in ways that implicitly degraded the individual fugitive and confirmed prevailing racial hierarchies in the British Atlantic world. While slaveholders recorded universal social characteristics, such as ethnicity, age, and height, they often emphasized those variations that made individuals more recognizable.[37] Common phenotypic descriptions ranged from the general ("very black" or "coal black") to the specific (late-eighteenth-century racial categories like "mulatto," "mustee," "sambo," and "quadroon").[38] These terms reflected the racialized hierarchy of the colonies, and as such differed from those used in the metropole, where slaveowners used the standard phrase "of a black complexion" to describe fugitive bondspeople.[39] What is more, Caribbean owners reproduced the language of early travel accounts by exaggerating phenotypic characteristics and commenting on the extraordinary nature of certain ostensibly "African" features, such "big" mouths; "remarkable thick lips"; "flat," "large," and "sunken" noses; and being "full eyed." Such descriptions became so commonplace as to form a stereotype of African bodies. Descriptions of Africans with missing or excessive extremities, uncommon bodily shapes, and facial features of supposedly anomalous size served two functions: to stigmatize all blacks with disability, and to reinscribe sixteenth- and seventeenth-century British perceptions of Africans as questionably human. Thus, the tension between the real debilitated enslaved body and its representation in runaway advertisements is key to understanding how the black body was understood in all its contradictions—as simultaneously weak, aggressive, stammering, undisciplined, wounded, hyper-able, and disabled—and the historically rooted relationship between racism and ableism.

"Loss of Life or Limb"

In the Barbados and Jamaica statutes, some of the most brutal corporeal punishments were reserved for runaway bondspeople.[40] The first comprehensive slave laws of Barbados (1661) and Jamaica (1664) encouraged the formation of "any number of men not exceeding twenty" to hunt down and "apprehend or take [runaways] either alive or dead."[41] These founding laws exonerated whites from disabling or killing bondspeople under punishment for running away or other misdemeanors. According to the 1661 Barbados law and the 1664 Jamaica law, "if any slaves under punishment" for "running away or any other crime or misdemeanor towards his said Master shall suffer in life or in member noe person whatsoever shall be accountable to any Law."[42] The parallel grouping of dismemberment and death suggests that as early as the mid-seventeenth century, dismemberment was both a common punishment against runaways and on a level with death in its brutality. Such laws reveal important insights into the place of disability, and in particular dismemberment, in slavery's economy of violence.

The changes to Barbados and Jamaica laws from the late seventeenth century throughout the eighteenth century testify to the increase in fugitivity in the island. Following an uncovered slave rebellion plot in 1675, the Barbados Assembly amended the law pertaining to runaways, declaring that "if any Negro or Slave after he hath lived in this Island for the space of Twelve months at least, shall run away from his Master or Mistress, and continue absent above the space of thirty days, such Negro or Slave shall suffer death for the same." According to the 1692 "An Additional Act to an Act, entitled 'An Act for the governing of Negroes'," the 1688 Barbados slave code did not include the aforementioned law because "after some Negroes had suffered death for running away," the law "was repealed, it being expected that others would have taken warning thereby, and not have been guilty of such offence for the future." In 1692, lawmakers reinstated the death penalty for runaways absent for thirty days or more, arguing that the "brutish and barbarous nature" of Africans and their descendants led "to their long absence from the service of their Owners, [where] they become desperate, and daily plot and commit Felonies and other enormities, not only to the terror and affrightment of the Neighbourhood, but the danger of the Island in general."[43]

The progression of Jamaica laws regarding runaways testifies to the fact that fugitivity had become the island's most pressing concern in the eighteenth century and that maiming was the key penal strategy employed against runaways for much of the century. According to the 1706–7 Jamaica law, runaways who surrendered would "be freed from all Corporal Punishment and Loss of Life or Limb" and "be transported from the island, and sold."[44] Still, bondspeople who had been in the island for one year and ran away for thirty days or more were "to be punished, by cutting off one of the feet of such Slave."[45] The punishment of fugitives fit the crime in that it attempted to impair the individual's mobility and prevent them from self-absconding in the future. By the mid-eighteenth century, lawmakers claimed that such punishments "have not proved effectual." In the 1749 "An Act to inflict further and other Punishments on runaway Slaves, and such as shall entertain them," lawmakers declared that fugitive bondspeople absent for six months or more be "tried for capital Offences" and "suffer Death, or such other Punishment as shall be inflicted."[46] By the 1788 Consolidated Act of the amelioration period, lawmakers turned to confinement to hard labor as punishment for runaways absent for six months or more; if the sentenced runaway escaped again, however, he or she was executed.[47] The amelioration law of 1788, while seemingly less brutal in its punishment of runaways, was in the final analysis a sentence of physical debilitation and eventual death through confinement to hard labor. Even in response to a heated attack on the institution of slavery, the 1788 law continued to confirm the supposed suitability of Africans and their descendants to enforced labor and legitimize the notion that black bodies were made to be broken.

The slave laws pertaining to runaways reflect the making of white disability in contrast to the making of black disability. In 1702, Jamaica lawmakers mandated that "in case any white person shall be disabled from getting his living by any wound or hurt in the said service," the individual "shall be paid by the Commissioner . . . the sum of twenty pounds per annum for and during his Natural Life."[48] Searching for runaways in Jamaica, an island with established Maroon societies, was a dangerous feat and could result in serious injury of whites. Yet, white disability in this context was treated as a consequence of protective service to the island and the maintenance of slave society. Defense of the state included tracking down runaway slaves, so whites who became disabled in this service were financially compensated as a testament to their service. The law further reveals the making of white disability and how male citizenship and productivity was defined. If an enslaved individual became disabled, slaveowners were not compensated because a bondsperson's worth as a productive laborer did not cease with impairment. Bondspeople continued to labor under the threat of violence—in the fields and boiling houses, as well as in less physically taxing positions such as carrying water to field laborers. Thus, black disability was constructed in such a manner that maintained blacks' supposed fitness for hard labor. In contrast, as free wage-earning workers, whites who became disabled were offered compensation. In compensating disabled whites, the 1702 law constructed the capturing of runaways as a service to the island and those injured as heroes worthy of compensation.

Slavery produced visually striking forms of discipline—ones that reflected how slaveowners used disabling conditions in an attempt to prevent the enslaved from moving freely. In Barbados, apprehended fugitives were imprisoned in the "cage" at the center of Bridgetown until slaveowners claimed them.[49] A runaway advertisement in 1783 described "a dark complexioned Indian fellow, nam'd James, about five feet six inches high, with a defect in one of his insteps."

James's owner, Samuel Mapp, offered a reward of ten shillings to whoever apprehended him and "lodge[d] the said fellow in the cage in Bridgetown." Advertisements that mentioned the cage were commonplace in Barbados newspapers well into the nineteenth century. An advertisement in 1815 opened with the following announcement: "Fifty shillings reward will be given for apprehending and lodging in the Cage, a yellow-skin man by the name Quashey, formerly the property of Elizabeth Clement, deceased."[50] The cage reinforced and perpetuated a cycle of broken and disabled enslaved bodies by limiting the individual's movement and publicly displaying their immobility, but it was by no means the only method of doing so.

In Barbados, the 1708 slave laws prohibited the removal of collars and manacles from enslaved people's bodies with a penalty of £10. Lawmakers acknowledged that "the inhabitants in this Island do often put Hooks and Rings, or Collars round their Negroes Necks and Legs that absent themselves and run away from their Master or Mistress's service, the better to distinguish them, so that hereby they may be apprehended and brought home." They continued by claiming that, as of late, such collars had been removed "by which means they [the enslaved] are not known, and thereby keep out much longer from their Master's and Mistress's service, to their great detriment and damage."[51] These iron collars often included projecting spikes to prevent the individual from moving into areas with trees or bushes. Fugitives were also made to wear iron shackles with projecting spikes around their ankles, which lacerated the skin of the opposing ankle if the individual ran. During his trip to Jamaica (1687–89), Hans Sloane explained that "for Running away . . . [masters] put Iron Rings of great weight on their [slaves'] ankles, or Pottocks about their necks, which are Iron Rings with two long Necks rivetted to them, or a spur in the mouth."[52] The spur, or "mask," was often used for insolence, a charge made by plantation authorities usually against bondswomen for language "crimes," which included uttering insulting or threatening songs and speaking patois or creole, which slaveowners struggled to understand.[53] The use of a spur or other manacle caused severe pain and prevented the sufferer from speaking, eating, and even swallowing.[54] Such measures made mutes of bondspeople but also caused physical trauma to the mouth.[55] Mentions of iron restraints were not uncommon in runaway advertisements. For instance, when Nancy ran away from her owner, Thomas Hobson, in 1781 she had on "an iron collar." In 1760, an enslaved carpenter named Kent ran away with several brand marks on his chest and shoulders and "a collar about his Neck." In 1797, Hamilton fled with "a chain and collar round his Neck" and was expected to be harbored in Kingston.[56] Chains were obviously material restraints that both exemplified chattel status and disabled the enslaved by severely limiting their movements. Collars and chains abraded the skin and caused open sores and infections, which could limit the body's ability to move freely long after the shackles were removed. Collars and chains also caused scars, which disfigured the skin and left a permanent reminder of enslavement. Further, the sheer physical impact of wearing a collar every day would have been undoubtedly debilitating.

Limiting bondspeople's freedom of movement went beyond enforced forms of physically damaging brutalization. Lawmakers imposed metaphoric disabilities as well. Before runaway advertisements became popular, the necessity of surveillance was widely appreciated by the white residents of the British Caribbean. The first comprehensive Barbados and Jamaica slave codes required that captives carry a "ticket," a written document that was authorized by the subject's owner or overseer, permitting the bondsperson to be temporarily absent from the plantation on "necessary business."[57] As Barclay argues, the use of such tickets, or "authorization papers," as they were sometimes called, "reflected slaveholders' desire to imagine and construct enslaved blacks as wholly dependent and limited cripples."[58] Outside of law, the enslaved were under constant surveillance—or at least the threat of surveillance—from drivers, watchmen, and slavecatchers, and they were forced to endure a culture of fear, the message of which was entirely transparent: all of white society was constantly on guard, watching and monitoring everything and everyone on the island.

At most authorization papers offered white residents the opportunity to indulge in a fiction of control and authenticity. The extent to which tickets were successful in preventing the enslaved from unauthorized absences is difficult to gauge, although runaway advertisements give us some indication.[59] For instance, in 1781 Jacob Hill placed an advertisement in the *Royal Gazette* for three runaways. According to Hill, Preston escaped four weeks ago. He was "of a yellow complexion; his breast very remarkable, appearing full, like that of a young girl; stout made; has very crooked legs, with a sore on one. . . . is marked on both shoulders IH, diamond on top." The second runaway was named Sam, who a few days prior "went in search of Preston with a ticket, but through a mistake did not mention when he was to return."[60] Sam took advantage of the ticket system to forge his own freedom and undermine the institution of slavery's attempts to limit bondspeople's movement. The promise of controlled mobility and identification also led to tickets being used as a means of undermining surveillance, through the increase of forgery. The increase in literacy among the enslaved in the early nineteenth century made forgery of written authorization more common; it was likely that this influenced the Barbados Assembly's exclusion of tickets from the 1826 slave code, and its decision to make forgery a capital offense punishable by death.[61] Bondspeople's consistent pursuit of freedom speaks to the ways in which limit, and by extension disability, were seized as meaningful forms of resistance to Atlantic slavery.

Runaway ads demonstrate that punishments that disfigured and impaired the enslaved were not just legal threats. As the visual evidence of punishments meted out on plantations, the marks of violence depicted or described in runaway advertisements activate one's imagination for the simple reason that they suggest what is absent—the act of violence itself.[62] Some advertisements specified that these identifying marks were the result of punishment, whereas others merely implied that violence had taken place. The clearest and most frequently employed indication of violence was mention of the whip. While flogging constituted a common punishment for both free and unfree laborers in the Caribbean as well as in the metropole, marks from the whip were specifically associated with blackness and the captive population of the British Caribbean.[63] The *Barbados Gazette and General Intelligencer* ran an advertisement in October 1787 describing a fugitive named Mary as having marks of the whip on her cheek.[64] Another, published in the *Supplement to the Royal Gazette* in 1795, wrote of a man named Ned who had a small scar on his cheek "by accident of a whip lash." Several years later in the *Barbados Mercury and Bridgetown Gazette*, George was said to have "very large scars on his shoulders, from some former severe whipping." It is worth noting that, writing in 1808 one year after the abolition of the slave trade, George's subscriber claimed that the marks of punishment inflicted onto George's body were "from *some former* whipping," the qualifiers clearly distancing the current owner from any form of violence or even prior knowledge of any violence. Such language suggests that slaveowners were aware of attitudinal changes toward slavery sweeping the Atlantic World and changed the language of runaway advertisements to avoid culpability. Others were simply said to have had "marks of punishment" on their bodies.[65]

Flogging not only disfigured enslaved people's bodies but could lead to physical impairment. Writing in the late eighteenth century, slaveowner Joshua Steele explained that the usual order of thirty-nine lashes was "more than sufficient, in many constitutions, to send [the enslaved] out of the world with a *locked jaw*, a convulsion commonly excited by great pain, in this climate."[66] Severe flogging could and did result in the death of bondspeople. Based on this knowledge, we can presume that, for those who survived, their bodies' ability to move and function in daily tasks would have been permanently compromised.

Disability presents itself "through two main modalities—function and appearance."[67] Marks of punishment, then, including brands and marks of the whip, had the potential to disable not necessarily through function but through appearance by making the so-called disobedience of the enslaved salient in slave society. Permanent disfigurement of the flesh created a visual indication of one's enslaved status and the body's relationship to the owner. When used as identifying marks in runaway advertisements, such marks functioned as a powerful surveillance that ultimately limited how and where individuals moved. Like disability, disfigurement carried stigma. Marks of punishment, such as the whip, inscribed individuals with so-called rebelliousness and, in doing so, decreased that person's worth on the open market. In devaluing commodified worth, such disfigurements had the potential to prohibit an enslaved person from escaping a particularly tyrannical owner or overseer through sale. By disfiguring the flesh of bondspeople, lawmakers and planters attempted to make black skin a living reflection of imperial and slaveholding power. There was also a normative or prescriptive element to this as well: the scarred body permanently memorialized individuals' experiences in slavery.

Thomas Thistlewood's diary vivid demonstrates the various ways enslaved bodies, and in particular those of "incorrigible" runaways, were marked with the signs of servitude and dispossession. Coobah, an enslaved woman who first ran away from Thistlewood's plantation in 1765 and then repeatedly starting in 1769, was flogged, put in chains and collar restraints, and kept in the stock overnight numerous times throughout her thirteen years on Thistlewood's plantation. She also suffered from smallpox and several bouts of venereal disease. In July 1770, Thistlewood "flogged her well and brand marked her in the forehead."[68] Her brand served as a means to render her body legible, and to fix her identity as criminal.[69] Coobah had become a liability to Thistlewood, and her absence deprived him of more than just one enslaved laborer when he was forced to order some of his other captives to search for her. In May 1774 Thistlewood sold Coobah to a planter in Georgia. Though this was in no way an escape from slavery, her constant acts of running away took her away from sugar production to what may have been a less hostile labor environment in Georgia.[70] Coobah entered this new place bearing marks of her servitude on her body, marks that displayed a fragmented personal history of her experiences in enslavement and attempts to self-emancipate. While Coobah's slavery-induced marks did not necessarily impair her, they provided a narrative of rebelliousness that could have caused her social stigma in her new environment and made her more prone to the violence that is often associated with disability. The permanent marks inflicted onto Coobah's flesh evoked power that held claim to the past, present, and future.

While the bodies of African-born captives testified to a past life of freedom, runaway advertisements turned these visible signs of a previous freedom into "scars" that stigmatized African past and degraded the memories that they represented. "Country marks" were commonly mentioned in runaway ads; the term referred to the scarification practiced among some sub-Saharan African groups, such as Senegambians, West Central Africans, and Ibos. To readers of the Barbadian and Jamaican press, reference to these marks signaled a host of derisive European stereotypes of certain African ethnicities, as well as the supposed rebelliousness of African-born captives. For the enslaved, however, such marks bore witness to their former lives in freedom and the ownership they once enjoyed over their own bodies. Slave society sought to juxtapose these country marks with the scars left by branding, such that many African-born bodies "engraved with cultural signs that bestow[ed] meaning, identity, and belonging" were then "reinscribed with new 'marks of civilization'" in the form of branding and punishment.[71] Slaveowners, thus, repurposed country marks for valuing the enslaved, and in the process gave different meanings than intended to country marks.

Dismembered limbs and extremities were frequently mentioned in runaway advertisements and although toes, feet, legs, hands, and arms were sometimes amputated or cut off because of sores, such amputations could also be evidence of punishments, particularly for runaways.[72] In 1717 the Jamaica Assembly made it illegal for masters to dismember captives on their own property, with the exception of runaways who were "to be punished, by cutting off one of the Feet of such Slave, or inflicting such other corporal Punishment as they [Justices of the Peace and Freeholders] shall think fit." Such law was in effect until the amelioration law of 1788. In 1783 a Jamaica planter described his runaway captive, Dan, as having "a wooden leg" because "he had his leg cut off for robbing the late Mr. John McDonald, then overseer of Drax Hall." John Tharp, another Jamaica planter, described his runaway Cuffee as "a desperate villain . . . [who] had his nose cropt for being formerly runaway." A Mr. Drummon told Olaudah Equiano that he cut off a bondsperson's leg for running away, which he said served its purpose since "it cured that man and some others of running away."[73]

Runaway advertisements reflected this violence. To deter running away, owners sadistically punished the enslaved and meted out "all kinds of abominations . . . such as deliberately crippling them and even sawing off their offending legs."[74] An advertisement published in the *Barbados Gazette and General Intelligencer* in 1788 read: "Absented from the subscriber, a negro man named Joe, formerly the property of Thomas Burton, Esq. deceased. He is about six feet high, one of his legs has been taken off above the knee, and he speaks very good English." In July 1789 a notice published in Jamaica described a female fugitive, Liddy, who had "lost her right hand above the wrist, and had an iron collar round her neck."[75] The iron collar on Liddy suggests that Liddy had previously run away from her owner; her amputated right hand may be indicative of a punishment for a criminal offense or of a labor accident.

Others were described as missing ears, toes, fingers, and teeth. For instance, on 10 February 1780, Dorothy Peake advertised for several runaways, including Kent, "a cooper by trade . . . [with] a piece taken off one of his ears, of middle age, is a well set fellow, rather bow-legged, and about 5 feet 7 inches." Kent's amputated ear was a common punishment in Caribbean slave societies although it was not specified in the laws of either Barbados or Jamaica. Missing toes were also common in runaway advertisements and could be an indication of punishment, disease, or labor accidents. A man named James was described as having "both his great toes cut off." Missing teeth were frequently mentioned in runaway advertisements. For instance, Sarah Gittens described Betty as "very bandy, has lost most of her teeth, one of the joints of the middle toe of her right foot, and has a scar on the inside of her left leg." Another advertisement referred to bondsman Billy Harwood as having "a black mark under his left eye from being blown by gunpowder, a scar upon his upper lip, two of his fore teeth out, and a scar on the throat." Like amputated toes, missing teeth could be caused by a variety of different circumstances—violence, labor accident, or malnutrition—however, slave narratives demonstrate that knocking one's teeth out was a common punishment inflicted on enslaved people for eating sugarcane. For instance, Ottobah Cugoano explained that "for eating a piece of sugarcane, some were cruelly lashed, or struck over the face to knock their teeth out." Some enslaved people, he wrote, "had their teeth pulled out to deter others, and to prevent them from eating any cane in the future."[76] Such violence would have caused immediate pain as well as long-term problems for enslaved individuals. For instance, loss of teeth would have significantly altered one's physical appearance as well as their daily lives, resulting in impaired chewing ability and therefore quantity of food intake, as well as speech difficulties. Runaway advertisements that detailed marks of punishments such as a brand, slit nose, cropped ears, missing teeth, or amputated legs made the otherwise invisible criminal act visible to the reading audience and, in doing so, increased the disabling power of marks of the flesh.

Disability in the Everyday

Sugar production was an incredibly disabling enterprise. Enslaved laborers were regularly dismembered, burned, and maimed in sugar production. For the previously mentioned Joe, having one leg "taken off above the knee" could have been punishment for a prior escape; it could also have been a forced amputation after an injury sustained working in the cane field. The boiling house—the architectural feature and work environment of the plantation that most resembled the factory—required the technical mastery of sugar boilers, who worked in extremely hot, loud, and dangerous conditions. Boilers were also susceptible to dismemberment from having their hands and arms caught in the mill, as well as from burns, which sometimes caused death. In his 1657 *True and Exact History of the Island of Barbados,* for example, Richard Ligon described the dangers of making and transporting rum. "We lost an excellent Negre" he wrote, "who bringing a Jar of this Spirit [rum], from the Still-house, to the Drink-room . . . not knowing the force of the liquor he carried, brought the candle somewhat nearer than he ought . . . and burnt the poor Nigre to death, who was an excellent servant."⁷⁷ Slavery produced overlapping and multifaceted forms of black disability.

The materially impoverished worlds in which the enslaved lived—lacking adequate food, clothing, and housing, and forced to work in unsanitary conditions—produced disabling illnesses. Runaway advertisements record several individuals described as being "defective in walking," "crippled," "crooked," "walk[ing] a little lame from a hurt on one of his legs," and "in a debilitated state." A "mulatto" man, Samuel Millar, was described as "afflicted to have the rheumatism in his arm."⁷⁸ In 1806, an enslaved girl named Clarissa was described as having "the third finger on her right hand crippled, a mark under her right eye, and has also the marks of punishment."⁷⁹ "Lameness," "crippled" limbs, and "abnormal" gaits were some of the most common forms of physical impairment displayed and described in Barbadian and Jamaican runaway notices but they were produced through a variety of circumstances.

Blindness also made regular appearances in runaway advertisements, though the condition did not necessarily impair one's ability to be productive on the plantation, where it was more common for bondspeople to experience a loss of vision due to environmental conditions. Blindness, missing eyes, or "sore eyes" could be caused by a vitamin A deficiency, infection, allergies, accident, or punishment. In 1795, a slaveowner advertised for his missing bondswoman named Stella, who was "generally known for having only one eye and a small leg." Enslaved individuals who became blind had to learn how to navigate their new reality and keep up with the demands of plantation labor. For instance, a 1791 runaway advertisement from Jamaica described Bob as a "stout able negro man . . . of the Congo country" who was "marked on one shoulder G.G." Bob was "blind of the left eye [and] has a large scar across his left cheek, which he got about sixteen years ago by the kick of a Mule, by which accident he came to lose his eye." According to the subscriber of the advertisement, Bob was a "most excellent swimmer and diver [and] has been occasionally employed as a fisherman and sailor negro."[80] Despite his disability, Bob clearly remained a productive laborer, one who was valued by his owner for his skills. The commonplace nature of these disabilities produced a naturalizing effect that blacks were inherently disabled and therefore suited for slavery.

In a social order predicated on black enslavement and white freedom, not all disabilities were created equal. Some impairments common among the enslaved did not constitute disabilities because planters found new ways to repurpose bodies that in other historical contexts, European industrial labor for instance, would have been disposed of because of their impairments. In some cases, disability made enslaved individuals more valuable without producing contradictions or fear of wasting a capable worker. Impaired sight, for instance, was common among watchmen, who were often recruited from old and infirm bondsmen whose disabilities made them unfit for field labor. Watchmen monitored the plantation grounds in search of runaways and other "criminal" behavior. In the night, explained one plantation management guide, "runaway negroes . . . are subject and too prone to rob and plunder the grounds of your negroes. Let therefore proper watch houses be built at due distances around the same, and the watch be prepared with a gun and watch dogs to give notice if any approach to commit their . . . robberys." In 1776, all three watchmen on the Newton plantation, at Christ Church, Barbados, were defined as "old," while on the Seawell plantation the head boiler and watchman, Obo, was described as "very old and weak with one eye." A notice for a female runaway, Sarah, mentioned that she had been "employed as a watch," and described her as "dim-sighted." As the plantation management guide put it, "old negroes that are past labour are fittest for such watchers, as they are not so subject to sleep as young and labouring negroes."[81]

Some runaway advertisements also described enslaved individuals' congenital abnormalities and testified to how the material conditions of slavery and lack of maternal care for enslaved mothers could result in disability at birth. W. Armstrong, for example, described Romeo as "without any marks only a natural one, which is, never having more than four toes on one of his feet." Toby and Blackwall were both described as "remarkable" for having six fingers on each hand. Another advertisement described a male fugitive named August, who had "his right leg and foot much decayed, being born so, and walks lame." In February 1789, George was distinguished by his "full mouth, uncommonly made, being much longer over the breast than the belly, broad thick feet; he must have been born with twelve fingers, and one being taken off from each hand, leaves a scar by the side of each finger."[82] George's description of course leaves unanswered questions—namely, the circumstances under which his fingers were cut off. But we can surmise that the amputation of two of his fingers suggests that being born with twelve fingers was viewed as an aberration in need of correction. More generally, such descriptions contributed to the long-standing English notion that African bodies were innately deviant and deficient, and the widespread display of African deformities in fugitive notices served to link blackness to a host of beliefs about Africans that extended to the body and mind.

Nowhere is this more apparent than in the language used to describe the bodies of female fugitives, which in British Caribbean runaway advertisements were most often described as simultaneously recognizable and deformed. In 1787 a Barbadian runaway referred to as "a black skin negro girl" was described by her owner as having "slim legs, a round belly, small or no breasts, round faced, silly looking, and her hair growing almost to her eyebrow; squints a little; and limps much, and has a crooked great toe, all on the right side." This description, although written for purposes of identification and apprehension, nonetheless reflected English perceptions of African bodies as grotesque, deficient, and abnormal. Similarly, on 30 December 1788, Philip Hackett, from Mox Hall estate in Barbados, advertised for his missing captive by evoking images of African women's abnormal femininity. According to Hackett, Rosetta was "four feet eleven inches high and seventeen inches over the shoulders, has a drowsy countenance, large thick lips, small fallen breasts, a round belly with her country marks cut in diamond, large buttocks, small legs, a very small foot, a small hand but somewhat hard from working with the hoe."[83] The exposure of Rosetta's body, particularly the description of her "fallen breasts," echoed sixteenth- and seventeenth-century European travel accounts that associated African women's nakedness with savagery. Moreover, the emphasis on her oddities of size—"large thick lips," "small fallen breasts," "round belly," "large buttocks," "small legs," "a very small foot," "a small hand"—imprinted her body with abnormalities, while the mention of her hand being "somewhat hard from working with the hoe" reinforced her body's supposed suitability to hard labor.

Runaway notices also conflated African phenotypic characteristics with physical abnormalities caused by malnutrition and vitamin deficiencies. For this reason some of the most common distinguishing marks used by slaveowners to identify bondspeople described their legs and feet. Runaways were described as "bow-legged," "knock-kneed," "splaw footed," "parrot toed," and "crooked in both knees."[84] These physical conditions manifested themselves most often in enslaved children and were a result of rickets, a disease caused by calcium and vitamin D deficiencies.[85] Plantation owners fed their bondspeople foods very high in starch, such as corn, rice, sugar, and plantain, which caused severe vitamin deficiencies and consequently often permanent physical deformities.[86] The repeated reproduction of such descriptions in British Caribbean newspapers suggested that Africans and their descendants were biologically, indeed racially, prone to these physical deformities. In fact, in 1774 the Anglo-Irish naturalist Oliver Goldsmith depicted African phenotypic characteristics and physical abnormalities caused by disease as racially specific deformities that defied the effects of geography and climate: "In the Negro children born in European countries, the same deformities are seen to prevail; the same flatness in the nose, and the same prominence of the lips. They are, in general, said to be well shaped; but of such as I have seen, I never found one that might be justly called so; their legs being mostly ill formed, and commonly bending outward on the shinbone."[87] Goldsmith's comment on the "ill formed" legs of Africans is likely a reference to the physical consequences of rickets; however, in associating these deformities with African phenotypic characteristics, Goldsmith suggested that they were "natural." He refuted the climatology theory of race by suggesting that not even European acclimatization could change the deformities of Africans and their descendants; he also denied that widespread forms of black impairment were caused by enslavement. Such *racialization* of deformity reflects the conflation of African phenotype with deformities caused by the brutal conditions in which the enslaved were forced to live. At the same time, Goldsmith relieved slaveowners, and slavery itself, of blame for physical deformities resulting from the malnutrition, overwork, punishment, and hostile living conditions the enslaved were forced to endure.

Disfiguring marks caused by disease and illness carried different implications for enslaved and free people. The marks left by smallpox had a disabling social effect on free women—namely, by adversely affecting their chances of marriage by making them less attractive to eligible suitors.[88] Marks of smallpox on the enslaved, by contrast, testified to the bondsperson's immunity to the disease, which made them more valuable on the open market but also more vulnerable to detection if they absconded.[89] An advertisement from Jamaica for the sale of captives from the ship *Loretta* described the enslaved as "CHOICE EBOE SLAVES which have had the small pox." Another notice from 1791 advertised for the sale of "Fourteen able seasoned FIELD NEGROES; who have had the yaws and smallpox; nine men and five women."[90] Bondspeople's immunity to such contagious diseases increased their market value and made them more prone to detection due to the highly visible effects of the disease on the face and body.

Montego-Bay, June 15, 1781.

FOR SALE, on Friday the 29th inst. in the harbour of Port Maria, the *Atalanta*'s entire cargo of 416 prime Gold-Coast SLAVES, which was advertised for the 13th inst. at this place, but obliged to be put off for want of purchasers, on account of the present scarcity of provisions.

Mures & Dunlop.

☞ The Atalanta will sail this day, with the fleet going to windward, under convoy of the Jamaica and Tobago.

St. Ann's, June 14, 1781.

FOR SALE, forty or more able, seasoned, Field Negro Men and Women, six Carpenters and Mill-Wrights, and two Taylors; who have all had the small-pox, and most of them have had the yawe.——For particulars, apply to RICHARD GRANT, Esq. Attorney-at-Law in Kingston, or of Mr. WILLIAM ROBERTSON, the Proprietor, in St. Ann's:——Who will also sell his PENN, called *THATCHFIELD*, with the Remainder of the Negroes, and the Stock thereon, on reasonable Terms.

FIGURE 6. For-sale advertisements often used language such as "prime" and "able" to advertise for supposedly ideal enslaved laborers. The images used in for-sale ads contrast with runaway ads in that the figures are often portrayed as unmoving, rooted to a spot with little to no scenic background. Such image implies that the figures are commodities, products to be surveilled, appraised, and purchased.

Psychological Wounding and Masquerade

Some of the marks of violence described in runaway advertisements hinted at the psychological wounds caused by enslavement. Runaway notices sometimes identified the aftermath of a bondsperson's suicide attempt.[91] Piere, a runaway from the Oxford plantation in the Jamaican parish of Saint Mary, was described by his owner as having "a scar on his throat, where he formerly cut it." On 15 August 1795, Henry Skerrett advertised in the *Royal Gazette* for his captive "Cuffee, a very black fellow, with three or four cuts in his throat; in the attempts he made to cut it through, he either willingly or wittingly failed." Solomon was likewise described as having "some scars on his throat, having attempted different times to cut it." In the same year, a young man named Charles escaped from his owner, Isaac Bernal Jr. The notice placed in the *Cornwall Chronicle* recorded that Charles's previous owner, Mr. Jackson, told Bernal that Charles had promised to "cut his own throat sooner than return to his Master."[92] While none of the runaway advertisements analyzed for this chapter describe bonds-*women* as having marks of attempted suicide, it may be that cutting one's throat represented a particularly masculine method of trying to kill oneself. Historians of slavery, after all, have shown that both enslaved men and women killed themselves to escape slavery.[93]

Fugitive notices are not the kind of primary source to indicate the origin of speech disorders, but we can reasonably speculate that many speech impediments were a result of the trauma caused by slavery. Fugitives' habits of speech—stammers, stutters, and other such impediments—were commonly used by owners to identify their missing bondsperson.[94] A fugitive bondsman named Rob was described as being "middle sized man, stammers in his speech, and had (when he went away) a sore on one of his legs." An advertisement from Jamaica in 1781 described "a Negro fellow named TOM, but called himself TOM DICKSON" who "has an impediment in his speech, and has lost his fore teeth, owning to a shot in his mouth." Another bondsman was described as "a tight well-made fellow, about 22 years of age, middle-sized, very busy hair, much pimpled in the face, hesitates and stutters much in his speech."[95] Such peculiarities might indicate that individuals' everyday contact with overseers, owners, and drivers, which was characterized by routine violence, may have caused trauma-induced speech blocks. However, it could be that stammers and stutters were used by bondspeople as a form of resistance in a similar manner as when bondspeople spoke what owners described as "bad" or "broken" English. "Bad" or "broken" English was an Africanized English employed by enslaved people as a form of resistance "to communicate the ideas, emotions, and sensibilities of persons of African descent."[96] The stutters, stammers, and impediments described in runaway advertisements could have also been used to bondspeople's tactical advantage—for example, to deflect owners' and overseers' demands by enacting disability.

Scars proved useful as identifying marks because they were thought to be immutable—they could be supplemented but never entirely removed.[97] Some fugitive bondspeople altered the scars and marks on their flesh in an attempt to evade identification. In 1794, a $15 reward was offered for the apprehension of Nimrod, a fugitive bondsman suspected of "endeavor[ing] to obliterate" the "WT" branded on both his shoulders and chest.[98] The information provided in runaway advertisements was, of course, liable to change—indeed, once a fugitive's appearance was committed to writing, she or he *had* to change as much as possible.[99] Fugitives most likely attempted to remove collars and chains, so owners always supplemented their descriptions with corporeal information. For instance, when Rachael G. Silvia stated that her missing captive Cinthia "had on a Chain, which it is supposed is taken off," she included information about her bodily appearance as well. In another notice, Prudence's owner warned that she might have changed her clothing in an attempt to disguise herself while a fugitive—a common practice for runaway bondspeople: Greenwhich tried to conceal the elephantiasis on his foot by wearing long trousers, while Lorain wore a handkerchief around his head to disguise "part of his right ear cut off."[100] Clothing could, thus, identify as well as camouflage the "distinguishing marks" that fugitive captives bore.

Disability as masquerade elicits questions about "passing." Disability passing is a complex topic that refers both to people concealing disability in order to avoid stigma, as well as to individuals exaggerating a condition in order to reap benefits from disability.[101] There were times when slaveowners and managers suspected that certain individuals feigned illness or impairment and were, therefore, skeptical of injuries and illnesses among the enslaved.[102] Masquerading as disabled, whether on or off the plantation, provided bondspeople opportunities to self-consciously shape their appearance. Erving Goffman's definition of passing as "stigma management" has been very useful to scholars of disability, who discuss passing as a strategy to conceal disability.[103]

But the attempt to alter one's identity and public appearance is undertaken for reasons that are historically specific.[104] While passing as able-bodied in the contemporary West represents an attempt to escape stigmatization and negative social stereotyping in an able-bodied world, passing as disabled in seventeenth- and eighteenth-century slave society offered fugitive bondspeople a certain amount of freedom. Feigning disability allowed them to use the changing physical and environmental context of freedom to adjust and renew their bodies. Runaway advertisements depicted fugitive captives not only "pretending to be something else . . . [but], in doing so, becoming something else."[105]

Disease, deformity, disfigurement, and impairment—in a word, disability—were widely displayed in newspapers across Barbados and Jamaica during the eighteenth and early nineteenth centuries. The identifying marks described in runaway advertisements changed over time, specifically with the amelioration period. Mentions of branding declined significantly in the last decade of the eighteenth century and early nineteenth century, whereas other forms of disfigurements, deformities, and disabilities increased. While branding in runaway advertisements waned in response to abolitionists' critique of branding as reflective of slavery's terror, in place of branding were a host of other disfiguring and disabling marks used in the identification and apprehension of fugitive bondspeople. Runaway ads further indicate that plantation authorities were aware of the antislavery discourse and responded to abolitionist attacks by using language of "former" whippings in order to evade responsibility for such violence. This change over time suggests that slaveowners changed the language used in runaway advertisements to avoid abolitionist critique but continued to uphold a culture of unchecked violence against the enslaved.

Runaway notices kept the enslaved in a "state of injury."[106] Such ads touted bondspeople's individual impairments. In displaying the wounds, disabilities, and scars produced by slavery, the advertisements did more than simply advertise for missing bondspeople. By displaying the injured black body, the notices reproduced early modern English notions of Africans as physically deficient and deformed, innately rebellious, and suited to a life of enslavement. Indeed, disability is key to understanding runaway advertisements as a means for black bodies to become racialized. Disability and blackness became inextricably intertwined and mutually constitutive forces that worked to further entrench the connections between racism and ableism.

The display of wounds in Caribbean fugitive notices was part of the long and overlapping history of the staging of race and disability for visual consumption. But what distinguishes these advertisements from other forms of display, such as freak shows and curiosity cabinets, is the terror they engendered. Runaway advertisements did not spark wonder like depictions of black bodies in earlier travelogues. Rather, fugitive notices reflected the fear with which white society associated the supposedly dangerous and disorderly enslaved population. These ads were above all a reflection of the plantocracy's anxiety over the need to sustain the institution of slavery. This fear expressed itself in the kinds of violence slaveowners imparted on the enslaved and their use of runaway adver-tisements to exert control over the enslaved through disabling terror. The ads were themselves disabling in that they acted as a form of widespread surveil-lance and policing measure that attempted to limit bondspeople's freedom of movement.

Lennard J. Davis argues that, "by narrativizing impairment, one tends to sentimentalize it and link it to the bourgeois sensibility of individualism and the drama of the individual story."[107] This warning notwithstanding, the violently marked fugitives whose experiences were recorded in runaway advertisements reveal dramatic personal stories of freedom and enslavement. The pervasiveness of impairment described in runaway advertisements illustrates the degree to which impairment and disability affected bondspeople, shaping their experi-ences of enslavement. Some measure of the brutality of these experiences is provided by the fact that individuals dared to run away despite their physical limitations, which in many cases significantly limited their physical mobility in the often inhospitable Barbadian and Jamaican hinterlands. In the context of slavery, the image of the black body was never just individual—it was, rather, emblematic of a collective body. But the marks recorded in runaway notices held different meanings for different readers.[108] For the slaveholding reading public, marks of punishment may have signaled, not cruel violence meted out to defenseless bodies, but rather the triumph of judicial order over violence and chaos.[109] For those uncomfortable with this simplistic narrative of slavery, such marks signaled a multilayered story of an individual's endurance of slav-ery and struggle for autonomy and self-emancipation. The rhetoric of runaway advertisements shows us how law, labor, and trauma were at work in slave societies and were revealed through the rhetoric of runaway advertisements. These ads did not simply catalog the disabling abuses of slavery, but through rhetoric they themselves were a disabling force in the sense that they perpetu-ated long-standing European notions of the enslaved as deformed beings.

CHAPTER 5

Bondsman or Rebel

*Disability Rhetoric and the Challenge
of Revolutionary Emancipation*

> Representation structures rather than reflects real-
> ity. The way we imagine disability through images
> and narratives determines the shape of the material
> world, the distribution of resources, our relationships
> with one another, and our sense of ourselves.
>
> —Rosemarie Garland-Thomson, "Disability and
>   Representation"

In his 1808 *History of the Rise, Progress, and Accomplishment of the Abolition of the Slave-Trade*, leading British abolitionist Thomas Clarkson described the Dolben Act (1788) as "the first bill that ever put fetters on that barbarous and destructive monster, the Slave-trade."[1] The Dolben Act was an amelioration reform that limited the number of captives one could carry on British slave ships and required that each vessel have a doctor to keep a register of captive and crew sicknesses and deaths.[2] Clarkson deployed both slavery and disability as metaphors to describe the slave trade as a "destructive monster" that necessitated confinement by iron shackles. Throughout the antislavery movement, abolitionists took up the rhetoric of monstrosity, long used by advocates of slavery to justify African enslavement, and flipped it on its head: the *real* monster, they argued, was the institution of slavery itself. To emphasize this point they seized on the image of the beaten, disfigured, and impaired enslaved person to evoke moral outrage and sympathy in their predominantly white, metropolitan audience. Abolitionists took advantage of the culture of sympathy and used disability to imagine a way to incorporate the black enslaved into the British body politic as *nonthreatening* free subjects. In the late eighteenth century, meanwhile, slavery advocates' earlier (fantastical) claims that Africans represented a "race of monsters" were dropped in favor of the growing philosophical and scientific interest in species difference.[3] Proslavery thinkers argued that Africans were intellectually incapable of freedom and increasingly claimed that they were a different species than human.[4]

An exploration of the relationship between disability, amelioration, and abolition in the period from the 1770s to the legal end of the slave trade in 1807 reveals that both opponents and supporters of slavery utilized notions of disability and invoked concepts of monstrosity to maintain the social and racial hierarchies of the eighteenth-century British Atlantic world.[5] Revolutionary emancipation, from Tacky's War in Jamaica (1760) to the Haitian Revolution (1791–1804), is key to understanding the place of disability in both anti and proslavery rhetoric in the age of abolition. Revolutionary emancipation gave rise to the gendered image of the armed, able-bodied, dangerous, and revolutionary black man, an image that circulated throughout the Atlantic World and haunted both sides of the slavery discourse. While some white abolitionists were drawn to the figure of the revolutionary black man, many were repelled. Antislavery campaigners emphasized in its place the figure of the broken and beaten bondsperson as a way of envisioning a subject who in her or his freedom presented no physical threat to white society. These two images embodied different paths to emancipation—the choice between revolutionary and armed rebellion on the one hand, exemplified by the Haitian Revolution, and emancipation as a process of imperial and legislated reform on the other.

As part of amelioration, abolitionists encouraged enslaved women to have children so that the enslaved population could reproduce itself naturally. The suppression of the slave trade would decrease planters' reliance on the slave trade as a means of reproducing an inheritable, monstrous race and labor force.[6] Planters continued to propagate the long-standing proslavery argument that African women did not feel pain in childbirth, which in turn testified to their supposed animality. In abolitionist propaganda, by contrast, the figure of the pained female body, in need of protection from long-term damage so that it might give birth and raise children, became a key means of displacing the figure of the armed, male rebel.

At the heart of the ameliorative effort to suppress slavery was the fear, held by people on both sides of the slavery issue, that the slave trade would only bring more future revolutionaries into the British colonies—a fear that only increased after the Haitian Revolution. That revolution transformed Saint

Domingue, the richest colony in the Caribbean, into the independent state of Haiti and exemplified enslaved resistance and self-liberation. Indeed, the figure of the rebel was impossible to ignore in the eighteenth-century British Atlantic world because it was a real threat to white society and imperial power. The pro and antislavery effort to suppress the intra-Caribbean slave trade, especially after the Haitian Revolution, was motivated by the same fear of black Haitian revolutionaries. This is not to reify being able-bodied as being in reality more capable of auto-emancipation but rather to demonstrate that the idea of black citizenship was framed in gendered and ableist terms. The able-bodied rebel was frightening, but that figure allows us to consider an interesting dichotomy.

The place of supposedly "disabled" and "able" bodies in competing ideas about modern citizenship was rooted in a sharp distinction between two models of emancipation: imperial humanitarianism and subjecthood, on the one hand, and revolutionary human rights and citizenship on the other. Abolitionists put forth humanitarian ideas of inclusion while implicitly rejecting the idea of human rights.[7] As such, the British abolitionist movement was fraught with hypocrisy, for while its members viewed the slave trade as a moral crime, they never espoused the idea that enslaved Africans were equal to, or deserved the same "rights" as, Britons. Jenny Martinez, for one, has rightly pointed out that the seeds of international human rights law were planted during the abolitionist era, particularly from the 1820s to the 1860s, when the first antislavery courts were established in Freetown, Havana, Rio de Janeiro, Suriname, Cape Town, Loanda, and New York.[8] But the rhetoric employed by abolitionists as part of their campaign to end the British slave trade demonstrates how, until quite recently, histories of disability and emancipation were severed from histories of human rights.

Early Antislavery Writings

If we are to understand the place of "disabled" and "able" bodies in the fight over slavery's existence, we must understand the antislavery sentiment that circulated prior to the abolitionist movement that coalesced in the 1780s. Of course, the first individuals to attack the institution of slavery publicly were the enslaved themselves. Indeed, in this respect, antislavery is as old as slavery itself. Enslaved people resisted from the very genesis of their capture and forced march, during the Middle Passage, and on the plantation. As scholars have demonstrated, the antislavery struggles of the enslaved also played a key role in the formal abolitionist campaigns against the slave trade and slavery. Among white Britons, there too were opponents of slavery from the very beginning of British overseas expansion; however, British antislavery thought was slow to develop into a political movement. In the seventeenth and early eighteenth centuries, most British people enjoyed the fruits of Caribbean slavery without having to face its social and cultural costs. Thus, during the early colonial period, the moral injustices of slavery were not a matter of widespread debate, since the desire to judge slavery critically "was tempered by an almost complete acceptance of the value of slavery to the colonies and to the empire." Still, several individuals, namely clergy from Protestant denominations who had seen human bondage for themselves, voiced their concern over the state of West Indian slavery.[9]

On the surface, these early antislavery writers did not engage with notions of disability, and yet, the moral and medical models of disability shaped their discussions of slavery in the British Atlantic world. In early modern England, the physical and moral were mutually constitutive, and religious and medical thinkers believed that to "cure" the physically deformed or disabled body one had to start with the soul.[10] The English perceived both blackness and disability as outward signs of inner immorality, and the idea that the corporeal was merely an outward reflection of one's inner goodness or sin remained influential well into the eighteenth century.[11] An early critic of slavery and founder of the Quakers in Ireland, William Edmundson traveled to Barbados, Antigua, Nevis, and Jamaica in 1671. In Jamaica he wrote a letter to the clergy warning them of God's imminent judgment of their support of slavery. Edmundson evoked disability as metaphor in his condemnation of clergymen, insinuating that one's inner sinfulness manifested itself through corporeal disabilities. He wrote, "is not your Flocks (as you call them) by that means fallen into grose diseases, as Rottenness of Heart, Unsoundness of Mind, Blindness and Deafness? ... And are they not fallen into Lameness of Feet and Hands? And cannot walk upright in *the just mans path, which is a Shining Light,* but stumbles at it."[12] Edmundson used disability as a metaphor to suggest that both the colonized and the colonizer suffer the effects of slavery's disablement.

Unlike in the late eighteenth and early nineteenth centuries, disabled bodies did not feature widely in early antislavery sentiment; in fact, the majority of early antislavery rhetoric was marked by an *absence* of real bodies. Instead, it emphasized the religious immorality of slavery and argued that religion would provide both colonists and their captives the means to transform slavery into a "redeemable" institution.[13] Religious thinkers made up a significant portion of early critics of slavery, and a key feature of their writing was the notion of sin. In a letter addressed to his fellow Friends, Quaker founder George Fox cautioned slaveowners, some of whom were Quakers, that planters would be held accountable for the spiritual failings of their bondspeople on Judgment Day.[14] Although this position lent itself to the notion that slavery itself was a sin, early antislavery sentiment did not advocate abolition. Rather, early abolitionists sought to make slavery more "humane" and to limit its expansion, all in an effort to save the souls of Africans and quell the prospect of insurrection and revolution.[15] For instance, in 1673 English theologian Richard Baxter offered a strong admonition of slavery when he argued that the trade represented "one of the worst kinds of thievery in the world" and that slave traders and owners alike were "fitter to be called incarnate devils than Christians." And yet, even with this powerful condemnation of the trade in humans, Baxter placed eternal salvation above immediate liberation by urging slaveowners to "make it your chief end in buying and using slaves, to win them to Christ, and save their souls . . . and let their salvation be far more valued by you than their service."[16] Thus, the first Britons to take an interest in the welfare of the enslaved advocated not for the liberation of enslaved bodies but for the salvation of souls.

The language of saving souls, however, contained within it an imperative to preserve the bodies of the enslaved from the disabling violence and abuse of slavery. Many early antislavery writers saw physical and spiritual liberty as one and the same.[17] Early antislavery writer Thomas Tryon argued that Caribbean slaveowners were "guilty not only of oppressing [enslaved] Bodies, but (as much as in them lies) of *damning [their] Souls.*"[18] Anglican minster Morgan Godwyn, who traveled to Virginia and Barbados in the mid-seventeenth century, stressed the Christian necessity of leading enslaved Africans to the Lord by drawing an analogy between physical health and spiritual health. He argued that to refrain from providing bondspeople "ordinary necessaries, [such] as *food,*" was just as "Barbarous and Inhumane" as "withhold[ing] from them the exercise of *religion*, and the knowledge of *God*, [which is] equally needful for the preservation of their *Souls.*" According to Godwyn, the popular belief among seventeenth-century slaveowners that Africans were not descendants of Adam led planters to justify their bondage and "disable them from all *Rights and Claims*, even to *Religion* it self." But Godwyn, like most early English critics of slavery, was not opposed to slavery itself. Rather, he advocated for the more humane treatment of bondspeople and for their conversion, arguing that a Christian bondsperson was more acquiescent than a heathen one.[19] Early opponents' concern for the souls of Africans reflected the belief that the suffering soul was intimately connected to the suffering body. The absence of bodies, therefore, did not preclude a concern for the physical state of Africans and their descendants in the British Caribbean.

In contrast to most of her contemporaries, Tory writer Aphra Behn depicted the figure of the broken and beaten black body to illicit sympathy from her white reading audience, while she simultaneously dispelled white fears of the *undisciplined* black male rebel.[20] Behn based her work on her experience in the British Atlantic colonies and used fiction to express her critique of slavery, revealing truths about slavery not articulated in traditional antislavery tracts. Although *Oroonoko* depicts the physical and psychological violence of slavery, such scenes portray vindicated acts of violence meted out onto those who transgressed the rules of slave society.[21] Prior to his execution, the titular character kills his wife, Imoinda, and unborn child to spare them from the traumas of slavery. Oroonoko is grief-stricken after Imoinda's death, which tortures him psychologically. Behn wrote that he "found his brains turn round, and his eyes were dizzy; and objects appear'd not the same to him [as] they were wont to do; his breath was short; and all his limbs surprised with a faintness he had never felt before." This depiction of the debilitating effects of psychological pain is followed by Oroonoko's gruesome physical torture and death, in which he is tied to a whipping post, flogged, and, with "an ill-favoured knife," castrated, and his ears, nose, and arms dismembered. All the while, Oroonoko is smoking a pipe and showing no sign of recognition of what is being done to his body. Shortly after his dismemberment, Oroonoko "gave up the ghost," and dies "without a groan or a reproach."[22] With Oroonoko's dismemberment and death, order and slaveholder power are restored in Suriname. Behn's focus on the enslaved body and the spectacle of disablement, particularly dismemberment, foreshadowed many elements of later antislavery writing in its depiction of the able-bodied black revolutionary man as a threat in need of violent containment. Behn seemed ultimately to sympathize with Oroonoko the captured prince but not with Oroonoko the rebel.

More than any other early antislavery text, Thomas Tryon's 1684 *Friendly advice to the gentlemen-planters of the East and West Indies* foreshadowed the abolitionist movement's emphasis of the broken, beaten, and suffering enslaved body and its preoccupation with the capacities and supposed differences of the black body and mind. Tryon was interested in corporeal realities and the physical consequences of slavery—violence, starvation, injury—and religious opposition was not a marked feature of his writings against slavery. In this way, Tryon's work can be seen as a transition from early antislavery writers' obsession with saving the souls of the enslaved and abolitionist writers' emphasis on the saving of enslaved bodies from the atrocities of slavery. Tryon was a hatter in Barbados for several years in the 1660s before returning to London. His *Friendly advice* was part travel narrative, part social critique of the institution of slavery. Tryon sought to expose slavery's corporeal destructiveness by framing his critique as a slave narrative delivered from the perspective of a fictitious bondsman. Through his first-person narration, Tryon's bondsperson paid great attention to the physical and psychological disabilities produced by slavery, including the brutalities of the Middle Passage, the violence inflicted onto bondspeople by plantation authorities, and the gendered nature of slavery's violence.

Tryon held slavery accountable for the psychological trauma suffered by captives and the sin of suicide that it caused among Africans. According to the fictional bondsman, at the moment of capture in sub-Saharan Africa, Africans were separated from their "nearest and dearest Relations, the kind Husband from this loving Wife, the tender Mother from her Helpless Babes, and Youth . . . snatcht from their mourning Parents, and that without any hopes of ever seeing one another again." The separating of families caused psychological trauma that led many captives to "chuse a miserable sinful Death, rather than such a wretched Life." He explains that "some have Hang'd, others Down'd themselves, some cut their own Throats, and procured to themselves the like violent Deaths."[23] In detailing the heart-wrenching scenes of children being separated from their mothers, Tryon illustrated the less visible, psychological disabilities produced by slavery and held slavery accountable for consequently provoking enslaved individuals to commit one of the gravest sins of early modern England: suicide.[24]

In his descriptions of the physical abuses of slavery, Tryon portrayed the enslaved as broken and nonthreatening victims of slavery's violence. Tryon's fictitious enslaved man explains that, at the hands of the captain and crew, the enslaved aboard the ship "have suffered so many violent Miseries and sore Oppressions, that we are thereby as poor, weak and feeble as Death, so that we can hardly either stand or go." The physical toll of the transatlantic journey, "rend[ers] us not capable to answer to Covetous ends of our new Masters" and "our afflictions are thereby doubled; for when our strength fails us, the inconsiderate and unmerciful Overseers make nothing to Whip and Beat us and the best words they can afford us are *Damn'd Doggs, Black ugly Devils, Idle Sons of Ethiopean Whores,* and the like." The bondsman continues on this point and argues that slaveowners deprived the enslaved of sufficient food, which "is first to make us *Cripples,*" after which planters "beat us with our *Crutches* for being Lame."[25] Here we see vividly illustrated one of the paradoxes of Atlantic slavery—that colonists purposefully debilitated enslaved bodies and then administered more disabling violence when the injured could not meet their labor expectations. Tryon's portrayal of the physical violence inflicted onto the enslaved onboard ship reassured white readers that the abuses of the Middle Passage were so great as to create "poor, weak, and feeble" captives in desperate need of whites to save their bodies and souls from slavery's disabling violence.

The disabling abuses of slavery continued on the plantation where, according to the fictional bondsman, his British Caribbean masters "slave us on in continual drudgery, till our Heart-strings crack, and our Nerves are enfeebled, and our Marrow is exhausted, and our Bones fall under their Burthens, and [we] . . . wish for Death rather than Life." The enslaved are overworked in the fields and at the mill, so much so that "our Hands and Arms . . . [are] crusht to pieces, and sometimes most part of our Bodies." Similar dangers befall those working in the boiling house, where "we are forced to stand and work at the Coppers, in the hot sulpherous Fumes, till Nature being overcome with weariness and want of proper Rest we fall into the fierce boyling Syrups." Disability did not necessarily offer enslaved individuals protection from the hostile labor expectations of slavery: "whether we . . . be well or sick, disposed or indisposed, it matters not, to Work we must go, under the Whip and the Spur, and the Sun's scorching Beams all the day long."[26]

Like his abolitionist successors, Tryon emphasized the gendered nature of slavery's disabling violence and the sexual terrorism of slaveowners. According to Tryon, pregnant bondswomen and new mothers "work equally with the rest, even until the very day of their delivery, or Birth of their Children" and after two or three days of rest, return to the fields with their infants in tow.[27] Tryon's description of enslaved women returning to the fields soon after birth emphasized the debilitating effects of childbirth. Tryon's emphasis on the pained bondswoman giving birth evoked the story of Genesis and suggested to his white English readers that black women, like their white counterparts, felt pain in childbirth and were, therefore, descendants of Eve.[28] Tryon denounced slaveowners who "gratifie their raging Lusts" by raping enslaved women and then making "perpetual slaves" out of their offspring. The bondsman asks, "what can be more hellish Cruelty, or greater Baseness, then for men to afflict their own Seed, to beget Children in their Drunkeness and Paroxisms of Lust, and then not care what becomes of them." Such slaveowners "make themselves Authors of their [children's] Miseries as well as of their Beeing, and instead of providing for, and well Educating them, to enslave and tyrannize over them, and leave them in that wretched condition to all Generations."[29]

In spite of their differing approaches, early opponents of slavery shared many of the same concerns as later abolitionists. They worried about the debased morals of British colonists and their refusal to teach and convert the enslaved to Christianity. And they condemned slavery not only on ethical grounds but also out of fear that the enslaved population might rise against whites. Unlike Behn and Tryon, the majority of these early opponents may not have focused on the corporeal realities of slavery, but neither did their works silence or deny such realities. In emphasizing spiritual salvation, early antislavery writers deployed a moral approach by insinuating that the "saving" of bondspeople's souls (and the "recovering" of colonists' souls) ultimately saved enslaved bodies, too, from the atrocities of slavery. By the eighteenth century, the prevalence of slave rebellions in the British Atlantic, combined with the development of a metropolitan culture of sympathy toward people with disabilities, greatly shaped debates about slavery and the place of "disabled" and "able" bodies in anti- and proslavery rhetoric.

Able-Bodied Revolutionaries and Disabled Bondspeople

During the first few decades of the eighteenth century, antislavery views were still largely ineffective; in the words of one scholar, they were "sufficient to raise moral doubts but unable to stimulate political action."[30] By the middle of the century, however, Quakers, spurred by their religious convictions, became the first religious group in the British Atlantic world to publicly oppose slavery.[31] These early objections "derived not from ideas about earthly equality but from the concept of equality before God."[32] And indeed, far from the radical egalitarianism that would characterize some later abolitionist thinking, Quakers and evangelicals almost always emphasized the danger slavery posed to white society.[33] These early polemicists therefore tried to convince politicians, members of the clergy, and other social and political elites that West Indian slavery was detrimental to the socioeconomic well-being of both the colonies and the metropole.[34] In the second half of the eighteenth century, both pro- and antislavery writers expressed concern over the security of the islands' white colonists. Their intention was to encourage Parliament to cut off the slave trade to the British colonies and to persuade planters to treat their captives better and perhaps implement measures that would lead to their eventual emancipation. Underlying these arguments was whites' fear of the figure of the black, male, rebel, which had gained renewed publicity in the aftermath of slave rebellion in the British Caribbean.

The move toward abolishing the slave trade was bracketed by two major slave rebellions: Tacky's War in Jamaica (1760) and the Haitian Revolution (1791–1804). Jamaica had a long history of enslaved and Maroon resistance leading up to the abolitionist period. From 1655 to 1740, a series of revolts ended with planters suing for peace and granting the Maroon rebels their freedom.[35] The last decade of this period is known as the first Maroon War, in which many bondspeople escaped into the mountainous and largely inaccessible regions of Jamaica.[36] The Seven Years' War (1756–63), which broke out roughly fifteen years later, stimulated the uprising known as Tacky's War, which resulted in the deaths of sixty whites and the loss of property estimated at £100,000, in addition to the cost of building new military defenses.[37] A string of revolts followed in 1761, 1765, and 1766.

Although enslaved resistance and Maroon warfare had set fear into the hearts of colonists since the seventeenth century, Tacky's War marked a turning point in how both opponents and supporters of slavery discussed revolutionary emancipation and the figure of the armed, black, male rebel.[38] The recently signed peace treaties with the Maroons in 1738–39 gave Jamaican colonists a false sense of security, and they were caught off guard by the 1760 rebellion. The insurrection reinforced planters' long-standing fear of Africans as the natural enemy of Europeans and the primary instigators of rebellion. Ordained Anglican priest and abolitionist James Ramsay, a former English naval surgeon, contended that "Master and slave are in every respect opposite terms; and the persons to whom they are applied, are natural enemies to each other." Nineteenth-century abolitionist Henry Broughman echoed such sentiments and conveyed the impression that the obverse nature of Europeans and Africans was evinced on their bodies: "the negroes . . . are the enemy most to be dreaded in America by all Europeans; they are the natural foes of those white men who are distinguished from them by indelible marks in body, and by marks almost indelible in mind." In his *History of Jamaica* (1774), planter and slavery advocate Edward Long argued that the "chief actors in the seditions and mutinies" in Jamaica, dating back to 1690, "were the *imported Africans*" who had been "banished [from] their country for atrocious misdeeds, and familiarized to blood, massacre, and the most detestable vices." According to Long in the years leading up to Tacky's War, Jamaica imported 27,000 Africans "and no small number of them had been warriors in Afric, or criminals; and all of them as savage and uncivilized as the beasts of prey that roam through the African forests."[39]

Long's *History of Jamaica* was widely read and cited among abolitionists, many of whom were greatly influenced by his notion that African-born bondspeople posed the greatest threat to the internal security of the islands. Leading abolitionist Thomas Clarkson cited Long's argument that imported Africans led the majority of slave rebellions, which led him to believe that "the

Slave Trade is the real cause of all West Indian Insurrections" and "that as long as it exists so long may these Insurrections be expected." In the aftermath of the Haitian Revolution, Long's arguments concerning the threat posed by African-born bondspeople became ever more persuasive to abolitionists in their campaign against the slave trade. After all, the revolution was the only slave revolt to end with emancipation and the overthrow of white power. The figure of the black male rebel, therefore, became an even greater threat to the slaveholding colonies of the Atlantic World. According to Clarkson, the fear of contagion from Haiti "in particular, . . . calls upon us to redouble" efforts to end the slave trade.[40] The fear of black insurgency caused by the Haitian Revolution even reached parliament, when in 1792 Prime Minister William Pitt proclaimed that "it is no small satisfaction to me, Sir, that among the many arguments for prohibiting the slave trade which crowd upon my mind, the security of our West India possessions against internal commotion . . . is almost the most prominent and most forcible." Pitt asked his opponents, "Why should you any longer import into those countries that which is the *very seed* of Insurrection and rebellion?" The enslaved, another abolitionist argued, "are ever ready to rise and wreak their vengeance on their injurious oppressors." By continuing the slave trade, West Indian planters were "bringing upon the Islands the engines of their own destruction."[41] By 1800 the fear of revolutionary emancipation and the figure of the black, male, rebel, exemplified by the Haitian Revolution, led a number of apologists to support creolization and the abolition of the slave trade.[42]

The last two decades of the eighteenth century saw the arming of enslaved Africans across the Americas as well as several enslaved insurrections in the eastern Caribbean, all of which gave the figure of the black, militarized, male rebel greater currency in the Atlantic World. The outbreak of the American Revolution, which lasted from 1776 to 1783, led to the arming of black loyalists in America, as well as the arming of more bondspeople in the British Caribbean than anywhere else in the Americas.[43] In Virginia thousands of indentured servants and enslaved individuals responded to the Earl of Dunmore's 1775 proclamation promising them freedom for taking up arms for the British.[44] At the time, Britain faced a severe shortage of soldiers and sailors but possessed a substantial enslaved population in its Caribbean colonies. Many planters, however, fearing the threat that armed bondspeople posed to white society, refused to recruit enslaved individuals for military service. The imperial government went ahead with its plans and recruited enslaved individuals from Africa instead. This exploitative "inclusion" required that black soldiers, even when manumitted, remain in the ranks on lifetime service.[45] The creation of the West India Regiments, which constituted the largest army of enslaved people of any

European empire between 1794 and 1833, helped perpetuate the image of the armed black soldier fighting for empire. And yet, "the very conditions that made the arming of slaves necessary, in particular acute shortages of white manpower, also made it a dangerous expedient in the perception of slave owners."[46] For instance, some Caribbean planters saw the revolutionary ideas emanating from America and the arming of black captives in the revolutionary war as catalysts in the major slave rebellion in Jamaica in 1776.[47] Thus, the tensions in Jamaica and throughout the Caribbean between planters and bondspeople started by the American Revolution, increased with the French Revolution in 1789, and reached a climax with the outbreak of the Haitian Revolution in 1791.[48] Following the Haitian Revolution, the eastern Caribbean witnessed widespread revolutionary insurgency. Enslaved rebellions and plots in Guadeloupe, Dominica, Saint Vincent, and Grenada all contributed to the long-established but newly heightened white fear of black militarism and revolutionary emancipation.

The American Revolution encouraged the growth of abolitionist sentiment in Britain, but it also posed a challenge for abolitionists who hoped to present a nonthreatening image of ameliorative reform. During the Revolutionary War, the thirteen colonies banned the international trade in Africans as a reflection of a much wider embargo on all things British.[49] The end of the American War of Independence in 1783 meant that slave ships could sail freely once again in the British Empire, while the loss of the American colonies provided the conditions for abolition to be more widely received among Britons. The end of the American Revolution caused a boom in the British slave trade and also marked the beginning of a rapid increase in abolitionist publishing. In the wake of Britain's loss of its American colonies, the abolitionist movement provided many with a unifying moral conviction, one whose popularity was in part a compensatory reaction to the feelings of national humiliation engendered by Britain's defeat in North America.[50] British abolitionists strove to parry the figure of the rebel by presenting amelioration as a process that would simultaneously serve the interests of the West Indian colonies, maintain the socioeconomic status quo, and protect the wealth that black colonial labor generated for England.

For many British abolitionists, the solution to the problem of how to frame abolition and amelioration was found in the form of the disabled, tortured enslaved body. In both written discourse and public speeches, abolitionists gave detailed accounts of enslaved individuals who had endured physical debilitation as a result of bondage. Opponents of the slave trade and slavery emphasized the human suffering involved in the Middle Passage and in the colonies not only through mortality statistics but also through stories of individual pain.[51] Indeed, so widespread were these depictions of individual suffering, particularly on the part of female bondspeople, that pain "appears as the defining aspect of their existence—often the only aspect of it that is mentioned at all."[52] Through lectures, petitions, parliamentary speeches, court trials, and free publications, tracts, and slave narratives, late eighteenth-century abolitionists inundated the public with evidence about the disabling violence of the slave trade and slavery. Abolitionists made sure to appeal to both literate and illiterate audiences by featuring images, such as the famous Brookes slave ship, in their propaganda strategies.[53] In their efforts to impress a largely free, white population unfamiliar with the brutal experiences of slavery, antislavery writers drew on disability to make the unfamiliarity of plantation life familiar to a British audience. While the majority of British people had little direct knowledge of plantation slavery in the Caribbean, they did understand the effects of impaired limbs, blindness, and disfiguring scars. Abolitionists used portrayals of enslaved disability to stir up moral indignation in their audiences over the physical impairment that accompanied West Indian slavery.

The use of disability in antislavery writings amounted to a propaganda strategy, one that reflected wider cultural shifts regarding ideas of pain, suffering, and sensibility. In eighteenth-century Britain, a growing emphasis on sensibility and humanitarianism promoted certain attitudinal changes toward the disabled. The wealthy believed they could atone for their worldly gains by giving charitably to people with disabilities or severe illnesses, whom they considered "objects of compassion."[54] A growing number of workhouses and infirmaries offered new institutional provision for the care of the disabled, while schools for deaf and blind children were established by the end of the century.[55] English Quaker Joseph Woods, the author of *Thoughts on the Slavery of the Negroes* (1784), understood and exploited the linkages between the disabled and the enslaved in eighteenth-century humanitarian thought. "The humanity of the present age," he wrote, "has established a great variety of institutions for the relief of . . . the sick, the lame, the blind, the insane; those whom disease or accident, united with poverty, have rendered helpless, become the objects of compassion and assistance to their more fortunate neighbours." But, as Woods astutely pointed out, individuals were far more likely to extend acts of benevolence and charity to those near at hand than those out of sight: "The relation of distant calamities, however terrible, of famines, of pestilence, of earthquakes, of counties desolated by war, produces indeed a temporary sympathy, but it is soon dispersed by cares or pleasures, which press for more immediate attention." Woods saw in West Indian slavery a timely example of how people can take comfort in abstraction, especially when self-interest is involved. Here is an evil, he wrote, "in which relief is withheld, though within our power because the scene of oppression is distant, and the hearts of those who are immediately engaged in it, are hardened by the powerful influence of avarice and habit, and because these very sufferings are the source of public revenue and private wealth."[56] Put simply, the plight of Caribbean bondspeople was out of mind because it was largely out of sight—not to mention the fact that it generated great wealth for Britain.

In the late eighteenth century, the language of "social rescue" peppered discussions of both disability and race. Efforts to relieve the sufferings of disabled and enslaved people, however, were framed as a humanitarian responsibility rather than in terms of the individual's inalienable human rights. As this chapter details, the distinction between human rights (the notion that all humans are born deserving certain treatment) and humanitarianism (the notion that humans are obligated to be concerned with the welfare of the human race) shaped British conceptualizations of black citizenship after the Haitian Revolution. Humanitarians and abolitionists treated both the disabled poor and the enslaved as though "restoration to physical health was a key means to restoring spiritual values."[57] In eighteenth-century Britain the treatment of people with physical and sensory impairments included a moral component as well, since infirmaries and hospitals that cared for the "sick and lame" sought not only to recover the bodies of the admitted but also to save their souls. What is more, supporters of provisional care for the disabled blended humanitarian rescue with civic advancement by arguing that, once relieved of their physical burdens, these individuals would return to the workforce and Britain would have fewer vagrants.[58]

Abolitionists made similar claims to social rescue, arguing that emancipation would free the enslaved from the devastating impairments of human bondage and lead to intellectual and moral improvement among Africans and their descendants. Thus, reforms aimed specifically at people with disabilities shared with abolitionist rhetoric a commitment to Enlightenment ideas of advancement, humanitarianism, and the free labor system. An anonymous article in the *Gentleman's Magazine* in 1780 claimed that if given the opportunity to "reap the fruits of their labour," the enslaved would no longer suffer the psychological and emotional disabilities caused by slavery, "their kind affections hav[ing] been animated, and their exertions of labour augmented."[59] If freed from slavery, abolitionists argued, Africans and their descendants could become independent, industrious, and, by implication, able-bodied yet obedient subjects. In his seventy-two-point *Sketch of a Negro Code*, originally drafted in 1780 for Home Secretary Henry Dundas and published in 1792, Edmund Burke argued that in slavery "the minds of men [are] crippled with . . . restraint [and] can do nothing for themselves."[60] Abolitionist William Wilberforce, who first brought the debate to abolish the slave trade to parliament, made similar connections between slavery/disability and freedom/ability. He argued that slavery "obstructs" the enslaved from rationality and intellectual ability, for "true liberty is the child of Reason and of Order." Abolitionists also ensured planters that improving the conditions of slavery and restoring the enslaved "from among the order of brutes" to the "level with the rest of the human species," was in planters' own financial interest. For with this, "their labour will be productive . . ." for "the labour of a man is always more productive than that of a mere brute."[61] Inherent in such arguments, of course, was the notion that able-bodiedness was a requisite for citizenship and social progress.

Slavery, however, kept Africans physically debilitated and dependent. Thomas Clarkson described the physical devastation wrought by enslavement from the moment of capture in sub-Saharan Africa until their pressing into sugar production in the Caribbean. In an "imaginary scene" in Africa that echoed Tryon's fictional narrative, Clarkson portrayed an "unhappy man" who could hardly keep up with the rest of the coffle because "his feet seemed to have suffered so much, either from the fetters, which had confined them in the canoe, or from long and constant travelling, for he was limping painfully along." The Middle Passage was so physically destructive, Clarkson argued, that once the human cargo reached the auction blocks of the Caribbean, many individuals carried little value as commodities on the open market. "Some of the wretched Africans are in so debilitated and hopeless a state," Clarkson explained "that no purchaser can be found." Here, Clarkson demonstrated one of the contradictions inherent in the slavery system: that slavery-induced disability produced useless bodies and, therefore, worthless laborers. He continued and hinted darkly that disabled people were simply killed or left to die at the end of a slave trading voyage: "From these considerations, they are left on hand, and become a burthen to the vessels . . . What becomes of them, the reader must be left to imagine. It is certain that they are not sold in the colonies, and it is equally certain that they are not taken home."[62] Clarkson linked able-bodiedness to worth and disability to helplessness; in doing so, he played to eighteenth-century fears of disability as a form of weakness and dependency. Slavery was so physically destructive that it made enslaved individuals wholly dependent and worthless.

By detailing the paradoxical nature of slavery-induced disability, abolitionists used disability and disability rhetoric to stimulate humanitarianism among the British public. They emphasized the contradictions inherent in a slave-owning culture that treated valuable laborers as exploitable and expendable commodities to highlight the sadistic and arbitrary nature of slavery's disabling violence.

James Ramsay served as a pastor in Saint Christopher, where he preached to his black and white congregation and, in contrast to many abolitionists of the late eighteenth century, based his writings on firsthand knowledge of Caribbean slave societies.[63] After three years in Saint Christopher, Ramsay resigned his position as pastor and returned home to England, where he continued to agitate for the abolition of slavery in the colonies and was very influential as an abolitionist. In 1784, he published two antislavery works that told of the physical and psychological disabilities caused by Caribbean slavery. The hardship of enslaved labor, according to Ramsay, rendered the enslaved "unprofitable, worthless, and deserving of [more] punishment." Concerned about a corresponding drop in productivity, some slaveholders therefore purposefully chose, as "an auxiliary to the lash," punishments that did not impair.[64] But as Joseph Woods pointed out, the slaveowner's self-interest was the only protection offered to enslaved bodies "till sickness or age render[s] [them] incapable of labour, but allows none of those comforts which alleviate the miseries of life."[65] Field labor, Ramsay argued, was a bondsperson's "greatest hardship" for he "can neither refresh, or indulge his wearied body. He is subjected by it to injury. He is placed in the jaws of trespass, and unavoidably made obnoxious to oppression, and stripes." As for the boiling house, Ramsay first appealed to concerns of British sugar consumers by arguing that the overworking of unfree laborers produced sugar that was "ill tempered, burnt in the boiler; and improperly struck." Switching approach, Ramsay then concluded by emphasizing the shock and lasting visual spectacle of disability. The mill, he wrote, "every now and then grinds off an hand, or an arm, of those drowsy, worn down creatures that fed it."[66]

Abolitionist depictions of slavery-induced disability, although intended to prove the humanity of the enslaved and garner British support of the abolitionist cause, echoed the much older tradition of European travelers' portrayals of "monstrous" Africans with missing limbs, eyes, and appendages so common in the sixteenth century (see chapter 1). Depictions of monstrosity are, thus, a key element of the continuities and discontinuities of racist thought that facilitate the shift from an emphasis on violence toward an emphasis on paternalism in European writings about slavery. Echoing the descriptions of African bodies in early European travelogues, as well as those found in colonial runaway advertisements, leading abolitionists such as James Ramsay and Thomas Clarkson depicted mutilated, disfigured, and impaired bondspeople, and in so doing invited their audience to read the black body as a spectacular text conveying the ultimate mark of enslavement: disability. Like many other abolitionists of his time, Ramsay emphasized the whip as the ultimate symbol of deliberate, calculated disablement. He argued that the whip could "effectively disable the culprit [the enslaved] for weeks." For bondspeople who committed "common crimes of neglect, absence from work, eating the sugarcane, [and] theft" the punishments included, "cart whipping, beating with a stick, sometimes to the breaking of bones, the chain, an iron crook about the neck, a large pudding or ring about the ancle, and confinement in the dungeon." Ramsay continued his depiction of the disabling punishments meted out onto enslaved individuals by emphasizing dismemberment as a reflection of slaveowners' sadistic violence: "There have been instances of slitting of ears, breaking of limbs, so as to make amputation necessary, beating out of eyes, and castration." According to Ramsay, "two chief judges have been celebrated for cutting off or mashing (so as to make amputation necessary) the limbs of their slaves." Thomas Clarkson used statistics and the sworn testimonies of military officers, planters, and captains, as well as runaway advertisements, as evidence of the mutilation suffered by bondspeople. He quoted a 1784 St. Christopher law "to prevent the cutting off or depriving any slave in this island of any of their limbs or members, or otherwise disabling them," which, Clarkson noted, was enacted in the first place because "some persons have of late been guilty of *cutting off and depriving slaves of their ears.*" Joseph Woods added to this depiction of sadistic torture when he notified his readers that slaveowners had "pepper and salt scattered on the wounds, for the purpose of increasing [the bondsperson's] pain."[67] The dismemberment of enslaved individuals was a powerful image in abolitionist works and reproduced the European notion that Africans and their descendants were not whole beings. In their vivid descriptions of brutal punishments for "minor" crimes, Ramsay and Clarkson sought to place the mantle of victimization on the enslaved, thereby detracting from the widely feared figure of the rebel.

Abolitionist imagery, in particular, demonstrates the representation of the enslaved as physically broken and, by implication, nonthreatening. The famous "slave medallion" made by potter Josiah Wedgwood in 1787 for the Society for the Abolition of the Slave Trade depicts a muscular black male enchained and on bended knee, his hands raised in supplication. Below the image are the words "AM I NOT A MAN AND A BROTHER?"[68] The Wedgwood image was extremely popular during the 1780s and 1790s, and it appeared in stationery, books, prints, paintings, newspapers, and as a ceramic figure.[69] The enslaved figure it depicts is undeniably muscular, but this reflects his body's purpose to labor, and not his militarization—a fact underscored by the presence of chains. He asks or begs for his freedom "from the safe position of his knees" so that "bestowing freedom upon [the enslaved] seemed . . . purely an act of humanity and will." As Marcus Wood argues, in the Wedgwood image, the black person becomes a "cultural absentee . . . a blank page for white guilt to inscribe." Accordingly, the image exemplifies abolitionists' depiction of black citizenship as a "crippled" form of citizenship, one achieved not through self-liberation, but through the bestowing of a humanitarian gift by the British people. Because the figure is on bended knee and in chains we do not know if he could run or walk, or if he moved with a limp. But regardless of whether it was part of a narrative of collective or individual suffering, it remained, in abolitionist rhetoric, a nameless and voiceless body, "an object afflicted, not . . . a subject capable of describing his or her affliction."[70] In emphasizing the debilitated and suffering bondsperson, abolitionists located the impetus for black rebellion in the feeling and reactionary body rather than in the thinking, planning, and politically conscious mind. Thus, abolitionists framed rebellion as a form of nonpolitics, and they deployed a new and "modern" language of disability in their representations of the tortured bodies of enslaved people to elicit Christian sympathy and divert British attention away from the threat of revolutionary emancipation. The power of such rhetoric rested precisely on its ability to display the black body as disabled, abject, and in need of white support. In this way, ironically, the racist paternalism that established and sustained the institution of slavery in the first place was perpetuated and reinforced.

In addition to the hobbled black captive, abolitionists offered an oppositional narrative of black citizenship in their depiction of the Haitian Revolution and the singular figure of Toussaint Louverture, the former captive turned revolutionary leader.[71] In the last years of his life, and especially after his death in 1803, British abolitionists mobilized Louverture "as an embodiment of the black republic, a symbol of the character and potential of the black race."[72] They celebrated Louverture as an individual militarized figure who embodied masculinity and valor, and who symbolized the tragedy of slavery. Antislavery writers marginalized the black masses, as well as the rebel leader (and independent Haiti's first ruler) Jean-Jacques Dessalines; instead, they centered their attention on a sentimentalized and (after 1803) conveniently deceased Louverture in order to erase Britain's defeat during the Haitian Revolution from British history and defuse the threat that black military success represented in the Atlantic World. Thus, the figure of Louverture was a viable component of the British abolitionist movement only because he was an antagonist of the French and not an obvious threat to Britain.

Unlike the Wedgwood image, and the countless depictions of broken and supplicating captives in abolitionist writings, Louverture was always shown standing, strong, and armed. For instance, in Scottish caricaturist John Kay's 1802 portrayal (fig. 7), Louverture is depicted as a strong, masculine, armed leader, directing his troops who stand at attention. The portrait of Louverture published in Marcus Rainsford 1805 work (fig. 8) similarly shows Louverture armed, standing in front of his well-ordered soldiers, and with the constitution

TOUSSAINT LOUVERTURE

FIGURE 7. John Kay's 1802 etching of Toussaint Louverture, repro-
duced in *A Series of Original Portraits and Caricature Etchings. With
Biographical Sketches and Illustrative Anecdotes* (Edinburgh: A & C
Black, 1877). Photo courtesy the British Museum.

FIGURE 8. J. Barlow's engraving of Toussaint Louverture, in Marcus Rainsford, *An Historical Account of the Black Empire of Hayti* (1805). Photo courtesy John Carter Brown Library, Box 1894, Brown University, Providence, R.I. 02912.

in one hand. Both images portray Louverture holding a large sword, symbolizing his military prowess, masculinity, and bravery. In both images he stands, wearing what most resembles a British uniform—the round hat with a cockade and plume, epaulets, the sleeves with chevrons, and the tasseled boots remind one of the uniforms worn by the exclusively white officers of the West India regiments.[73] In this way, abolitionists valorized Louverture as a black, able-bodied, and militarized rebel. Through Louverture, antislavery writers engaged with and romanticized the figure of the able-bodied, former captive who rises to lead an army to emancipation—even if, ultimately, the figure at the heart of the Wedgwood seal remained their preferred symbol of black suffering.

This ambivalence toward the figure of the militarized black man existed in the North American context as well. John Singleton Copley's painting *The Death of Major Peirson* (1783) depicts the shooting of its eponymous subject during France's final attempt to invade Jersey in 1781 (fig. 9). The black man shown in the painting was Peirson's slave, Pompey, who avenges his owner's death by shooting the French sniper. Pompey wears the uniform most often associated with Lord Dunmore's Royal Ethiopian Regiment, a loyalist force of ex-slave fugitives formed by Dunmore in 1775 in Virginia, and the first regiment

FIGURE 9. John Singleton Copley, *The Death of Major Peirson, 6 January 1781* (1783). Photo courtesy Tate Gallery.

of African-descended people officially enlisted by the British army in this period. The painting offers a powerful yet ambivalent image of blackness. Like the portrait of Louverture, it suggests that able-bodiedness was central to black masculinity. But while on the one hand, the depiction of Pompey in his uniform avenging his master's death could support a proslavery stance, since it shows black loyalty to British masters, on the other, this could support an antislavery perspective by depicting Pompey as the "real" hero in this violent battle scene. Either way, the painting reflects much of the ambivalence of the era, as well the tension between freedom and subservience that was bound in the image of the black, armed, and able-bodied man.

Animals, Monsters, and the Unhuman

Prior to the 1770s, advocates of slavery saw no reason to organize a systematic defense of slavery: they were "comfortable in their belief that the status quo would be maintained [and therefore] produced reactive rather than proactive arguments to antislavery accusations."[74] An exception was Nevis clergyman Robert Robertson, an apologist for Caribbean slaveowners who published three proslavery responses between 1730 and 1740.[75] Robertson argued that the reason planters did not Christianize the enslaved was because of the innate "dullness, defects, corruptions and perverseness of the Slaves." Such deficiencies, he claimed "are not to be surmounted in a human Way," but instead by slavery and "the Faithfulness and Diligence of their [enslaved Africans'] Instructors, supported by due Authority." Robertson concluded by asserting that the supposed defects of Africans and their descendants were so powerful that even "the sense they have of their slavery does not lie so deep as some imagine."[76] The use of intellectual disability as justification for African enslavement would become a hallmark of proslavery defenses. Antiabolitionists came down clearly on the side of claiming that geographic and biological evidence affirmed that Africans were animals rather than humans in the latter decades of the eighteenth century.

By the late eighteenth century, West Indian planters' political power had reached its height, with a number of absentee planters playing a significant role in defending slavery and the interests of the British Caribbean plantocracy. The Society of West Indian Planters and Merchants had responded to the antislavery movement only when it became obvious that Prime Minister William Pitt was paying particular attention to the arguments put forth by William Wilberforce, and once Pitt approved a parliamentary inquiry into the slave trade.[77] The society and its supporters never attempted to justify the conditions on board British slave ships—the horrors involved were impossible to defend. Instead, proslavery propagandists justified the Middle Passage as a necessary precondition for the wealth generated through African labor on the plantations, without which Caribbean planters and British citizens alike would suffer. Even the enslaved benefited from plantation slavery, they argued, for life in the sugar colonies was much better than the "barbarous" African societies they came from.[78]

In defending slavery, these writers, like their abolitionist opponents, argued that Africans were a threat to the security of the British Empire. Proslavery writers expressed their fear of the able-bodied black male rebel most explicitly in their discussions of slave revolts in the Atlantic World. They condemned the black rebel through depictions of torture and the restoration of colonial authority. Jamaican planter Bryan Edwards described the torture and execution of rebels in the aftermath of Tacky's War.[79] Despite being burnt and "hung up alive in irons and left to perish in this dreadful situation," one rebel "uttered not a groan, and saw his legs reduced to ashes with the utmost firmness and composure." Likewise, the other rebels "never uttered the least complaint."[80] Like Aphra Behn before him, Edwards depicted the aftermaths of slave revolts in which order is restored to plantation society only after rebels were "broken" and "disobedient" bodies were tortured and executed.

The last three decades of the eighteenth century marked a new phase in slavery's relationship to monstrosity as proslavery polemicists moved away from older arguments about African monstrosity in favor of scientific arguments that more explicitly dehumanized Africans and linked them to animals. Implicit in this animalization of Africans and their descendants was the claim that Africans were intellectually deficient. At the very peak of slave rebellions in the Caribbean, proponents of slavery attempted to deny enslaved Africans' ability to self-govern by stripping blacks of any vestige of humanity. For instance, Thomas Thicknesse compared African bodies to animals to undermine Africans' political relevance and to justify their enslavement. Thicknesse's first experience in the colonies was in Georgia in 1735; he later became captain of an independent company in Jamaica, thanks to his friend and first prime minister of Great Britain, Sir Robert Walpole.[81] In his *A Year's Journey*, Thicknesse described Africans in the following terms: "Their face is scarce what we call human, their legs without any inner calf, and their broad, flat foot, and long toes (which they can use as well as we do our fingers) have much the resemblance of the Orang Outang, or Jacko, and other quadrupeds of their own climate."[82] Such arguments abandoned much of the earlier anthropological uncertainty with which Africans were associated in the sixteenth- and seventeenth-century English consciousness.

According to proslavery writers, Africans' intellectual incapacities prevented them from transcending their savage, animal nature and entering the realm of self-government. Edward Long argued that Africans possessed a "bareness of Genius and in general a weakness of intellect, little disposition to industry, nor genius of ye fine arts; the brute appearing to predominate and efface the human rational being." He claimed that Africans could not govern, nor even imagine self-liberation, because their minds were ruled by beastliness. Those from Guinea, he wrote, possessed "a very confined intellect [and] many appear perfectly stupid. . . . They never think, have no memory, of what is past is just as unknown to them as what is to come."[83] This was, ultimately, an argument for African disenfranchisement and disablement. "Whatever great personages this country [the African continent] might anciently have produced," Long argued "they are now every where degenerated into a brutish, ignorant, idle, crafty, treacherous, bloody, thievish, mistrustful, and superstitious people even in those states where we might expect to find them more polished, humane, docile, and industrious."[84] When analyzed from the standpoint of disability, proslavery writers' claims were often far more scientifically sophisticated than later scholars would admit. Here, for example, Long accepted the possibility of a glorious, if ancient, African past marked by "great personages." But in emphasizing the degree to which African civilization had degenerated, Long opened up the scientific possibility that the opposite of degeneracy—that is, the path taken by Europeans—was evolution. Thus, in proslavery writing, there was a clear effort to draw on scientific evidence that human life in Africa was of great antiquity, even if writers like Long twisted the scientific evidence into a racist narrative of degeneracy.

In the 1780s, Long began revisions for a second edition of his *History*, in which he attempted to demonstrate that Africans were fundamentally different from Europeans, not only in terms of physical *appearance*, but their actual biological make-up. The second edition never appeared, but Long's manuscript notes demonstrate the development of a particularly modern antiblack racism.[85] He claimed that he had been "informed by a . . . physician" who had "anatomised several bodies of negroes, that the substance of their brain is covered with a dusty coloured membrane, impregnated no doubt from the same source of their more internal cuticulam membrane." Such knowledge, according to Long, "incontestably proves" that black skin color "is not caused by the action of the solar rays, but by a peculiar liquor which their internal organs are formed to secrete which agrees with the assertions of other anatomists." According to this logic, Africans' biological deviations were evidence of their *natural* enslaved status. Africans, he argued, "seem to be of all making the . . .

servant of Aristotle—Some men . . . are born to be slaves that is seem adapted and intended by nature for servitude."[86] Clearly, Long's theories developed alongside an emerging pseudoscientific racism in the late eighteenth century.

Proslavery writers also argued that these biological deviations posed a threat to "civilized" British culture. Philip Thicknesse, for example, expressed disgust at Britain's mixed-race population and argued that "a little race of mulattoes, mischievous as monkeys, and infinitely more dangerous" was infecting the British population. Here again he drew a straight line from animals to Africans: "there is not on earth so mischievous and vicious an animal as a mule, nor in any humble opinion a worse race of men than the negroes of Africa." In direct response to the Somerset ruling, Thicknesse argued that Africans should not be allowed free in Britain, since they would only "propagate their mischievous race among us. We have wicked streams, and *streamers* of human blood among us already."[87] Again, the fear of the monster, so prominent in early European travel accounts, resurfaces but by the late eighteenth century the "nature" of what was once referred to as a monster had been decided: it is an animal.

Both Thicknesse and Long linked African deviance to intellectual disability by ascribing to Africans simian characteristics. Thickness claimed that "not one [African] was ever born with solid sense; yet all have a degree of monkey cunning, and even monkey mischief, which often stands them in better stead than sense," while according to Long, African "genius (if it can be so called) consists along in trick and cunning, enabling them, like monkies and apes, to be thievish and mischievous, with a particular dexterity."[88] Proslavery writers expressed the same fear of the monster as pre- and early colonial writers had, but for these later writers their subject's "nature" was now deemed more animalistic than fantastical. The emphasis on the ape emerged in the late eighteenth century, part of natural historians' effort to fix the border between human and animal.[89] Both Long and Thicknesse depicted Africans as animal-like—savage, wild, and lacking intelligence—while also demonstrating an acceptance of the similarities between human and animal, and they offered evolution as a possible explanation for the development of these two indistinct categories.[90]

Antislavery writers responded to proslavery arguments about Africans' ostensible intellectual limitations. Joseph Woods, while he acknowledged that intellectual disparities existed among individuals, countered that "the inferiority which is attributed to the whole race of negroes probably arises from that depression of mind which accompanies a state of slavery, and from the discouragement thrown in the way of every liberal inquiry, rather than from any original, intellectual defect." James Ramsay offered a similar rebuttal by arguing that there was no "essential difference between European and African mental powers," and that if the enslaved appeared intellectually stunted it was because they were crippled by their bondage. "Oppression," Ramsay wrote "makes wretches stupid, and their stupidity becomes their crime, and provokes their farther punishment." For Ramsay, proslavery depictions of the enslaved as inherently criminal—liars, thieves, murderers—reflected the fact that the legal disabilities imposed on the enslaved meant that criminal behavior was their only opportunity for self-determination. "The truth is," he wrote, "a depth of cunning that enables them [the enslaved] to over-reach, conceal, deceive, is the only province of the mind left for them . . . to occupy." Likewise, in the final section of his work, Ramsay specifically responded to the arguments made by Long in his *History of Jamaica*. He began by addressing the long-held belief that Africans constituted a distinct species. "If allowed to be a *distinct* race," Ramsay wrote, "European pride immediately concludes them as an *inferior* race, and then it follows, of course, that nature formed them to be slaves to their superiors." From this logic, "the master . . . fairly concludes himself loosed from all obligations, but these of interest, in his conduct towards them." Ramsay continued and skillfully pointed out the connection between enslaved Africans' perceived intellectual disability as cause and justification for the *real* physical, emotional, and psychological disabilities they endured in enslavement. For Ramsay, Long's assertion that Africans' skin color and corporeality testified to their intellectual and moral inferiority was "a precarious foundation for genius." If Africans did have "less capacious skulls," if their "calves of the legs [were] less fleshy, and elevated more towards the hams," it was because "climate, diet, and various modes of life have great power over the features, form, and stature of man."[91]

And yet, despite insisting that these intellectual deficiencies were produced rather than innate, Ramsay nonetheless maintained that Africans were incapable of successfully entering into immediate emancipation; as he put it, freedom could offer the enslaved able-bodiedness only if "gentle [and] slow in its progress." The enslaved, moreover, were not intellectually capable of freedom, being "ignorant" and in such a "helpless condition . . . that full liberty would be no blessing to them." Such racist and class-based paternalism toward bondspeople would become a hallmark of white abolitionist writings into the nineteenth century and reflect the intertwining of race and able-bodied citizenship. The enslaved, Ramsay argued, "need a master to provide and care for them" while they transition into freedom. Liberty must keep "pace with the opening of their minds."[92] Gradual, rather than immediate, emancipation—at best a work in progress in many abolitionists' minds—would free the enslaved from the devastating impairments of bondage, bestowing in a timely and conservative manner the "gift" of able-bodiedness.

Ramsay's writing shows that assumptions about Africans' intellectual incapacities did not emanate solely from advocates of slavery. The abolitionist poet Hannah More also used similar concepts to further her antislavery stance, but in a way that linked blackness to disability as defect and limit. In reference to enslaved Africans, More wrote:

Tho' dark and savage, ignorant and blind
They claim the common privilege of kind;
Let Malice strip them of each other plea,
They still are men, and men shou'd still be free.[93]

Clearly, More, who associated blackness with savagery and equated intellectual and sensory impairments with deficiencies, used the links between race and disability to forward her arguments.

While their numbers were very small, the narratives of ex-slaves, more than any other form of antislavery propaganda, challenged proslavery claims that Africans were incapable of intellectual advancement. British abolitionists were on constant lookout for witnesses that might advance their campaign against the slave trade, and yet they evinced little interest in the testimonies of the thousands of ex-slaves living in Britain in the late eighteenth century—and this in spite of the fact that they knew and worked alongside ex-slaves like Olaudah Equiano.[94] Indeed, it is profoundly ironic that as the abolitionist movement gathered pace, the evidence of Africans' intellectual capabilities was on ample display throughout the Atlantic World, in the form of the growing number of slave rebellions, to be sure, but perhaps most powerfully in the successful publications of ex-slave abolitionists. During the 1770s and 1780s, the writings of Phillis Wheatley, Ignatius Sancho, Ottobah Cugoano, and Olaudah Equiano figured greatly in the ongoing antislavery debate in Britain. Equiano and Cugoano were especially successful in this regard. In response to proslavery claims that Africans and their descendants were intellectually deficient, Equiano argued that the institution of slavery was itself disabling; for example, in a powerful passage he claimed that

When you make men slaves, you deprive them of half their virtue, you set them in your own conduct, an example of fraud, rapine, and cruelty, and compel them to live with you in a state of war; and yet you complain that they are not honest or faithful! You stupefy them with stripes, and think it necessary to keep them in a state of ignorance; and yet you assert that they are incapable of learning; that their minds are such a barren soil or moor, that culture would be lost on them; and that they come from a climate, where nature . . . has left man alone scant and unfinished, and incapable of enjoying the treasures she hath poured out for him![95]

The emphasis placed on refuting proslavery arguments about Africans' intellectual deficiencies demonstrates that intellectual ability became a mark of humanity during debates over slavery's existence.[96] The narratives of former bondspeople suggest, for instance, that only through acquiring the ability to write in a European language could one "prove" one's humanity.[97] Equiano held slavery responsible for the so-called intellectual deficiencies and criminal behavior of enslaved Africans. Equiano critiqued the hypocrisy of the institution of slavery, which kept the enslaved "in a state of ignorance" while condemning them for being "incapable of learning."

To be sure, pro- and antislavery writers arrived at very different conclusions when it came to calculating the threat posed by a free black population in England. But both sides relied on the assumed linkages between race and disability. In proslavery propaganda, the histories of race and disability overlapped not just in language or metaphor, but rather in *real* parallel ways. For instance, in his manuscript notes, Edward Long suggested a violent solution to African slavery. Africans' inner and outer deficiencies, he argued, "deforms the beauty of this globe," so much so that Africans "deserve to be exterminated from the . . . earth."[98] Opponents of slavery did not go as far as to suggest a proto-eugenics solution to the "problem" of blacks in the metropole. But this did not necessarily mean that they would argue for equality. Granville Sharp, for example, one of the first and most influential abolitionists in Britain, opposed the slave trade and slavery, but his writings reveal that he had reservations about what to do about the problem, and these reservations were motivated partly by his unease over the presence of a large population of black people in England. It was a "real and national inconvenience," argued Sharp, "to increase the present stock of black servants in this kingdom, which is already too numerous." The presence of blacks in England took jobs and food away from the white poor and, therefore, "the public good seems to require some restraint of this unnatural increase of black subjects."[99] In his 1786 letter to the archbishop of Canterbury, Sharp commented that Lord Mansfield's verdict in the Somerset case of 1772 "deterred slave-holders from bringing with them such swarms of Negro attendants to this island [England]."[100] Thus, one of Sharp's main issues with slavery was that it brought people of African descent to England in the first place, where Sharp felt they did not belong.

In the late 1780s and 1790s, Sharp, along with Olaudah Equiano, was among a small group of abolitionists to establish the colony of Freetown, in Sierra Leone, as a free black territory. It attracted thousands of former slaves from around the British Empire—black loyalists from Nova Scotia, Jamaican Maroons, the black poor of London, and some of those eventually liberated from the slave trade. The project constituted a form of social engineering, one that reflected Sharp's belief that whether free or enslaved, blacks were fundamentally different than whites. Of the over ten thousand black people (most of them servants) living in London at the end of the eighteenth century, the English Parliament managed to convince only about 350 of them to relocate to Sierra Leone.[101] The abolitionist establishment of Freetown implicitly accepted proslavery arguments about the necessity of the geographical separation of races. For although the passage to Freetown was couched in humanitarian rhetoric, it was in fact a violent scheme developed to rid England of its black population.

Bondswomen, Childbirth, and Monstrosity

In addition to written propaganda, proslavery planters and lawmakers responded to abolitionists' attacks on slavery by implementing new laws intended to make the institution more "humane." Between 1788 and 1807, the Parliament of London passed a series of acts, collectively known as the Consolidated Slave Acts. Intended to ameliorate slavery's most harmful effects and limit disability among the enslaved, the acts also promoted creolization by encouraging enslaved women of childbearing age to have children. Passed over several years, the laws were intended to placate the growing antislavery lobby in England, and they resolved to regulate and improve the social conditions of bondspeople but they were not fully implemented in large part due to the established planter culture of unchecked power.

During the first phase of the amelioration era, as the 1788–1807 period came to be known, planters paid ever closer attention to bondswomen, not out of concern for the health and well-being of these individuals, but rather out of their own economic interest. Foreseeing that the slave trade might very well end, stopping the *importation* of slaves, planters focused their efforts on reproducing the enslaved population through birth.[102] In their effort to exploit the reproductive abilities of bondswomen, planters set in motion a number of measures to increase the overall health of women still in their childbearing years. In the debates over the slave trade abolition, proslavery advocates encouraged planters to promote "the annual increase of the Slaves by birth. And likewise to grant freedom to every female Negro, who has born and reared up five children to the age of seven years."[103] Jamaica's 1792 slave code officially intended to "obviate the causes which impeded the natural increase of the negroes gradually to diminish the necessary of the slave trade; and ultimately to lead to its complete termination."[104] Women of childbearing age were therefore exempt from field labor, and they were often relocated to work environments that planters perceived as less threatening to their prenatal health, such as the cattle pen or great house, where they would work as domestic laborers.[105] Bondswomen who birthed a certain number of children were entitled to greater food allowances. Planters even hired medical practitioners to regularly care for pregnant women.[106] Despite these changes, planters nevertheless viewed punishment, even of pregnant women, as a necessary part of plantation management. What is more, planters did not consider punishment a thwarting of the goal of increasing through birth the number of bondspeople. For instance, by "whipping across the shoulders or burying their wombs in the ground, slaveholders roused bondswomen into submission and still benefited from their reproductive capacity."[107] Although many of these reforms were not administered in any practical way, the Jamaica Assembly's cooperation to reform slavery, at least on paper, consistently subverted abolitionist criticism in Britain, which prolonged the struggle for the abolition of the slave trade.[108]

The new policies of the amelioration period revived the principle of maternal inheritance, but in novel ways.[109] As it became clear that the slave trade's days were numbered, enslaved women's reproductive ability became essential to the institution's future. Trading patterns changed significantly in the late eighteenth century, in part because of this increased emphasis on reproduction, which also saw the introduction of a new tax relief for the importation of bondswomen under the age of twenty-five. In tandem with these changes, the Jamaica Assembly in 1797 passed an act adding £10 tax for the importation of women over the age of twenty-five.[110] Slavery's defenders and opponents each tried to capitalize on black women's fertility, though in different ways: for slaveowners it "symbolized hereditary slavery, [while] for abolitionists it symbolized the conduit through which a free laboring population could be propagated." Moreover, antislavery writers argued that if slaveowners provided better physical and emotional care for their captives, bondspeople's overall health would improve, leading to the birth of new generations of blacks who would, over time, "acquire [the] habits of free people, thereby naturally eliminating the continued need for bonded laborers."[111] Still, abolitionists were critical of the laws that exploited the reproduction of enslaved women. Such acts were "*A bounty from the Parliament of Britain* that shall make the fortune of any man, or set of men, who shall bring them over as slaves, in order that they may be used for breeding slaves!"[112] Abolitionists also emphasized the failure of natural increase among the enslaved—a population that, for obvious reasons, exhibited low birth rates and high death rates. This was in many ways a logical response to the gendered nature of Caribbean slavery, based as it was on the principle of maternal inheritance.

Supporters of slavery interpreted bondswomen's failure to reproduce as an innate deficiency. They claimed that African women's fertility was stifled by licentiousness, which lead to widespread venereal disease and subsequent infertility.[113] Dr. Jesse Foot, whose work was paid for by the Society of West Indian Merchants' anti-abolition subcommittee, argued that it was impossible to thwart "the libidinous practices of negroes," for "a young negro man will have as many wives as his will prescribes, or his fancy in succession suggests," and "the women who entertain promiscuous connections are never fruitful." Planter Bryan Edwards expressed similar beliefs when he wrote that the enslaved "hold chastity in so little estimation, that bareness and frequent abortions, the usual effects of a promiscuous intercourse, are very generally prevalent among them." The notion that Africans were "abnormally" sexual was connected back to the treatment of bondswomen as "'monstrous labour units' who could just as easily drop a child at will and soon after return to toil at the most arduous field tasks."[114]

Edward Long, for one, claimed that enslaved women could birth multiple babies at once "without a shriek or scream."[115] And yet, according to planters, white women's experience of childbirth was accompanied by extreme pain— evidence, they claimed, of these women's humanity and their supposed *unfitness* for servitude. Slavery advocates claimed that African women, since they were something other than human, were immune to pain, while abolitionists acknowledged that they did, in fact, suffer during childbirth. Thus, pain in childbirth became a crucial sign of humanity, and immunity to pain a defining feature of the animal. The figure of the pained, prostrate female giving birth also became a key means, in abolitionist discourse, of displacing the black male rebel.

Just as proslavery writers began modifying their thinking on African monstrosity—which, as we saw, they increasingly linked with animality—abolitionists, too, assumed the language of monstrosity, but with a significant difference: they argued that monstrosity was located not within the individual African, but the institution of slavery itself. In referring to slavery as a monstrosity, abolitionists relied on older notions of disability that evoked evil, deformity, and depravity. For instance, in a letter to Thomas Clarkson, fellow abolitionist Samuel Taylor Coleridge wrote that "no evil more monstrous has existed upon earth."[116] Others referred to slavery as a "cruel monster," and the slave trade as "the monstrous trade."[117] Antislavery writers like James Ramsay also used monstrosity in their direct attacks against slaveowners, overseers, and merchants—and in so doing turned the concept against the very people who espoused it in the first place. For example, referring to the 1781 Zong massacre, in which the slave ship's captain Luke Collingwood threw overboard 131 African captives, Ramsay asked: "Can humanity imagine that it was meant, in any possible circumstances, to submit the fate of such numbers of reasonable creatures to the reveries of a sick monster?"[118]

Antislavery writers employed notions of disability as well, which they used to foster a patriotic conviction among their readers that slavery contradicted what it meant to be English. For instance, one writer argued that when slavery is finally abolished, this "should be followed up with an impeachment of those monsters of cruelty that the national Honour may be vindicated & that posterity may not think that even in the eighteenth century we were a nation of savages."[119] For this author, monstrosity and savagery defined slavers, and not the enslaved. In his *Essay on Slavery and Commerce*, Thomas Clarkson used disability to play on a sense of national pride. He distinguished between *true* English citizens, who exhibited charity toward the disabled, and those who claimed English citizenship but whose involvement in slavery, in Clarkson's opinion, made them monsters and negated their English citizenship.[120] Clarkson, in conversation with the "unhappy African," explained that men involved in slavery "are not *Christians*. They are *infidels*. They are *monsters*. They are out of the common course of nature." By contrast, "their countrymen at home ... support the sick, the lame, and the blind. They fly to the succour of the distressed. They have noble and stately buildings for the sole purpose of benevolence. They are in short, of all nations, the most remarkable for humanity and justice."[121] For Clarkson, care for the disabled was the sign of Englishness; violence against the enslaved was the sign of the monster.

By calling slaveowners and merchants monsters, Clarkson suggested not only that such individuals were evil and morally depraved, but also that they did not belong in England. In Clarkson's text this national culture of charity, sympathy, and kindness to the disabled came to define, in moral terms, what it meant to be English in the late eighteenth century. Clarkson linked the social, economic, and political oppression experienced by England's disabled citizens to that of the enslaved and, in doing so, yoked humanitarianism to Englishness. All the while he remained silent on, and implicitly rejected, the more fixed idea of human rights. For abolitionists, revolutionary able-bodies fought for human rights and equal citizenship, and English abolitionists effectively rejected those after the American Revolution. Humanitarian ideas of citizenship were what abolitionists offered to the enslaved, predicated on the assumption that theirs was a "crippled" form of citizenship.

Both anti- and pro-slavery propagandists during the first wave of British abolition (1788–1807) relied on disability to relay the horrors of Atlantic slavery and to detract from the figure of the armed and able-bodied black male rebel. Used in this way, disability came to facilitate the incorporation of Africans and their descendants into the English body politic while blunting the radical potential of this otherwise profound challenge to the status quo. The use of racialized disability rhetoric also helped abolitionists reconcile antislavery sentiments with racism and calls for reform with the widespread opposition to revolution. Supporters of slavery, by contrast, claimed that Africans were intellectually disabled and, as such, were more akin to animals than humans. Such arguments served to deny blacks' political relevance in the Atlantic World while promoting the notion that the enslaved were a threat that needed to be contained and controlled through enslavement.

The different ways in which these writers utilized disability reflected contemporary attitudinal changes on both sides, especially as relates to race, slavery, and disability. The specter of the rebel body haunted the late eighteenth-century Atlantic World. In the wake of the Haitian Revolution, the figure of the black male rebel, present in both pro- and antislavery writings and images, shaped representations of freedom and the possible routes out of enslavement. The contrast between the supplicant, disabled bondsperson and the threatening, able-bodied black male represented different forms of emancipation. These competing forms presented a choice—between revolutionary and armed rebellion and emancipation as a process of imperial and legislated reform.

Conclusion

On 31 July 1838, Jamaican missionary and abolitionist Reverend William Knibb celebrated the emancipation of the enslaved at a service in Falmouth, Jamaica. Earlier that year, nearly 800,000 men, women, and children of African descent were set free throughout the British Empire. Though slavery had been abolished in 1834, a four-year period of apprenticeship followed during which enslaved individuals between the ages of six and sixty labored for their former owners. Knibb's congregation celebrated the end of slavery in the British Empire with a funeral service. They placed an iron collar, a whip, and a set of chains in a coffin bearing the inscription "Colonial Slavery, died July 31st, 1838, aged 276 years," and then they sang:

> The death-blow is struck—see the monster is dying,
> He cannot survive till the dawn streaks the sky;
> *In one single hour*, he will prostrate be lying,
> Come, shoutt o'er the grave where so soon he will lie.

When midnight struck, Knibb shouted, "the monster is dead; the Negro is free."[1]

As the celebratory words sung by Reverend Knibb and his congregation suggest, the figure of the "monster" continued to inform debates about slavery well into the nineteenth century. Disability is key to how slavery and the unfinished work of emancipation continued to haunt former slave societies. The abolition of slavery throughout the Atlantic promised a world in which the capitalist and racist marketplace would no longer determine black life. And yet, in the decades following emancipation, the reverberations of slavery and the circularity of the devaluation of black life remained. In the post-emancipation British Caribbean, the use of legislative coercive power continued to try to deny former bondspeople choice in terms of where they lived, where they worked, and for what wages. The new vagrancy laws, the riot acts, and the masters and servants acts worked together to restrict emancipated people's freedom of movement by effectively preventing emigration so that people could not move around to find work elsewhere.[2] Although legally free, ex-slaves continued to suffer from the disabling legacies of slavery as they were subjected to a new system of domination that would keep them in a subordinate and dependent relationship with their former owners. Thus, life that was once bought and sold continued to be treated as though it could be reduced to surplus and disposed of.

Reverend Knibb's use of the term "monster" to describe slavery testifies to the historical intersections between disability and colonialism.[3] By uncovering the ways in which disability is represented in cultural discussions of monstrosity, how the enslaved experienced the embodiment of disability, how disability was institutionalized through the legal codes that defined slavery, and how the discourse of disability affected both pro- and antislavery discourse in the abolitionist era, we can better understand that slavery did more than build the national wealth of the metropole. The enduring legacies of slavery extend to ideas about black bodies, the aligning of interests and shaping of identities, and to viewing black bodies in particular ways.

This book illustrates the importance of the space between fitness and death to the enslaved experience. The slave trade and plantation slavery, specifically the sugar-producing colonies of the British Caribbean, are the historical underpinnings of systematized and violent African diasporic impairment. Slavery is key to understanding not only the corporeality of disability but the conceptual and interpretive meanings ascribed to it in the sugar-producing colonies of the British Caribbean. Scholars of slavery have long emphasized violent death as an integral aspect of Atlantic slavery.[4] This book, however, focuses on the space between fitness and death, a liminal space of physical and psychological debilitation resulting from the intrinsic violence of enslavement itself. Plantation slavery in the English Caribbean was an extremely disabling system of exploitation and degradation. The processes of capture, forced march, imprisonment, and forced migration that characterized the slave trade, together with the hostile living and working conditions found on Caribbean sugar plantations, often resulted in long-term emotional, psychological, sensory, and physical impairment.

The prevalence of impairment, disfigurement, and deformity on Barbadian and Jamaican sugar plantations shows that the colonial Caribbean challenges traditional Eurocentric timelines of disability history, which maintain that disability in its modern sense emerged with the onset of industrialization in nineteenth-century Europe and North America.[5] Indeed, slavery reveals the Western-centric bias of premodern versus modern by examining the emergence of modern notions of disability and the disabled body alongside the development of an English antiblack racism. Disability challenges scholars of African slavery in the Americas to rethink how the racist ideology about Africans and their descendants developed in the early modern era, and how the brutalized and traumatized slave body became a site through which disability in its modern connotations were understood.

The shared histories of race, disability, and slavery in the Atlantic World therefore offer a transnational and comparative basis for seeing the global intersections between colonialism and disability. The place of the monster and of monstrosity is key to understanding the emergence of Atlantic slavery and early antiblack racism. *Between Fitness and Death* shows that even before the rise of the Atlantic slave trade, precolonial and early colonial European writing often equated Africans and their descendants with animality and monstrosity. The origins of English antiblack racism reveal a long and complicated cultural legacy that was permeated with the belief in the subhumanity of Africans and their descendants.[6] English antiblack racism was expressed differently than nineteenth-century racism since it emerged long before the late Enlightenment.[7] During the fifteenth and sixteenth centuries, European understandings of race and skin color were greatly influenced by notions of monstrosity and deformity, which portrayed Africans, and in particular African women, as monstrous beings.[8] These ideas served to normalize and mute opposition to African dispossession in the English Atlantic world.

Slavery relied on the ever-present humanity of the enslaved. As it existed in the English Caribbean, slave law—from the earliest comprehensive codes of the mid-seventeenth century to the amelioration laws of the late eighteenth and early nineteenth centuries—deliberately constructed the enslaved as somehow both human and animal, and yet not fully either. This anthropological ambiguity is crucial to understanding the disabling forms of slavery. Lawmakers did not want to distinguish between the human and the animal because the intersection between these two categories defined the space of the monster, which was human but a suspect form of humanity. By not resolving the tension between the human and the animal, lawmakers and slaveowners alike could recognize the humanity of the enslaved but effectively disable it by treating them like animals. Slave law constructed a disabled legal category that suspended Africans between the human and the animal as a means to contain and profit from racial monstrosity. Perhaps more than any other legal principle, maternal inheritance demonstrates lawmakers' ability to deliberately recognize the humanity of the enslaved in order to systematically disable it. In this way slave law created a lesser and destructible form of humanity that mothers passed on to their children.

Situating Atlantic slavery, and specifically the slaveholding colonies of the British Caribbean, as key to the development of modern understandings of disability and the disabled body, uncovers plantation slavery in Barbados and Jamaica as a preeminent site of disability and demonstrates that disability among the enslaved became an ultimate expression of British racism. Caribbean sugar production was an industrial enterprise, one that was highly modern for its time. It was also physically debilitating. Enslaved laborers were at constant risk of becoming disabled by the hostile environments they lived in, the capricious yet institutionalized violence of owners and overseers, and the dangerous labor conditions in which they were forced to work. The impairments they endured did not necessarily constitute disabilities because, as forced laborers, their bodies were put to work, under the threat of the whip, until they were literally of no use to plantation production.

The marks inflicted onto the bodies of bondspeople were displayed in runaway advertisements in Barbados and Jamaica. Written by plantation owners or managers, these ads relied on the physical description of burns, sores, amputated limbs and extremities, whether marks of punishment or marks of disease, to aid in the apprehension of fugitive bondspeople. Runaway advertisements worked to perpetuate the long-standing notion that Africans and their descendants were deformed and disfigured beings, while at the same time disabling the enslaved by extending the power of the law and slaveholders' ability to limit bondspeople's movement.

The very real specter of revolutionary emancipation in the eighteenth-century Atlantic World, from Tacky's War in Jamaica (1760) to the Haitian Revolution (1791–1804), is key to understanding disability's place in both anti- and pro-slavery rhetoric. In abolitionist propaganda, writers argued that whites' brutal treatment of the enslaved provoked the black majority to rebel and commit atrocities against white men, women, and children. These writers placed the figure of the enslaved individual, beaten and broken, at the center of their works in order to counteract the figure of the "strong" armed, and threatening black rebel as a way of envisioning a potentially free black subject who was not a threat to the British Empire. Proslavery writers, by contrast, argued that abolitionists' revolutionary ideas of emancipation were the catalysts of slave uprisings. Advocates of slavery came increasingly to use sophisticated scientific arguments to bolster their claim.

Colonialism changes the way we think about disability. Scholars of disability have argued that disability is a universal human condition: each of us will likely acquire certain disabilities at some time in our lives.[9] And yet, in spite of its universality, disability must be understood within specific historical contexts. As Herbert Muyinda reminds us, when it comes to understanding histories of disability, "place matters."[10] Histories of disability and colonialism must remain attentive to different patterns of colonial exploitation and racialization and the distinct legacies of disablement that they have produced. There are specificities to the history of disability and African enslavement that cannot simply be transferred to all other colonized contexts. *Between Fitness and Death* illustrates that plantation slavery in the Caribbean should be considered among one of history's most disabling systems of exploitation. Plantation slavery, which expanded rapidly during this period due to sugar production in the Caribbean, became one of the most traumatizing forms of human bondage. The dismemberment, scarring, and mutilation that was a routine part of the experience of enslavement marked the enslaved body with symbolic power of the slave-master relationship; the punished body became a kind of text that told a story of both blacks' supposed rebellious nature and of a refusal to accept one's enslavement.

Notes

Introduction

1. *Athenian Mercury*, 23 May 1691, original emphasis. *Athenian Mercury*, 26 September 1691, original emphasis.

2. They more or less dismissed both the climatological theory—that black skin color was caused by the sun—and the curse of Ham theory—that blackness was the notorious mark of the divinely cursed descendants of Noah's son Ham.

3. *Athenian Mercury*, 11 May 1691. *Athenian Mercury*, 23 May 1691. But the question remained whether the mother or the father had more influence on intergenerational resemblance. In their answer to whether a "natural defect in the parent" is "communicated to the child by the particles of the semen or otherwise," the editors answered: "Fancy may have a great share here, as well as in the former Cases, and the Defect of the Father be so strongly fixed on the Mothers Mind, as to impress it on the Child. Natural defect seem an unphilosophical term, for all Defects are monstrous, and as such unnatural. Accidental Defects indeed there may be, and we find daily are, but if this proceeds from the Male Parent, by the Particles of the Semen, such Defects are only in Quality, not Quantity. Stuttering parents, have, it's true, had Children troubled with the same Defect; but this we look upon rather to proceed from Imitation, than any other case." The male role in producing supposedly deformed children was, therefore, accidental, and it resulted in individual rather than collective or racial defects.

4. *Athenian Mercury*, 26 September 1691, original emphasis.

5. Roxann Wheeler's 2000 study of race in eighteenth-century Britain argues that although British culture utilized a "physical typology" of human differences, such differences

were not seen as innate facts but products of environment and climate. Wheeler argues that more important than physical differences were a range of "proto-racial," sociocultural discourses that distinguished Christian Europeans from heathen savages. For Wheeler and others, the "racializing" idioms of eighteenth-century Britain should not be confused with the "racist" ideologies of the nineteenth century. See *Complexion of Race,* 9–11, 271, 301. For more on the question of which came first, slavery or racism, see chapter 1 of this book.

6. See as examples, Edward Topsell, "Of the Ape," in *Historie of foure-footed beastes*; Richard Jobson, *Golden Trad*; "The first voyage made by Master William Towrson March-ant of London, to the coast of Guinea . . . in the yeere 1555," in Hakluyt and Goldsmid, *Principal Navigations*; Herbert, *Some yeares travels.*

7. Jordan, *White over Black,* 232.

8. For recent works that have likewise examined the archive of slavery through a new lens, see S. Turner, *Contested Bodie*; Muskateem, *Slavery at Sea*; Fuentes, *Dispossessed Lives.*

9. In previous studies, scholars of Caribbean slavery approach disability among the enslaved primarily as a medical pathology, which treats disability as an individual char-acteristic and not a category for exploring power itself. See for instance, Higman, *Slave Populations*; Handler, "Diseases and Medical Disabilities . . . Part I" and "Diseases and Medical Disabilities . . . Part II."

10. See, for instance, Wheeler, *Complexion of Race*; J. Morgan, *Laboring Women*; K. Hall, *Things of Darkness*; Kidd, *Forging of Races*; Molineux, *Faces of Perfect Ebony.*

11. See, for instance, D. Davis, *Inhuman Bondage* and *Problem of Slavery*; Dayan, "Legal Slaves"; Burnard, *Mastery, Tyranny, and Desire.*

12. For a complementary critique of how slavery reveals the Western-centric bias of the premodern versus modern distinction see Paton, *No Bond but the Law,* and V. Brown, *Reaper's Garden.*

13. James, *Black Jacobins,* 392.

14. Mintz, *Sweetness and Power,* 143–49. For instance, in the eighteenth and early nine-teenth centuries, sugar did not make a significant caloric contribution to the English working-class diet because it was used mainly in tea. However, during the second half of the nineteenth century, the caloric contribution of sugar increased and cheap sugar became the most important addition to the British working-class diet. Mintz, *Sweetness and Power,* 48–49.

15. Of course, some advertisements for missing bondspeople included descriptions of individuals who were *not* injured, debilitated, or scarred, however such notices were rare. The absence of slavery-induced marks on the enslaved body could indicate that the individual was a newcomer to slavery in the Americas or that she or he was a skilled bondsperson who faced fewer labor related risks in their daily lives.

16. For examples of scholarship on English perceptions of Africans and their bodes, see, Jordan, *White over Black*; Boose, "Getting of a Lawful Race"; K. Hall, *Things of Darkness*; A. Vaughan and V. Vaughan, "Before Othello"; J. Morgan, *Laboring Women*; C. Smith, *Black*

Africans. For a disability analysis of English descriptions of African bodies and minds see, Kennedy, "Let Them Be Young"; Kennedy and Newton, "Haunting of Slavery."

17. Mel, "Playing Disability," 99.

18. Activists in the Union of the Physically Impaired Against Segregation (UPIAS) first developed the social modem of disability in Britain in the 1970s. The social model reads disability not as an individual physical state of being (i.e., impairment) but as a social state of being (a *process* of disablement). In academic scholarship, Vic Finkelstein (who came to disability studies following his exile from South Africa for antiapartheid activities), Colin Barnes, and Michael Oliver produced the first academic discussions of the social model of disability. For scholarship on the theoretical models of disability and the scholarly debates surrounding them see, Finkelstein, *Attitudes*; Barnes, "Disability Studies"; Oliver, "Conductive Education"; Barnes and Oliver, *New Politics*; Goodley, *Disability Studies*; T. Shakespeare, "Social Model."

19. On the disposability of enslaved bodies, see Muskateem, *Slavery at Sea*, 3.

20. Drawing on what Achilles Mbembe calls "a state of injury," I explore the ways in which Atlantic slavery produced impairment. This is key to understanding the commodification of enslaved Africans in the English Atlantic world. Mbembe, "Necropolitics."

Chapter 1. Imagining Africa, Inheriting Monstrosity

1. For a discussion of race and religion as hereditary conditions in early English discourses about blackness and slavery, see Goetz, *Baptism*, esp. chapters 4 and 5.

2. There has been a great deal of scholarship on medieval and early modern European notions of monstrosity, as well as European understandings of race and in particular blackness. This chapter draws on these rich historiographies and analyzes primary sources familiar to studies of race and slavery but through a disability lens to examine the linkages between the development of antiblack racist thought and understandings of deformity and disability in the emerging world of Atlantic slavery. Although scholars of slavery have shown how European discourses of monstrosity connect with understandings of gender, sexuality, race, and ethnicity, they have passed quickly over the disability or deformity that underpins the category of monstrosity. See, for instance, J. Morgan, *Laboring Women*, esp. chapter 1; Molineux, *Faces of Perfect Ebony*, particularly chapter 3; Curran, *Anatomy of Blackness*; Delbourgo, *Collecting the World*, esp. chapter 2; Jordan, *White over Black*; Wheeler, *Complexion of Race*.

3. Lund, "Laughing at Cripples," 94.

4. D. Turner, introduction, 5.

5. Stagg, "Representing Physical Difference," 23. The term *monster* derives from the Latin word *monstrare*, meaning to show or demonstrate, and the French word *monere*, meaning to warn. See Sharpe, "England's Legal Monsters," 110.

6. Dunthorne, "How to Approach a Monster," 111.

7. Raynalde, *Byrth of Mankynde*, 6.

8. Stagg, "Representing Physical Difference," 20, 25.

9. Brammal, "Monstrous Metamorphosis," 6.

10. Fissell, *Vernacular Bodies*, chapter 2.

11. Brammall, "Monstrous Metamorphosis," 12; Fissell, *Vernacular Bodies*, chapter 2.

12. Historians have referred to medieval and early modern monsters as "mixtures," "prerogative instances," and a "confusion of categories." See Dunthorne, "How to Approach a Monster," 1113; Clark, *Thinking with Demons*; Daston and Park, *Wonders*.

13. Although enslaved people shared a precarity with other master-less men, such as seventeenth- and eighteenth-century seamen, race ultimately distinguished the perpetual enslavement and shipment of Africans as unfree laborers in the Americas from conditions of servitude and status still prevalent among English servants, apprentices, and sailors.

14. Shildrick, "Maternal Imagination," 244.

15. The principle of maternal inheritance was applied to the English Caribbean colonies and held that the status of the mother determined the status of the child. The principal of legal inheritance was applied in the English Atlantic colonies after the 1656 Elizabeth Keys case in Virginia. Keys, an indentured servant of African descent living in Virginia, sued for freedom "after the overseers of her late master's estate classified her and her son as *negroes* (Africans or descendants of Africans) rather than an indentured servant with a freeborn child." In court, Keys and her attorney, William Grinstead, gave three interrelated arguments: Keys was a baptized Christian; Keys's father was an Englishman; and her father had bound her as an indentured servant for nine years, which period had passed. Keys's assertion of mixed African and English ancestry was based on English common law, which mandated that a child inherited her father's condition. Following Keys's freedom suit, in December 1662 the General Assembly of Virginia corrected the inconsistencies in its use of the word *slave* by declaring that the status of the mother determines the status of the child, irrespective of the status of the father. For scholarship on the Elizabeth Keys case and the principle of maternal inheritance, see Handler, "Custom and Law"; Banks, "Dangerous Woman," 799; K. Brown, *Good Wives*; Goetz, *Baptism*; J. Morgan, "Partus sequitur ventrem"; M. Newton, "Returns to a Native Land"; Dorsey, "Women without History"; Hartman, "Belly of the World"; Billings, "Case."

16. Jennifer L. Morgan argues that sixteenth-century English travelogues about Africa, in particular William Towrson's, "gave readers only two analogies through which to view and understand African women—beasts and monsters." (*Laboring Women*, 28). I argue, in contrast, that the animal and monster were not separate categories of understanding but inextricably intertwined and it was precisely the animal component of the monster that gave monstrosity so much power in justifying the exploitation and dispossession of Africans and their descendants in the world of Atlantic slavery.

17. K. Thomas, *Man and the Natural World*, 39.

18. Ramesey, *Mans Dignity*, 97.

19. "The second voyage to Guinea set out by Sir George Barne, Sir John Yorke, Thomas Lok, Anthonie Hickman and Edward Castelin, in the year 1554. The Captain whereof was M. John Lok," in Hakluyt and Goldsmid, *Principal Navigations*, np.

20. Brammall, "Monstrous Metamorphosis," 7.

21. Thomas, *Man and the Natural World*, 135.

22. Freedman, "Medieval Other," 2.

23. Garland, *Eye of the Beholder*, 160.

24. Africanus, *A Geographical Histories of Africa*, 42.

25. Thomas, *Man and the Natural World*, 38.

26. Bacon, *Works of Lord Bacon*, 1:158. For a discussion of the importance of clothing and supposed connection to savagery, see Kupperman, "Presentment of Civility."

27. Wheeler, *Complexion of Race*, 19; Thomas, *Man and the Natural World*, 38–39.

28. *Complete Geographer*, 196.

29. Morgan *Laboring Women*, 26.

30. Ibid., *Laboring Women*, 21–23; Bucher, *Icon and Conques*; Chaplin, "Natural Philosophy"; Pratt, *Imperial Eyes*.

31. Columbus, *Journal of Christopher Columbus*, 160–65.

32. Drawing on Las Casas's work, English travelers produced some of the most widely circulated information about Spanish colonization of Hispaniola. See C. Smith, *Black Africans*, 1.

33. Lowe, "Stereotyping," 43.

34. Ibid., 31–32, 47. Morgan, *Laboring Women*, 17.

35. Münster, *Treatyse*.

36. Marees, "Description and Historicall Declaration," 927.

37. Hacket, *Summarie*.

38. Braude, "Sons of Noah," 116.

39. Mandeville, *Voyages and Travailes*. Attributed to the fictional John Mandeville, this work contained information from a variety of earlier travel narratives and encyclopedias. By 1500 it had been translated from the original French into German, Italian, Dutch, Spanish, Irish, Danish, Czech, and Latin.

40. J. Burton and Loomba, *Race in Early Modern England*, 70.

41. Raleigh, *Discovery*, 110–11.

42. Curran, *Anatomy of Blackness*, 7.

43. K. Hall, *Things of Darkness*, 11.

44. Ibid., 9.

45. Cited in Boucher, *Cannibal Encounters*, 15.

46. Greenblatt, *Marvelous Possessions*, 22–23.

47. Curran, *Anatomy of Blackness*, 83.

48. Ibid., 111.

49. "The second voyage . . . M. John Lok," np.

50. J. Burton and Loomba, *Race in Early Modern England*, 158.

51. Fryer, *Staying Power*, 14–18.

52. Indagines, *Briefe introductions*, 68.

53. J. Burton and Loomba, *Race in Early Modern England*, 89.

54. Abbot, *Brief Description*, 177.

55. Best, *True Discourse*, 55. For other discussions of George Best's theories on the origins of black skin color, see K. Hall, *Things of Darkness*, 12.

56. Best, *True Discourse*, 54.

57. Sweet, "Iberian Roots," 148–50. For a discussion of the curse of Ham theory and Puritanism in the Anglo-Atlantic World, see Whitford, "Calvinist Heritage."

58. Cited in Sweet, "Iberian Roots," 148.

59. Sweet, "Iberian Roots of American Racist Thought," 148.

60. Godwyn, *Negro's & Indians advocate*, 14, original emphasis.

61. Boose, "Getting of a Lawful Race," 44.

62. Braude, "Sons of Noah," 105.

63. Caliban's ambiguous humanity foreshadows Africans' indeterminate status in the English Caribbean for, as Melanie J. Newton argues, everything Caliban inherits from his absent father and his mother, the witch Sycorax, "blurs the boundary between human and animal and fits him for enslavement (a deformed and possibly animal shape, lack of honour and civility, a servile yet violent nature, and unnatural sexual desires)." M. Newton, "Returns to a Native Land," 115. For other studies on Caliban in anticolonial writing, see A. Vaughan and V. Vaughan, *Shakespeare's Caliban*; Lindsay, "Which First Was Mine Own King"; Goldberg, *Tempest in the Caribbean*; Jackson, *Creole Indigeneity*, esp. chapter 2; Nixon, "Caribbean and African Appropriations"; A. Vaughan, "Caliban"; and Loomba, *Shakespeare, Race, and Colonialism*, 38.

64. W. Shakespeare, *Tempest*, 2.

65. W. Shakespeare, *Tempest*, 2.2.28–32.

66. Curran, *Anatomy of Blackness*, 43–44; Delbourgo, *Collecting the World*, 72.

67. Miller, "Fowls of Heaven," 58.

68. Topsell, "Of the Ape," in *Historie of foure-footed beastes*, 3–4.

69. J. Burton and Loomba, *Race in Early Modern England* 166.

70. Jobson, *Golden Trade*, 52.

71. J. Morgan, *Laboring Women*, 29.

72. Anon, *Female Monster*, 7.

73. Jones, *Engendering Whiteness*, 21.

74. J. Morgan, *Laboring Women*, 31–35.

75. "The first voyage made by Master William Towrson Marchant of London, to the coast of Guinea . . . in the yeere 1555," in Hayluyt and Goldsmid, *Principal Navigations*, 6:184.

76. Fritze, 'Herbert." Herbert had significant connections to powerful individuals in England who helped finance slavery and the slave trade. He served as the attendant to captive Charles I in 1647, was knighted by Cromwell in 1658, and was later made a baronet under Charles II. His financial ties to slavery and the slave trade testify to the linkages between capitalism and emerging antiblack racism.

77. Herbert, *Some yeares travels*, 18. In the early modern period, *dugge* referred to a woman's breast, used most often in reference to suckling.

78. Herbert, *Some yeares travels*, 19.

79. Salih, "Filling Up the Space"; L. Davis, *Enforcing Normalcy*, 40, 55, 67, 82.

80. Herbert, *Some yeares travels*, 19.

81. Ibid., 21. My thanks to Matthew Sears for his translation from the original Latin to English.

82. D. Smith, "Brief Introduction," ii, xxiii.

83. See also Shaw, *Everyday Life*, 83–84.

84. Ligon, *True and Exact History*, 91.

85. Ibid., 75, 168.

86. Ibid., 60, 62, 64, quotation on 52.

87. Ibid., 29.

88. Albrecht Dürer (1471–1528) was a German painter, printmaker, mathematician, and art theorist. His *Vier Bücher von Menschlicher Proportion* ("The Four Books of Human Proportion"), published posthumously in October 1528, greatly influenced Renaissance aesthetic discourse. See Parshall, "Great Knowledge."

89. Ligon, *True and Exact History*, 81.

90. J. Morgan, *Laboring Women*, 154.

91. Camille A. Nelson, "American Husbandry."

92. Ibid., 8.

93. Kristeva, *Powers of Horror*, 4.

94. Beckles, *White Servitude*; Linebaugh and Rediker, *Many-Headed Hydra*, 44.

95. Beckles, "Plantation Production," 44.

96. Blackburn, *Making of New World Slavery*, 240–41.

97. Palmié, "Toward Sugar and Slavery," 139.

98. Cited in Puckrein, *Little England*, 77.

99. Coke, *First part*, n.p.

100. Ibid.

101. Blackburn, *Making of New World Slavery*, 230.

102. Blackstone, *Commentaries*, 390. Blackstone wrote: "Of all tame and domestic animals, the brood belongs to the owner of the dam or mother; the English law agreeing with the civil, that 'partus sequitur ventrem' in the brute creation, though for the most part in the human species it disallows the maxim. And therefore in the laws of England, as well as Roman, 'si equam meam equus tuus praegnantem fecerit, non est tuum sed meum natum est' [If my mare be in foal by your horse, it is not your foal but mine] (390).

103. The connection between matrilineality and the inheritance of enslaved status was expressed in colonial Mexico by the Castilian concept of *limpieza de sangre* (purity of blood) and the emerging *sistema de casta* (society of castes), in which access to economic resources and political rights was dependent on the ostensible purity of one's bloodline. Spanish fears and anxieties over slavery and the *limpieza de sangre* were projected onto women's reproductive sexuality as a means of containing genealogical contamination and maintaining the racialized social order of the Iberian Atlantic World. See Martínez, *Genealogical Fictions*; Twinnam, *Purchasing Whiteness*; Martínez, "Black Blood"; Socolow,

Women of Colonial Latin America, 7–9; Verena Stolcke, "Invaded Women"; Seed, *To Love, Honor, and Obey,* esp. 146–50; Pike, *Linajudos and Conversos.*

104. As a form of legal disablement, the maternal inheritance principle could not rob women of knowledge about how to control their own reproduction. African women, especially midwives, knew and used knowledge of contraception and plants as abortifacients. See Sheridan, *Doctors and Slaves,* 225–28; Bush, "Hard Labour."

105. Patterson, *Slavery and Social Death,* 7.

106. Scholars continue to debate whether Europeans perceived skin color as the primary mark of human difference before the late eighteenth century. In other words, what came first, slavery or racism? My findings in this regard align with those who argue that the ideological bases for antiblack racism were established long before the late Enlightenment, in the fifteenth, sixteenth, and seventeenth centuries. For more on this question see, for example, Sweet, "Iberian Roots"; Braude, "Sons of Noah"; J. Morgan, *Laboring Women* and "Some Could Suckle over Their Shoulder"; Chaplin, *Subject Matter*; Kopelson, *Faithful Bodies*; K. Brown, *Good Wives*; Wheeler, *Complexion of Race.*

107. Tryon, *Friendly advice,* 190, 115, 116.

108. Godwyn, *Negro's and Indian's Advocate,* 13, 14, 30.

109. Thomas, *Man and the Natural World,* 135.

110. T. Browne, *Pseudodoxia Epidemica,* 462–68, 466, 477–78. See Colin Kidd, *Forging of Races,* 67–68. For other discussions of Sir Thomas Browne, see Hall, *Things of Darkness,* 12–13.

111. Mc Elligott, 'Crouch.'

112. R. Burton, *View of the English Acquisitions,* n.p.

113. Behn, *Oroonoko,* 81.

114. The anonymously penned thirteenth-century poem "Cursor Mundi" tells of four Saracens whose supernatural conversion cured both their inner immorality and outer blackness. See Loomba and Burton, *Race in Early Modern England,* 65–67.

Chapter 2. Between Human and Animal

1. 1661 Barbados Slave Code. Lawmakers in Jamaica replicated this passage in 1664, despite not having an enslaved population large enough to warrant such trepidation. See 1664 Jamaica Slave Code.

2. 1661 Barbados Slave Code, preamble.

3. Cover, "Violence and the Word," 1601, 1609.

4. *Act of assembly of the island of Jamaica . . . the Consolidated Act* (1788). Both Barbados and Jamaica's founding slave codes (1661 and 1664) contained such wording, which remained in the slave laws throughout the colonial period.

5. Kristeva, *Powers of Horror.*

6. Agamben, *State of Exception,* 109.

7. These theories of pain, suffering, and alienation put forth by Kristeva, Agamben, and Cover are useful for understanding disability in the context of Atlantic slavery, although

their works do not engage with blackness or Atlantic slavery. This absence does not invalidate these theories or make them irrelevant to the study of slavery and disability, but it demonstrates the ways in which histories of slavery have conditioned blackness as a space of ambivalence and ambiguity in European thought. Modern social and political theories have themselves been constituted "in a field of pain and death" that reenacts slavery's violence through a refusal to engage with blackness as a form of humanity. This silencing of blackness and slavery in modern theory is reflective of the relationship between history, the archive, and power, as well as modern theory's reluctance or unwillingness to acknowledge slavery as the basis for theorizing about wider human experience.

8. For a discussion of how the English slave codes contributed to the development of racial categories see Amussen, *Caribbean Exchanges*, esp. "Right English Government," 162–232.

9. Nirmala Erevelles, *Disability and Difference in Global Contexts: Enabling a Transformative Body Politic* (New York: Palgrave, 2011), 55–56.

10. Blackstone, *Commentaries*, 107.

11. Dunn, *Sugar and Slaves*, 227. By the seventeenth century, when the English began colonizing and settling North America and the Caribbean, slavery had not existed in England for centuries. See Tomlins, *Freedom Bound*, 418–20. Rugemer, "Development," 432. Bradley J. Nicholson notes that slavery was introduced in England in 1547 but was repealed two years later. See Nicholson, "Legal Borrowing," 42.

12. "Barbados, 1651," articles 21 and 22.

13. Lazarus-Black, "John Grant's Jamaica," 156. See also N. Hall, "Judicial System." In 1651, prior to the comprehensive slave code, the proprietary governor of Barbados, Francis Willoughby, and the commissioners of the Commonwealth of England signed the Charter of Barbados and together both parties agreed that "all Laws made heretofore by general Assemblies, that are not repugnant to the Law of *England*, shall be good; except such as concern the present difference." "Barbados, 1651," articles 21 and 22.

14. Dunn, *Sugar and Slaves*, 227.

15. Scholars of slavery have demonstrated the various ways in which slave law was bent and broken by both slaveowners and the enslaved themselves. See for instance, Shaw, *Everyday Life*; M. Newton, *Children of Africa*; Paton, *No Bond but the Law*; V. Brown, *Reaper's Garden*.

16. Watson, *Slave Laws*, 63.

17. Jenny Shaw stresses that long-standing English notions of difference, particularly those between Irish Catholic servants and their English Protestant masters, were significantly challenged and changed with the onset of African slavery in the English Caribbean. English colonists' shifting hierarchies of difference were reflected in legislation. See Shaw, *Everyday Life*, esp. chapter 1, "'An Heathenishe, Brutish and an uncertaine, dangerous kind of People:' Figuring Difference in the Early English Atlantic," 15–43; Beckles, "Riotous and Unruly Lot"; Amussen, *Caribbean Exchanges*, 17–18.

18. Amussen, *Caribbean Exchanges*, 122.

19. The titles of these laws are referenced in later laws. For a detailed timeline of these laws, see Handler, "Custom and Law," 242–47.

20. Amussen, *Caribbean Exchanges*, 124–26; Handler, "Custom and Law," 249. The degree to which indentured servants and enslaved Africans shared an overlapping experience of forced labor is debated by scholars. See Amussen, *Caribbean Exhanges,* 126–29; Beckles, "Riotous and Unruly Lot."

21. 1673 Jamaica Slave Code.

22. Ibid.

23. Amussen, *Caribbean Exchanges*, 130.

24. Gaspar, "With a Rod of Iron," 346.

25. 1661 Barbados Slave Code.

26. Susan Dwyer Amussen argues that the 1661 slave code determined the distinctions between free/unfree and white/black. See *Caribbean Exchanges*, 129–35.

27. Amussen, *Caribbean Exchanges*, 133.

28. Gaspar, "With a Rod of Iron," 352; Tomlins, "Transplants and Timing," 389.

29. 1661 Barbados Slave Code; 1664 Jamaica Slave Code. Jerome Handler has found that in the Barbados laws of the 1650s "status distinctions along 'racial' lines were legally recognized" in the 1650s Barbados laws." See Handler, "Custom and Law," 245. By 1700, the Tainos had vanished from Jamaica. See Wilson, "Performance of Freedom," 50–51.

30. Fisher, "Atlantic Indian Slavery." My thanks to Linford Fisher for sharing this work with me. In English North America, Virginia was the only southern colony to prohibit Indian enslavement; however, repeated confirmation of the law implies that it was not followed. For Fisher's published work on Indian slavery, see, for example, *Indian Great Awakening*; "Why Shall Wee Have Peace"; "Dangerous Designes." Also see C. Snyder, *Slavery in Indian Country*, 78.

31. "Negro, n. and adj.," OED Online, www.oed.com, accessed 5 May 2014.

32. *Negro's & Indians advocate*, 36.

33. Paton, "Punishment," 927.

34. 1661 Barbados Slave Code; Amussen, *Caribbean Exchanges*, 132.

35. While in Roman law, slaves were the legal property of their owners, they were for certain purposes human, for others a thing. See Watson, *Slave Laws*, 22.

36. A Declarative ACT upon the Act making Negroes Real Estate, in *Acts Passed* (Hall); *Laws of Barbados*.

37. Goveia, *West Indian Slave Laws*, 28.

38. An Act to prohibit the Inhabitants of this Island from employing, their Negroes or other Slaves, in selling or bartering (1708), in *Acts Passed* (Hall).

39. My sincerest gratitude to Linford Fisher for sharing with me his transcription of the 1676 Act. *Acts and Statutes*, 135–38. Also see Fisher's discussion of the 1676 act to prohibit the Indian Slave Trade from New England to Barbados in "Dangerous Designes," 99–124.

40. "An Act for the Governing of Negroes" (Barbados, 1688), in *Acts Passed*.

41. 1661 Barbados Slave Code, preamble.

42. "Act for the Governing of Negroes" (1688).

43. *Acts and Statutes*; "Act for the Governing of Negroes" (1688).

44. "Act for the Governing of Negroes" (1688).

45. Ibid.

46. Whites' fear of the taking of white women in the aftermath of a rebellion was a constant feature of the white imagination. After Bussa's Rebellion in Barbados in 1816, colonial authorities in Barbados claimed that the rebels planned "to put to death all the white men who came into their possession; but they were not to kill the white women, who were to be reserved for their own purposes." Barbados House of Assembly 1818, 56–57. Quoted in M. Newton, "King v. Robert James," 586.

47. Goveia, *West Indian Slave Laws*, 28.

48. 1664 Jamaica Slave Code; very similar language was used in the 1661 Barbados Slave Code, the difference being that owners convicted of such crime were expected to pay to the "publique treasury three thousand pounds of Musso Sugar but if hee shall kill another mans hee shall pay unto the owner of the Negro double the vallue and unto the publique Treasury five thousand pounds of Musso sugar." See 1661 Barbados Slave Code, clause 20. "Musso" was probably short for Muscovado sugar.

49. Rugemer, "Development," 448–49.

50. 1696 Jamaica Slave Code. In her research on Jamaican court records, Diana Paton found that no white individual was ever convicted of the crime of "wantonly" killing an unfree person in the island's history. See "Punishment," 949, fn. 16.

51. Dunn, *Sugar and Slaves*, 245. Amussen, *Caribbean Exchanges*, 138.

52. Paton, "Punishment," 927–28.

53. 1661 Barbados Slave Code; 1664 Jamaica Slave Code.

54. 1661 Barbados Slave Code. The law is repeated, in slightly different language in the following slave codes: 1664 Jamaica Slave Code; "The Acts of Assembly and Laws of Jamaica, Abridg'd under Proper Heads" (1684), in *Abridgement of the Laws*; "An Act for the Governing of Negroes" (1688), 115; *Laws of Jamaica*.

55. Gaspar, "With a Rod of Iron," 348.

56. Handler, *Unappropriated People*, 34–39. Handler notes that self-purchase was recognized in custom in the eighteenth and nineteenth centuries, however, never in law.

57. "An Act for the encouragement of all Negroes and Slaves, that shall discover any conspiracy," in *Acts Passed* (Hall).

58. Handler, *Unappropriated People*, 30.

59. "An Act for the encouragement of such Negroes and other Slaves, that shall behave themselves courageously against the Enemy in time of Invasion (1707), in *Acts Passed* (Hall).

60. Gaspar, "With a Rod of Iron," 344.

61. "An Act for the further Encouragement of Parties, and more Speedy Reduction of Rebellious and Runaway Slaves" (1706–7), in *Laws of Jamaica*.

62. "An Act to make free several negro and mulatto slaves, as a reward for their faithful services in the late rebellion" (1760), in *Acts of Assembly* (1787). Another enslaved man named Jack was freed for his role in suppressing Tacky's Rebellion, see "An Act to make

free a negro slave, named Jack, the property of Peter Thomas, of the parish of Saint Mary, planter, for his faithful services to the public" (1762), in *Acts of Assembly* (1787).

63. Handler, *Unappropriated People*, 67–68.

64. Ibid., 68.

65. An Act for amending An Act of this Island, entitled, 'An Act for the governing of Negroes;' and for providing a proper maintenance and support for such Negroes, Indians or Mulattoes . . . (1739), in *Acts Passed* (Hall).

66. "An Act for Regulating the Manumission of Negro, Mulatto, and other Slaves; and to oblige the owners to make a provision for them during their lives" (1774), in *Laws of Jamaica*.

67. *Act of Assembly*.

68. Ibid.

69. Goveia, *West Indian Slave Laws*, 27.

70. M. Newton, *Children of Africa*, 37.

71. Ibid., 36.

72. R. Davis, *Holy War*, 40–41.

73. Blackburn, *Making of New World Slavery*, 4.

74. Kristeva, *Powers of Horror*, 4.

75. Butler, *Bodies*, 3.

76. Kristeva, *Powers of Horror*, 1.

77. M. Newton, "Returns to a Native Land," 115.

78. Dorsey, "Women without History," 166.

79. M. Newton, "Returns to a Native Land," 115.

80. Jones, *Engendering Whiteness*, 159; J. Morgan, "Paartus Sequitur Ventrem," 13–14.

81. Amussen, *Caribbean Exchanges*, 125–26.

82. J. Morgan, *Laboring Women*, 14.

83. British colonial slave law's construction of the enslaved as monstrous had precedents in medieval and early modern English law. Beginning in the thirteenth and surviving until the mid-nineteenth century, English law defined the legal category monster as a human/animal hybrid and the body as "the ultimate bedrock of what it means to be human." Sharpe, "England's Legal Monsters," 101. Sharpe notes that references to monsters can be found in Henry de Bracton, *On the Laws and Customs of England*, 2:2, 2:21, 2:203–4; 3:151, 3:221, 4:198, 4:227, 4:361, 4:362 (see Sharpe, 101, fn. 14). The first English legal texts to refer to monsters were the thirteenth-century works of Bracton and those of an author known only as Britton. Sharpe, "England's Legal Monsters," 113. In *On the Laws*, Bracton defined monsters as "those procreated perversely, against the way of human kind, as where a woman brings forth a monster or a prodigy." Both Bracton and Britton claimed that monsters were produced through bestiality, and English lawmakers stipulated that the offspring of such a union were "not reckoned among children" and, therefore, were not entitled to the inheritance laws of English people. Bracton, *On the Laws*, 2:31. The English, therefore, rejected as incompatible with their legal tradition the Roman legal principle that "where childlessness precluded inheritance the birth of a monster counted as a child." Sharpe, "England's Legal Monsters," 108.

84. Bracton, *On the Laws*, 4:361.

85. Sharpe, "England's Legal Monsters," 114.

86. Swinburne, *Brief Treatise*, 168–69.

87. Sharpe, "England's Legal Monsters," 125.

88. Godwyn, *Negro's & Indian Advocate*, 24.

89. Godwyn, *Negro's & Indian Advocate*, 24–26, 24.

90. Hartman, *Lose Your Mother*, 103.

91. Patterson, *Slavery and Social Death*, 5.

92. Thomas Thistlewood Papers.

93. Jordan, *White over Black*, 156.

94. Natalie Zemon Davis's study of slave law and punishment in colonial Suriname shows that emasculation was practiced on the royal eunuch of the kingdom of Oyo for immoral sexual acts such as adultery, incest, and bestiality. Castration, however, had no precedent in English law. See N. Davis, "Judges," 937.

95. Scholars of slavery have argued that castration was *not* sanctioned in the slave laws of Barbados and Jamaica. See for instance, Dunn, *Sugar and Slaves*, 240; Jordan, *White over Black*, 154–55. Edward Rugemer's discussion of "gelding" demonstrates that some territories (e.g., South Carolina) legislated the castration of two-time male runaways, whereas Barbados and Jamaica laws made no reference to castration, although there is evidence that planters practiced it, particularly against male rebels. See Rugemer, "Development," 455.

96. 1661 Barbados Slave Code; 1664 Jamaica Slave Code. Emphasis added.

97. *Member* was distinct from *limb* in the 1661 Barbados slave code and the 1676 supplemental act, as well as the 1664, 1673, and 1678 codes of Jamaica. By 1688 (Barbados) and 1692 (Jamaica), *member* becomes synonymous with *limb*. See 1661 Barbados Slave Code; *Acts and Statutes*; "A Supplementall Act to a former Act"; 1664 Jamaica Slave Code; 1673 Jamaica Slave Code; 1678 Jamaica Slave Code.

98. My thanks to Melanie Newton for helping me articulate this understanding of slave law. Personal communication, 5 November 2018.

99. MacGregor, "Sloane."

100. Sloane, *Voyage*, 1:lvii.

101. Siebers, "Sexual Culture," 40.

102. Jordan, *White over Black*, 156.

103. Buisseret, *Jamaica*, 274–79. Equiano, *Interesting Narrative* 94–95.

104. Behn, *Oroonoko*, 140.

105. Godwyn, *Negro's & Indians advocate*, 41.

106. Fuentes, *Dispossessed Lives*.

107. For studies on crime and punishment in early modern England, see Spierenburg, *Spectacle*; Innes, "King's Bench Prison"; Walker, "Imagining the Unimaginable," "Everyman," and *Crime*; Kermode and Walker, *Women*.

108. In England criminals were whipped and paraded through the streets as a spectacle. Until the end of the eighteenth century, both men and women were stripped naked from the waist up when whipped. Punishments common to England but not the Caribbean included the pillory and stocks. See Spierenburg, *Spectacle*.

109. See V. Brown, *Reaper's Garden*, and Paton, "Punishment."
110. 1696 Jamaica Slave Code.
111. The 1696 Jamaica Slave Code stated that in cases "of any Felony, Burglary, Robbery, Burning of Houses, Canes, rebellious Conspiracies, or any other capital Offence whatsoever," the justice of the peace "shall give sentence of death, transportation, dismembering or any other punishment, as they in their judgement shall think meet to inflict, and forthwith, by their Warrant, cause immediate Execution to be done by the common, or any other Executioner; (Women with child only excepted, who are hereby repriv'd till after delivery) and if they judge not the criminals to die for any Crime, but to receive corporal punishment; and that the owner as recompence, pay unto the party or partied injur'd, a certain sum of money; thath then in case the owner or owners refuse to pay the said sum, the said justices and freeholders may adjudge the said criminal or criminals to the party or parties injur'd, his, her or their heirs for ever."
112. Leslie, *New and Exact Account*, 42.
113. Paton, "Punishment," 937–41.
114. *Debate on a Motion*, 86.
115. N. Davis, "Judges," 937.
116. "Act for the Governing of Negroes" (1688), 118, original emphasis.
117. 1696 Jamaica Slave Code.
118. An Act for the punishment of Run-away Slaves, and of Slaves who shall willfully entertain, harbour and conceal any Run-away Slaves (1731), in *Acts Passed* (Hall), 139.
119. S. Browne, "Digital Epidermalization," 139.
120. Thomas Thistlewood Papers.
121. *Act of Assembly*, 13–14.
122. 1661 Barbados Slave Code; 1664 Jamaica Slave Code.
123. 1673 Jamaica Slave Code.
124. 1678 Jamaica Slave Code.
125. An Act for the better Government of Slaves and free Negroes (1702), in *Laws of Jamaica* (1716), 135–39.
126. Godwyn, *Negro's & Indians advocate*, 13.
127. *Laws of Jamaica* (1716).
128. Cunningham, *Imaginary Betrayals*, 7–8.
129. Paton, "Punishment," 939–40.
130. Goveia, *West Indian Slave Laws*, 19–35.
131. 1661 Barbados Slave Code; 1664 Jamaica Slave Code.
132. 1696 Jamaica Slave Code.
133. The law stated: "AND be it further enacted by the Authority aforesaid, That no Slave shall be dismembered at the Will and Pleasure of his Master, Owner, or Employer, under the Penalty of One hundred Pounds; to be recovered in any Court of Record against the Person who shall dismember, or order the dismembering of such Slave or Slaves as aforesaid; one Half whereof shall be to his Majesty, his Heirs, and Successors, for and towards the Support of the Government of this Island, and the contingent Charges thereof; the

other Half to such Person or Persons who shall inform and sue for the same." See "An Act for the more effectual punishing of Crimes committed by Slaves" (1717), in *Acts of Assembly passed in the island of Jamaica; from 1681, to 1737, inclusive*, 107.

134. "Cruelty attending the Slave Trade as at present practiced on Negro Slavery," *Gentleman's Magazine*, October 1780, MS3248, Wellcome Library, London.

135. Long, *History of Jamaica*, 2 497.

136. Thomas Thistlewood Papers.

137. Dovaston, *Agricultura Americana*, 62.

138. "The Acts of Assembly and Laws of Jamaica" (1684). This law was based on the 1661 Barbados Slave Code, which stipulated the same.

139. 1661 Barbados Slave Code and 1664 Jamaica Slave Code. "It farther ordeyned and enacted by the authoritie aforesaid that whatsoever ——— Negro shall at any time of his accord take upp any Runaway Negro that have beene out about twelve Monethes shall have for his soe doeing five hundred pounds sugar to bee paid by the owner." For more see Shaw, *Everyday Life*, 37.

140. *Laws of Jamaica*.

141. 1696 Jamaica Slave Code.

142. V. Brown, *Reaper's Garden*, 144.

143. Thomas Thistlewood Papers.

144. Brown, *Reaper's Garden*, 28.

Chapter 3. Unfree Labor and Industrial Capital

1. MS523/288, Newton Papers.

2. Prince, *History*, 21.

3. Finkelstein, *Attitudes*; Oliver, *Politics of Disablement*; Barnes, *Cabbage Syndrome*.

4. L. Davis, *Enforcing Normalcy*, 74.

5. For a complementary critique of how slavery reveals the Western-centric bias of the premodern versus modern distinction, see Paton, *No Bond but the Law*, and V. Brown, *Reaper's Garden*.

6. Mintz, *Sweetness and Power*, 46.

7. Sheller, *Consuming the Caribbean*, 107.

8. Dunn, *Sugar and Slaves*; Higman, *Slave Populations*; V. Brown, *Reaper's Garden*; Smallwood, *Saltwater Slavery*.

9. MS523/270, Newton Papers.

10. Mbembe, "Necropolitics," 21, original emphasis.

11. Erevelles, *Disability and Difference*, 39.

12. Rediker, *Slave Ship*, 7.

13. Hartman, *Lose Your Mother*, 119.

14. Ibid., 180.

15. Ibid., 119, 44.

16. B. Wood, *Slavery*, 129.

17. Spillers, *Black, White*, 206.

18. I draw on Erving Goffman's concept of stigmatization in Goffman, *Stigma*. Goffman traces the term *stigma* to the branding of Greek slaves, when it referred to "bodily signs designed to expose something unusual and bad about the moral status of the signifier." In the Christian era, stigma referred to both "bodily signs of holy grace" and "bodily signs of physical disorder." Goffman concludes that the term has come to apply more to the "disgrace" itself than to the bodily markings.

19. Hartman, *Lose Your Mother*, 80.

20. Morrison, *Beloved*, 61, cited in Hartman, *Lose Your Mother*, 80.

21. Hartman, *Lose Your Mother*, 80.

22. Smallwood, *Saltwater Slavery*, 60.

23. Rediker, *Slave Ship*, 10.

24. Erevelles, *Disability and Difference*, 40.

25. Smallwood, *Saltwater Slavery*, 81–82.

26. Falconbridge, *Account*, 22.

27. Muskateem, *Slavery at Sea*, 39; 45

28. J. Newton, *The Journal of a Slave Trader*, 29, 17, 56.

29. Medical log of slaver the "Lord Stanley." Hereafter referred to as RCS MS0003.

30. Smallwood, *Saltwater Slavery*, 136–37. On the *Lord Stanley*, the majority of those afflicted by such conditions died despite Bowes's medical attention.

31. RCS MS0003.

32. Ibid.

33. Ibid.

34. Ibid. According to Alexander Falconbridge, it was acceptable practice for the purchaser (the slave ship captain) to return disabled or "defect" captives within a day of the sale. After the first day, however, such reexaminations were not permitted.

35. Africans became captives through various means, see Muskateem, *Slavery at Sea*, 31–33.

36. RCS MS0003.

37. Boster, "'Epeleptick' Bondswoman," 272–73.

38. Smallwood, *Slavery at Sea*, 120.

39. RCS MS0003.

40. J. Newton, *Journal*, 48.

41. Falconbridge, *Account*, 18.

42. Hartman, *Lose Your Mother*, 184–85. Muskateem, *Dispossessed Lives*, 136; Smallwood, *Saltwater Slavery*, 87, 150, 169, 173–77; Nielsen, *Disability History*, 41–48; H. Thomas, *Slave Trade*, 376, 378, 386, 311.

43. Rediker, *Slave Ship*, 10.

44. Diptee, *From Africa to Jamaica*, 4–5.

45. Sloane, *Voyage*, 1:liii.

46. *Supplement to the Royal Gazette* (Jamaica), 1–8 July 1780.

47. Dovaston, *Agricultura Americana*, 249, 280, 280–81, 246.

48. Baynton, "Disability."

49. Dovaston, *Agricultura Americana*, 245. See also Sloane, *Voyage*, 1: liii.

50. Curran, *Anatomy of Blackness*, 55; Roberts, *Slavery and the Enlightenment*, 210–11.

51. Curran, *Anatomy of Blackness*, 55.

52. Vincent Carretta claims that Equiano's account of his early life is "probably ficti-cious" (Carretta, *Equiano*, xvi). His argument and "proof" has been widely discredited by scholars of Atlantic slavery. See, for instance, the exchange between Paul Lovejoy and Carretta in *Slavery and Abolition*; Lovejoy, "Autobiography and Memory"; Carretta, "Response to Paul Lovejoy"; and Lovejoy, "Issues of Motivation." See also Byrd, "Eboe, Country, Nation."

53. See chapter 5.

54. Equiano, *Interesting Narrative*, 12.

55. Sloane, *Voyage*, 1:lviii.

56. Dovaston, *Agricultura Americana*, 246. Thornton, "War," 182.

57. Patterson, "Slavery and Slave Revolts"; "Slave Revolts"; Wilson, "Performance of Freedom."

58. Anon, *Great Newes*, 9. For secondary works that discuss these revolts and the Coro-mantee connection, see Handler, "Slave Revolts and Conspiracies"; Sharples, "Hearing Whispers"; Beckles, "Slave Drivers' War"; Shaw, *Everyday Life*.

59. Olmos and Paravisini-Gerbert, *Creole Religions*, 161.

60. Fick, *Making of Haiti*; Dubois, *Avengers*; Weaver, *Medical Revolutionaries*.

61. "Superannuated, adj. and n.," OED Online, www.oed.com, accessed 12 June 2017.

62. "Infirm, adj.," OED Online, www.oed.com, accessed 12 June 2017.

63. "Invalid, adj.2 and n.," OED Online, oed.com, accessed 12 June 2017.

64. MS523/288, Newton Papers.

65. Ibid.

66. Prince, *History*, 17.

67. Engels, *Condition*, 101–13, 8–11.

68. Dunn, *Sugar and Slaves*, 67–74; Beckles, *Natural Rebels*, 42–44, 119–27; Blackburn, *Making of New World Slavery*, 254.

69. Long's Collection, 41.

70. Dunn, *Sugar and Slaves*, 60.

71. Higman, *Slave Populations*, 615–17.

72. Cited in ibid., 614.

73. Jamie L. Bronstein argues that British workers were the first to experience the physi-cal consequences of industrialization. See *Caught in the Machiner*, 3.

74. Dovaston, *Agricultura Americana*, 125.

75. S. Turner, "Home-Grown Slaves," 40.

76. Follet, "Heat, Sex," 512.

77. Bush, "African Caribbean Slave Mothers," 79.

78. Ibid., 82.

79. S. Turner, *Contested Bodies*, 85, 141, 180, 253.

80. Journal of Somerset plantation.

81. S. Turner, *Contested Bodies*, 8–10.

82. Follet, "Heat, Sex," 511.

83. Barclay, "Mothering the 'Useless,'" 137, 135.

84. MS523/275, Newton Papers.

85. See the 1818 returns of Barbados, The Return of John Rycroft Best.

86. MS523/270, Newton Papers.

87. Dovaston, *Agricultura Americana*, 286–87.

88. Hogarth, *Medicalizing Blackness*.

89. Dovaston, *Agricultura Americana*, 270.

90. Richard Ligon wrote that in the seventeenth century illnesses in Barbados were "more grievous, and mortality greater by far than in England, and these diseases many times contagious." According to Ligon, the "black ribbon for mourning . . . is much worn there." See Ligon, *True and Exact History*, 173.

91. Handler, "Diseases and Medical Disabilities . . . Part I," 22.

92. Ibid., 12.

93. Dovaston, *Agricultura Americana*, 253, 256.

94. Helen Meekosha has made a similar argument about indigenous people in Australia. See Meekosha, "Decolonising Disability."

95. Prince, *History*, 25. Saint Anthony's Fire, or erysipelas, was a highly contagious disease characterized by intense inflammation of the skin and mucous membranes and high fever. See Kiple, *Caribbean Slave*, 93–97.

96. Prince, *History*, 22, 20.

97. Woodbridge, *Vagrancy*, 23.

98. Lees, *Solidarities*, 19.

99. Williamson, *Poverty*, 2.

100. Lees, *Solidarities*, 63.

101. Runaway advertisements, in particular, point to bondspeople's masquerading of disability to escape detection from owners and the rest of white society. See chapter 4.

102. *Supplement to the Royal Gazette* (Jamaica), 1–8 July 1780.

103. Groebner, *Who Are You?*, 90.

104. Dea H. Boster argues that in the Antebellum South, the enslaved exaggerated and feigned disability to discourage their purchase and to avoid performing particular forms of labor. See *African American Slavery*, 42, 89, 115.

105. Paul Gilroy's concept of the Black Atlantic as a "counterculture of modernity" might be usefully applied here. See Gilroy, *Black Atlantic*, 1–40.

Chapter 4. Incorrigible Runaways

1. *Savanna-la-Mar Gazette* (Jamaica), 9 September 1788.

2. "Man-Boy" referred to males ages eleven to eighteen. Plantation agents categorized young enslaved people into four categories—infants, children, boys and girls, and man-boys and women-girls. Such categories shaped understandings of slave childhood and

indicated an individual's supposed readiness for labor. During amelioration, plantation authorities increasingly emphasized these developmental stages as they sought to reproduce the slave population naturally. See S. Turner, *Contested Bodies*, 214; Muskateem, *Slavery at Sea*, 38.

3. For an in-depth study of country marks and what they reveal about African ethnicities and the transatlantic slave trade see Gomez, *Exchanging Our Country Marks*.

4. For examples of studies on runaway advertisements in the Atlantic World, see Heuman, *Out of the House of Bondage*; Prude, "To Look Upon the 'Lower Sort'"; Waldstreicher, "Reading the Runaways"; Franklin and Schweninger, *Runaway Slaves*; Fuentes, *Dispossessed Lives*; Charmaine Nelson, "Ran Away from Her Master." Recently, a number of scholars and institutions have produced online databases of runaway advertisements, including but not limited to these: the Documenting Runaway Slaves Project (runaway slaves.usm.edu), which includes seven collections (Arkansas, Louisiana, Mississippi, Jamaica, Bahamas, British Guiana/Suriname); Freedom on the Move (freedomonthe move.org); Saint Domingue (marronage.info); Canada (https://earlycanadianhistory .ca); Connecticut (http://runawayct.org/about); Maryland (http://www.afrigeneas .com/library/runaway_ads/balt-intro.html); and Slavery Adverts 250 (https://twitter .com/SlaveAdverts250).

5. The majority of newspapers that have survived are from the late eighteenth and early nineteenth centuries. I have included only paid advertisements, submitted to the newspapers by plantations owners or overseers, and not those submitted by jailers and workhouse administrators. All of the runaway advertisements are original; I have not counted repeat notices as part of this collection. For a full list of newspapers in circulation in Barbados and Jamaica during this period see Practor, *Colonial British Caribbean Newspapers*.

6. For a discussion of the psychological impact of slavery, specifically of the Middle Passage, see Muskateem, *Slavery at Sea*, esp. chapter 5, "Battered Bodies, Enfeebled Minds," 106–30.

7. Longmore and Umanski, *New Disability History*; Muyinda, "Negotiating Disability."

8. The yaws began with swelling of the skin, bone, and cartilage and could deform and disable the hands, feet, and legs of the individual sufferer. Handler, "Diseases and Medical Disabilities . . . Part 1," 22.

9. Clarkson, *Essay*, 145.

10. Clarkson, *Negro Slavery*, 95, original emphasis.

11. M. Wood, *Blind Memory*, 83.

12. Sharon Block argues that the meanings of black, white, and red used by colonists to describe bondspeople in eighteenth-century North American runaway advertisements were reflective not of racial identities but Europeanists' understanding of humoral theory. According to Block, complexion was not static, neither was it associated with skin color or race in the pre-nineteenth-century British colonies. See, Block, *Colonial Complexions*. In contrast, my research aligns with Kim F. Hall, Jennifer L. Morgan, Rana Hogarth, and

other scholars who argue that race and antiblack racism developed over the course of the early modern period, from the sixteenth to the eighteenth centuries.

13. The term *social uniform* is from Fanon, *Black Skin*, 86.

14. "An Act for the Governing of Negroes" (1692), in *Acts Passed* (Hall), 130.

15. Handler, "Escaping Slavery," 184.

16. Heuman, "Runaway Slaves,"; Handler, "Diseases and Medical Disabilities . . . Part 2," 183–84.

17. Barclay, "Greatest Degree," 35. MS523/276, Newton Papers. Melville Hall Estate Papers.

18. 1661 Barbados Slave Code; 1664 Jamaica Slave Code) By 1688, Barbados law had changed from "keeper of the prison" to "the Keeper of the Cage," which reflected the island's use of the cage as a form of imprisonment for fugitives until owners laid claim to them.

19. 1661 Barbados Slave Law, clauses 1, 4–21 (excepting clause 17). Similar wording can be found in the 1664 Jamaica Slave Code, clauses 4–12, 17–19.

20. 1673 Jamaica Slave Code.

21. 1678 Jamaica Slave Code.

22. *Act of assembly*, 17.

23. British colonial newspapers were part of a transatlantic "news revolution," such that by the mid-eighteenth century, newspapers had become a central feature of everyday life, not just in European cities but in colonial ones as well. To these were added advertisements seeking criminals, fugitives, and missing persons through the dissemination of detailed physical descriptions. Dawson, "First Impressions," 278.

24. For a discussion of the power of the everyday in race making, see Holt, "Marking."

25. A vast literature deals with making race in the Atlantic. See, for instance, Hogarth, *Medicalizing Blackness*; Jenny Shaw, *Everyday Life*; Wheeler, *Complexion of Race*; J. Morgan, *Laboring Women*; Chaplin, *Subject Matter*; Curran, *Anatomy of Blackness*; K. Hall, *Things of Darkness*; Kidd, *Forging of Races*; Hannaford, *Race*.

26. *Public Advertiser* (London), 13 November 1761.

27. G. Morgan and Rushton, "Visible Bodies," 47.

28. *Public Advertiser* (London), 14 February 1759.

29. Fryer, *Staying Power*, 25. Fryer writes that "the higher up the social scale the owner was, the less did the slave have to fear physical violence, if only because the rich paid good money for their slaves and were careful to protect their investment" (25).

30. For a discussion of descriptions of sailors' bodies, in particular tattoos, in Britain's American colonies, see Newman, "Reading the Bodies."

31. *London Evening Post*, 23–25 January 1755. *Morning Post and Daily Advertiser* (London), 16 October 1788.

32. For instance, in reference to the cruel punishments ordered by her mistress, Mary Prince wrote: "To strip me naked—to hang me up by the wrists and lay my flesh open with the cow-skin, was an ordinary punishment for even a slight offence." See Prince, *History*, 15.

33. Prude, "To Look upon the 'Lower Sort,'" 137.

34. *Barbados Mercury*, 19 October 1784.

35. Scholars of slavery have analyzed runaway advertisements to reveal information about runaways. For instance, Gad Heuman has shown that the majority of runaways were skilled males, and that in general more African-born fugitives were apprehended than creole ones. Both field and skilled laborers ran away, and owners advertised for both, though it was more common for skilled bondspeople to flee successfully. Heuman's research has also revealed that owners who resided closer to cities with access to the local newspapers advertised more frequently than those who lived in rural areas. Thus, the presence of skilled and domestic fugitives in runaway advertisements was a reflection of the greater tendency for such advertisements to be placed by owners who lived in or near towns, since nonagricultural and domestic labor strongly characterized enslavement in urban and other non-rural contexts. See Heuman, introduction, 4–5. Mary Turner has shown that enslaved individuals of mixed black and white descent could more easily pass as free if they were fortunate enough to make it to a town and find a means of supporting themselves. See M. Turner, *Slaves and Missionaries*, 48.

36. Gad Heuman's claim that runaway advertisements are an "unbiased" source for the study of runaways and the nature of slavery in the Caribbean (see Heuman, introduction) seems to dismiss the significance of the fact that depictions of runaways reflected owners' and overseers' perceptions of the individual fugitive, which were likely influenced by longstanding racist ideologies about black bodies and minds. David Waldstreicher offers an alternative perspective, arguing that "runaway advertisements, in effect, were the first slave narratives—the first published stories about slaves and their seizure of freedom" (see Waldstreicher, "Reading the Runaways," 247.) Waldstreicher's argument highlights the narrative aspect of runaway advertisements but does not critically examine the practical and ideological purposes that the advertisements served. Ex-slave narratives were influenced by the politics of abolition, whereas runaway advertisements were influenced by slaveowners' racism and capitalist self-interest in regaining their human property. While runaway advertisements offer perhaps a more candid insight into the abuses of slavery, the volition of the enslaved, and their relationships to kin, runaway notices were written for drastically different purposes than abolitionist publications.

37. Prude, "To Look Upon the 'Lower Sort,'" 140.

38. *Supplement to the Royal Gazette* (Jamaica), 1–8 April 1780; *Supplement to the Royal Gazette* (Jamaica), 22–29 September 1781; *Supplement to the Royal Gazette* (Jamaica), 18–25 April 1795.

39. G. Morgan and Rushton, "Visible Bodies," 46.

40. Prior to 1655, at least eleven Barbados laws dealt with Marronage, while sixteen of the twenty-three clauses that comprised the island's 1661 slave code pertained to runaways. These laws limited bondspeople's freedom of movement by restricting where, when, and with whom the enslaved could move beyond the plantation grounds.

41. 1661 Barbados Slave Code. Similar wording can be found in the 1664 Jamaica Slave Code.

42. 1661 Barbados Slave Code; 1664 Jamaica Slave Code.

43. An Additional Act to an Act, entitled "An Act for the governing of Negroes" (1692), in *Acts Passed* (Hall), 130–31.

44. "An Act for the further Encouragement of Parties, and more Speedy Reduction of Rebellious and Runaway Slaves" (1706–7), in *Laws of Jamaica*, 378.

45. "An Act for the more effectual punishing of Crimes committed by Slaves" (1707), in *Acts of Assembly, passed in the island of Jamaica; from 1681, to 1737, inclusive*, 107–8.

46. "An Act to inflict further and other Punishments on runaway Slaves, and such as shall entertain them" (1749), in *Acts of assembly* (1787), 2:23. This specific act applied to enslaved individuals eighteen or older who had either been born in the island or resided there for three years or more.

47. *Act of assembly*, 24–25.

48. "An Act for the more effectual raising Parties, to pursue and destroy Rebellious and Runaway Slaves" (1702), in *Laws of Jamaica*, 440.

49. By the mid-eighteenth century, other towns in Barbados had cages to keep fugitives before transferring them to the main cage in Bridgetown. Handler, "Escaping Slavery," 205.

50. *Barbados Mercury*, 25 October 1783. *Barbados Mercury and Bridgetown Gazette*, 8 January 1805.

51. "An Act to prohibit the Inhabitants of this island from employing, their Negroes or other Slaves, in selling or bartering (1708), in *Acts Passed* (Hall), 185.

52. Sloane, *Voyage*, 1:vii.

53. This form of gendered torture derived from sixteenth-century English use of the scold's bridle, a torture device used against unruly or quarreling women, supposedly to tame the tongue. See Boose, "Scolding Brides."

54. Branagan, *Penitential Tyrant*, 271.

55. For a discussion of American slave law and metaphoric disabilities see Barclay, "Greatest Degree."

56. *Gazette of Saint Jago-de-la-Vega* (Jamaica), 15–22 November 1781. *Kingston Journal*, 29 November 1760. *Daily Advertiser* (Jamaica), 22 February 1797.

57. 1661 Barbados Slave Code.

58. Barclay, "Greatest Degree," 36.

59. Handler, "Escaping Slavery," 185.

60. *Supplement to the Royal Gazette* (Jamaica), 27 January–2 February 1781.

61. Handler, "Escaping Slavery," 185.

62. Groebner, *Defaced*, 28.

63. More research is needed to determine a timeline of the shift from flogging as a punishment meted out to a variety of laborers, to the association of whip marks with black bodies. In the Caribbean, flogging was not solely reserved for the enslaved; it was used against free people of color until after emancipation. However, Diana Paton's study shows that by the late eighteenth century, the association between enslaved status and flogging was well entrenched in Jamaican society. See Paton, "Punishment," 938–39.

64. *Barbados Gazette and General Intelligencer*, 3–6 October 1787.

65. *Supplement to the Royal Gazette* (Jamaica), 23–30 May 1795. *Barbados Mercury and Bridgetown Gazette*, 17 December 1808. *Barbados Mercury and Bridgetown Gazette*, 3 June 1806.

66. Dickson, *Mitigation of Slavery*, 1:147.

67. L. Davis, *Enforcing Normalcy*, 11.

68. Thomas Thistlewood Papers. The use of branding on "raced" bodies was not isolated to the colonial Caribbean. Across the British Empire, the branding of colonial subjects served as a form of punishment, deterrence, and as a means of registering an individual as a criminal. Clare Anderson's study of penal practices in British India, for example, shows that the godna, a type of brand or tattoo on the criminal's forehead that detailed its bearer's crimes, characteristics, and sentence, was administered by colonial authorities in the first half of the nineteenth century as a key part of state building. See Anderson, *Legible Bodies*, 2.

69. For a discussion of scars as markers of the commodification of the enslaved see Fuentes, *Dispossessed Lives*, 14–19.

70. The labor and material conditions of enslavement in North America were generally less physically taxing than in the Caribbean; however, much of this depended on what kind of crop was grown. For instance, rice cultivation was as, if not more, physically destructive to enslaved bodies as sugar production. See Blackburn, *Making of New World Slavery*, 459–83.

71. Cole and Haebich, "Corporal Colonialism," 294.

72. Higman, *Slave Populations*, 294.

73. Goveia, *West Indian Slave Laws*, 29. *Cornwall Chronicle* (Jamaica), 12 July 1783. *Cornwall Chronicle* (Jamaica), 26 March 1786; in the laws of Jamaica, the cutting of the nose or nostrils was a punishment reserved for enslaved individuals who "shall offer any violence to any Christian as by striking or the like" (see 1661 Barbados Slave Code and 1664 Jamaica Slave Code). Equiano, *Interesting Narrative* 95.

74. Shyllon, *Black Slaves*, 12.

75. *Barbados Gazette and General Intelligencer*, 2–5 July 1788. *Royal Gazette* (Jamaica), 8 July 1789.

76. *Supplement to the Royal Gazette* (Jamaica), 1–8 April 1780. Ibid. *Barbados Gazette and General Intelligencer*, 29 March–2 April 1788. *Barbados Mercury and Bridgetown Gazette*, 16 January 1808. Cugoano, *Thoughts*, 11.

77. Ligon, *True and Exact History*, 141.

78. Ibid.

79. *Barbados Mercury and Bridgetown Gazette*, 3 June 1806.

80. Kiple, *Caribbean Slave*, 90. *Supplement to the Royal Gazette* (Jamaica), 26 April–2 May 1795. *Daily Advertiser* (Jamaica), 15 December 1791.

81. Dovaston, *Agricultura Americana*, 278–79, JCBL. MS 523/276, Newton Papers. *Supplement to the Royal Gazette* (Jamaica), Saturday 1–8 April 1780. Dovaston, *Agricultura Americana*, 279.

82. *Supplement to the Royal Gazette* (Jamaica), 24 June—1 July 1780. *Daily Advertiser* (Jamaica), 29 January 1791; *Barbados Gazette and General Intelligencer*, 25–29 October 1788. *Supplement to the Royal Gazette* (Jamaica), 23–30 September 1780. *Barbados Gazette and General Intelligencer*, 11–14 February 1789.

83. *Barbados Mercury*, 12 April 1788. Ibid., 30 December 1788.

84. The terms "splaw footed" and "parrot toed" were not race specific, but they demonstrate the power of language in forging conscious and unconscious analogies between disability and animality.

85. Handler, "Diseases and Medical Disabilities . . . Part 2," 183.

86. Ibid.

87. Goldsmith, *History*, 86.

88. Bennett, "Inoculation," np.

89. Handler, "Diseases and Medical Disabilities . . . Part 1," 5.

90. *Jamaican Gazette*, 3 January 1765. *Daily Advertiser* (Jamaica), 7 July 1791.

91. There has been a lot of work on suicide among enslaved people in the Caribbean and North America and particularly suicide as resistance. See, for instance, Bush, "Defiance or Submission?" and "Hard Labour"; Bell, "Slave Suicide"; T. Snyder, *Power to Die*; R. Browne, *Surviving Slavery*.

92. *Supplement to the Royal Gazette* (Jamaica), 8–16 April 1780. Ibid., 8–15 August 1795 (Jamaica). Ibid., 4–11 April 1795. *Cornwall Chronicle* (Jamaica), 22 January 1795.

93. V. Brown, *Reaper's Garden*; Hartman, *Lose Your Mother*.

94. For instance, *Royal Gazette*, 1–8 April 1780 (Jamaica); *Supplement to the Royal Gazette*, 4–11 April 1780 (Jamaica); *Daily Advertiser*, Monday, 3 January 1791 (Jamaica); *Kingston Journal*, 24 October 1761; 21–28 July 1781; 11 March 1780 (Jamaica); *Barbados Mercury and Bridgetown Gazette*, 21 May 1806 (Barbados).

95. *Barbados Mercury and Bridgetown Gazette*, 21 May 1806. *Supplement to the Royal Gazette* (Jamaica), 21–28 July 1781. *Supplement to the Royal Gazette* (Jamaica), 1–8 September 1787.

96. Gomez, *Exchanging Our Country Marks*, 177–80, 14.

97. Groebner, *Who Are You?*, 97.

98. *Royal Gazette* (Jamaica), 3–10 January 1795.

99. Groebner, *Who Are You?*, 90.

100. *Royal Gazette* (Jamaica), 31 January–7 February 1789; *Supplement to the Royal Gazette* (Jamaica), 27 October–3 November 1781.

101. Brune and Wilson, *Disability and Passing*, 1–2.

102. Boster, *African American Slavery*, 114–15.

103. Goffman, *Stigma*. For discussions of passing and disability, see Brueggmann, "It's So Hard to Believe" and "Interlude 1"; Kleege, "Disabled Students"; Michalko, *Difference*; and Siebers, "Disability."

104. See Tobin Siebers's discussion of Eve Kosofsky Sedgwick's work on closeting in "Disability," 2.

105. Waldstreicher, "Reading the Runaways," 244.

106. Mbembe, "Necropolitics," 21.

107. L. Davis, *Enforcing Normalcy,* 3–4.

108. Fuentes, *Dispossessed Lives,* 16.

109. Groebner, *Defaced,* 30.

Chapter 5. Bondsman or Rebel

1. Clarkson, *History,* 1:560.

2. Hochschild, *Bury the Chains,* 154.

3. Fryer, *Staying Power,* 261.

4. This chapter does not intend to intervene in the ongoing discussion about the Thomas Clarkson thesis or Eric Williams's decline thesis. Rather, it is concerned particularly with the crucial part that discourses of disability played in abolitionist debates. To that end, it is less concerned with *why* abolition happened when it did and for what reasons, than with *how* and *why* the debate was framed in a particular way, and what kinds of emancipatory futures were either enabled or foreclosed by the mobilization of disability rhetoric in the debate over abolition.

5. D. Turner, *Disability,* 147.

6. See M. Newton, *Children of Africa*; Ferrar, *Freedom's Mirror*; Johnson, *Fear.*

7. Fergus, "Dread of Insurrection." On the humanitarian element of the abolitionist campaign, see also D. Davis, *Problem of Slavery* and *Inhuman Bondage*; Drescher, *Econocide*; D. Davis, *Inhuman Bondage*; C. Brown, *Moral Capital,* 4–18, 57–58, 230, 156, 301, and 314; Oldfield, *Chords of Freedom.*

8. Martinez, *Slave Trade,* 85.

9. C. Brown, *Moral Capital,* 51, 40, 43; quotation on 36.

10. D. Turner, *Disability,* 58.

11. Ibid., 36.

12. Edmondson, *Letter,* 4.

13. Jordan, *White over Black,* 195.

14. Fox, "For the Governor."

15. C. Brown, *Moral Capital,* 55.

16. Baxter, *Christian Directory,* 559, 560.

17. D. Davis, *Problem of Slavery,* 308.

18. Tryon, *Friendly advice,* 139. For a discussion of Thomas Tryon and the construction of race, see Goetz, *Baptism,* 108–9.

19. Godwyn, *Negro's & Indian advocate,* 78–79, 14, 147.

20. Salih, "Putting Down Rebellion," 66.

21. For a lengthy discussion of ameliorative texts' depictions of punishment of the insurrectionary black slave body, see Salih, "Putting Down Rebellion," 64–86.

22. Behn, *Oroonoko,* 137, 140.

23. Tryon, *Friendly advice,* 81–82, 108.

24. For a discussion of slavery and suicide in early North America, see T. Snyder, *Power to Die.*

25. Tryon, *Friendly Advice,* 85, 194.

26. Ibid., 88, 89, 104–5.

27. Ibid., 103–4.

28. Shaw, *Everyday Life*, 33

29. Tryon, *Friendly advice*, 128–29, 129.

30. C. Brown, *Moral Capital*, 40.

31. In America, the Quakers Anthony Benezet and John Woolman preached to their fellow Friends that slavery was blasphemous and implored them to abandon slavery or suffer damnation. The antislavery pamphlets of the American Quakers were extremely influential on the other side of the Atlantic, as British evangelical Christians experienced their own religious revivalism that emphasized the New Testament teachings of equalitarianism. See Ryden, *West Indian Slavery*, 158.

32. Jordan, *White over Black*, 194.

33. Ibid., 196.

34. Swaminathan, "Developing the West Indian Pro-slavery Position," 41.

35. Patterson, "Slavery and Slave Revolts," 289.

36. Taylor, "Planter comment," 244.

37. Ibid., 145; Fergus, "Dread of Insurrection," 758; Long, *History of Jamaica*, 2:462.

38. The uncovered conspiracies in Barbados (1692), Antigua (1739), and Jamaica (1776), in addition to countless other acts of rebellious and potentially insurrectionary behavior on part of the enslaved, left planters in a "state of perpetual unease." See C. Brown, *Moral Capital*, 76.

39. Ramsay, *Essay*, 173; Broughman, *Inquiry*, 301; Long, *History of Jamaica*, 2:444, 2:442.

40. Clarkson, *True State*, 7, 8.

41. *Debate on a Motion*, 149–50, 7, 99.

42. My analysis of Tacky's War as it relates to abolitionist rhetoric and creolization as an ameliorative reform strategy is indebted to Claudius Fergus's excellent essay, "Dread of Insurrection," esp. 758–59.

43. P. Morgan and O'Shaughnessy, "Arming Slaves," 180.

44. Carey and Kitson, introduction, 5.

45. Buckley, *Slaves in Red Coats*.

46. Morgan and O'Shaughnessy, "Arming Slaves," 181.

47. Ibid., 182.

48. It is worth noting that two of the key actors in the Haitian Revolution, Henri Christophe and Jean Baptiste Pointe du Sable, fought in the American Revolution as part of French expeditionary forces.

49. Most of the slave ships arriving in the thirteen colonies were British, and even those that were American had been purchased by the Royal African Company. For more on the slave embargo see Blackburn, *American Crucible*, 136–37, 143–44.

50. Hochschild, *Bury the Chains*, 130.

51. Perry, "Traffic," 85.

52. Ibid., 96–97.

53. Walvin, introduction, 8; Walvin, "Slave Trade," 172. Historians of literacy in early modern England argue that there was a sharp increase in literacy in England around 1780

and that approximately 50 to 75 percent of English folks were literate in the late eighteenth century. See Laquer, "Cultural Origins."

54. D. Turner, *Disability*, 43.

55. Ibid., 7.

56. Woods, *Thoughts*, 5, 6, 6–7.

57. D. Turner, *Disability in Eighteenth Century England*, 43.

58. Ibid., 43–44, 6–7.

59. "A West Indian" (author), "Cruelty attending the Slave Trade as at present practiced on Negro Slavery," *Gentleman's Magazine*, October 1780, 458ff. MS3248, Wellcome Library.

60. Burke, *Sketch*, 173. Burke's publication was not an explicit condemnation of the slave trade nor slavery. However, it was consulted by politicians when drafting the act to abolish the slave trade in 1807.

61. *Debate on a Motion*, 9, 144, 144.

62. Clarkson, *Essay*, 42, 60, 60.

63. M. Smith, *Thomas Clarkson*, 31–32.

64. Ramsay, *Essay*, 62.

65. Woods, *Thoughts*, 8–9.

66. Ramsay, *Essay*, 62, 64, 64.

67. Ibid., 71, 85–86, 86. Clarkson, *Abstract*, vii, original emphasis. Woods, *Thoughts*, 8.

68. Guyatt, "Wedgwood Slave Medallion," 93.

69. M. Wood, *Blind Memory*, 22.

70. Colley, *Britons*, 376. M. Wood, *Blind Memory*, 22, 216.

71. Britain became involved in the Haitian Revolution in 1793, when it invaded Saint Domingue in the hopes of profiting from the civil war in the French colony, only to be defeated in 1798 by Louverture's troops. When the British withdrew from Saint Domingue, they offered to make Louverture king of Hispaniola and help defend the island from the French. Louverture refused, and yet the British never ceased depicting him as an ally in their ongoing war against the French. For more on British representations of Louverture, see Pierrot, "Our Hero."

72. Clavin, "Race, Rebellion," 2–3.

73. Pierrot, "Our Hero," 582–96.

74. Swaminathan, "Developing the West Indian Pro-slavery Position," 41. The Somerset case of 1772 propelled proslavery writers into a concerted defense of the institution and led to a decades-long debate over slavery and abolition in the English Atlantic world. Though Lord Mansfield's decision to free James Somerset had a very restricted intention: to respect English law, which had no precedent for slavery in England, while still upholding the rights and powers of slaveholders. Antislavery activists advertised it as a triumph for their cause, and in doing so significantly expanded the case's implications. Mansfield's ruling ultimately overturned two previous opinions regarding the legality of slavery in England, and although it had little immediate effect on the practice of slavery in the British Empire, abolitionists questioned planters' ability to reconcile their proslavery stance with the morals of metropolitan Britons. In response to this, the first legal decision against the institution of slavery, a more cohesive proslavery position began to form.

75. C. Brown, *Moral Capital*, 33.

76. Robertson, *Letter*, 21.

77. M. Turner, *Slaves and Missionaries*, 5–6.

78. Ibid., 195–96.

79. See also Sarah Salih's discussion of the depiction of rebellions in antislavery writings in "Putting Down Rebellion."

80. Edwards, *History Civil*, 2:61.

81. K. Turner, "Thicknesse."

82. Thicknesse, *Year's Journey*, 2:102.

83. C. E. Long Papers, 41.

84. Long, *History of Jamaica*, 2:354.

85. Historians do not know why Long's second edition was never completed, only that he spent much time revising it for a subsequent edition. See K. Morgan, "Long."

86. Long, "Revisions to Edward Long's *The History of Jamaica*."

87. Thicknesse, *Year's Journey*, 110.

88. Ibid., 103; Long, *History of Jamaica*, 2:377.

89. Salih, "Filling Up the Space," 96–97; Thomas, *Man and the Natural World*, 19, 47, 57, 112, 125–44, 289.

90. See also Salih's discussion of Georges Louis Leclerc, Comte de Buffon, and Edward Long in "Filling Up the Space."

91. Woods, *Thoughts*, 12–13. Ramsay, *Essay*, 195, 209, 197, 212.

92. Ramsay, *Essay*, 118.

93. H. More, *Slavery*, ll. 137–40.

94. Hochschild, *Bury the Chains*, 133.

95. Equiano, *Interesting Narrative*, 104.

96. K. Thomas, *Man and the Natural World*, 132.

97. Salih, introduction, xiv–xv.

98. C. E. Long Papers, 44.

99. Sharp, *Representation*, 74–75; 109–10.

100. Hoare, *Memoirs*, 263.

101. Fryer, *Staying Power*, 196, 203. There is a vast historiography on the Sierra Leone project. See for instance, Fett, *Recaptured Africans*; Byrd, *Captives and Voyagers*; Everill, *Abolition and Empire*.

102. Carey and Kitson, introduction, 2.

103. *Debate on a Motion*, 137.

104. Quoted in M. Turner, *Slaves and Missionaries*, 6–7.

105. S. Turner, "Home-Grown Slaves," 45.

106. Ibid., 47.

107. Ibid., 52–53.

108. M. Turner, *Slaves and Missionaries*, 6–7.

109. The Jamaica Assembly instituted their own reforms to the Jamaica slave codes in 1787, 1789, and 1792. In their place were issued several new laws offering bondspeople

protection from sadistic punishments that had long impaired and disfigured their bodies. See chapter 2 for a more detailed discussion.

110. S. Turner, "Home-Grown Slaves," 41, 44.

111. Ibid., 42.

112. *Debate on a Motion*, 108.

113. Ryden, *West Indian Slavery*, 199.

114. Foot, *Defence*, 96–97, 101. Preston, *Letter*, 16. S. Turner, "Home-Grown Slaves," 49.

115. Long, *History of Jamaica*, 2:380. Also cited in S. Turner, "Home-Grown Slaves," 49. For other secondary source discussions of the European belief that African women did not feel pain in childbirth, see Delbourgo, *Collecting the World*, 73.

116. Samuel Taylor Coleridge to Robert Southey, [February 1808], in *Unpublished Letters*, 1:395.

117. Dickson, *Mitigation of Slavery*, JCBL; letter from John Dun on slavery, 15 February 1792, MS.2227, Boston Public Library.

118. Ramsay, *Essay*, 35.

119. Letter from John Dun.

120. For more on how abolitionists drew on concepts of national ideology to condemn slavery and those involved, see Ryden, *West Indian Slavery*, 158–59.

121. Clarkson, *Essay*, 43–44.

Conclusion

1. Hochschild, *Bury the Chains*, 348.

2. M. Newton, *Children of Africa*, 229–30.

3. Disability scholars have noted that disability is often used as a metaphor by scholars of colonialism, while scholars of colonialism have likewise mooted that colonialism is often drawn upon by scholars of disability to describe experiences of dispossession, exclusion, and oppression. See for instance, Barker and Murray, "Disabling Postcolonialism"; and Sherry, "(Post)colonizing Disability."

4. See for example, Muskateem, *Slavery at Sea*; V. Brown, *Reaper's Garden*; R. Browne, *Surviving Slavery*.

5. See also Michael Rembis, "Challenging the Impairment/Disability Divide: Disability History and the Social Model of Disability," unpublished article shared with permission of the author (2019).

6. See Jordan, *White Over Black*, 43. Critiques of Jordan include K. Brown, "Native Americans," and Westhauser, "Revisiting the Jordan Thesis."

7. See, for instance, K. Hall, *Things of Darkness*, 2.

8. J. Morgan, *Laboring Women*, 14.

9. L. Davis, "Crips Strike Back," 502; Garland-Thomson, "Feminist Disability Studies," 1568; McRuer, *Crip Theory*.

10. Muyinda, "Negotiating Disability," 99.

Bibliography

Archival Sources

ABBREVIATIONS

AAS   American Antiquarian Society. Worcester, Massachusetts.
FLL/UWI   Faculty of Law Library. University of West Indies. Cave Hill, Barbados.
JCBL   John Carter Brown Library. Brown University. Providence, Rhode Island.

NEWSPAPERS

Athenian Mercury (London). Online access.

Barbados Gazette. AAS; JCBL.

Barbados Gazette and General Intelligencer. Bridgetown Public Library. Bridgetown, Barbados.

Barbados Mercury. AAS; Bridgetown Public Library, Bridgetown, Barbados.

Barbados Mercury and Bridgetown Gazette. Bridgetown Public Library. Bridgetown, Barbados.

Cornwall Chronicle (Jamaica). National Library. Kingston, Jamaica.

Cornwall Chronicle, and Jamaica General Advertiser. AAS.

Daily Advertiser (Jamaica). AAS.

Diary and Kingston Daily Advertiser. AAS.

Gazette of Saint Jago-de-la-Vega (Jamaica). AAS.

Gentleman's Magazine (London). Wellcome Library. London, UK.

Jamaica Courant. JCBL; AAS.

Jamaica Gazette. AAS.

Jamaica Mercury. AAS; National Library, Kingston, Jamaica.

Jamaica Mercury and Kingston Weekly Advertiser. Boston Public Library. Boston, Massachusetts.

Kingston Journal. AAS.

London Evening Post. Online access.

Morning Post and Daily Advertiser (London). Online access.

Public Advertiser (London). Online access.

Royal Gazette (Jamaica). AAS; JCBL; National Library, Kingston, Jamaica.

Saint Jago Intelligencer (Jamaica). AAS.

Savanna-la-Mar Gazette (Jamaica). AAS.

Supplement to the Jamaica Mercury. Boston Public Library. Boston, Massachusetts.

Supplement to the Kingston Journal and Universal Museum. AAS.

Supplement to the Royal Gazette. Library of the Society of Friends. London, UK; National Library of Jamaica.

Weekly Jamaica Courant. AAS.

OTHER ARCHIVAL SOURCES

1661 Barbados Slave Code. An Act for the better ordering and governing of Negroes. Barbados, 1661. FLL/UWI. Microfilm.

1664 Jamaica Slave Code. An Act for the punishing and ordering of Negro Slaves. Jamaica, 1664. Microfilm. FLL/UWI.

1673 Jamaica Slave Code. An Act for the better ordering and governing of Negroes in Laws and Acts by Sir Thomas Lynch at Jamaica in February 1673. KJ715 2000. Microfilm. FLL/UWI.

1678 Jamaica Slave Code. An Act for Governing Slaves in Laws Transmitted to Jamaica in 1678. Microfilm. FLL/UWI.

1696 Jamaica Slave Code. An Act for the better Order and Government of Slaves. Microfilm. FLL/UWI.

Acts pass'd in the General Assembly 1694 & 1695 ... Reported 1698. Jamaica, 1694–95. Microfilm. FLL/UWI.

Dickson, William. *Mitigation of Slavery in Two Parts*. Marginal inscriptions Codex Eng 209 3—size flat. JCBL.

Dovaston, John. *Agricultura Americana: or improvements in West-India Husbandry Considered. Wherein the present system of Husbandry used in England is Applied to the Cultivation or growing of Sugar Canes to advantage*. 2 vols., Codex Eng 60, manuscript. [1774]. JCBL.

Journal of Somerset Plantation, 1782–1796. MS 229. National Library. Kingston, Jamaica.

Laws Enacted by Sir Thomas Lynch at Jamaica in February 1673–1674. Jamaica, 1674. FLL/UWI.

Laws Transmitted to Jamaica in 1678. Jamaica, 1678. FLL/UWI.

Letter from John Dun on slavery. 15 February 1792, MS 2227. Boston Public Library. Boston, Massachusetts.

C. E. Long Papers. Add. 18270. British Library. London, UK.

Edward Long. "Revisions to Edward Long's *The History of Jamaica, Volume II*." Add. MS 12405, ff. 335r-346v, C. E. Long Papers, Manuscripts Reading Room, British Library, London.

Medical log of slaver the "Lord Stanley" 1792 by Christopher Bowes. RCS MS0003. Royal College of Surgeons. London, UK.

Melville Hall Estate Papers 25th March 1772. ADD 35155 a.5. British Library. London, UK.

Misc. Notes on Long's *Jamaica*. British Library. London, UK.

Newton Papers. Main Library. University of West Indies. Cave Hill, Barbados.

The Return of John Rycroft Best. Mcfm562–1818-000. Newton Papers.

Supplementall Act to a former Act Entitled an Act for the Better Ordering and Governing of Negroes, dated Aprill 21, 1676. *Acts and Statutes of the Assembly, 1650–1682 ("Transcript Acts")*. Barbados Department of Archives, n.d.

Thomas Thistlewood Papers. James Marshall and Marie Louise Osborn Collection, Beinecke Rare Book and Manuscript Library. Yale University. New Haven, Connecticut.

Published Primary Sources

Abbot, George. *A Brief Description of the Whole World*. London, 1664.

Act of assembly of the island of Jamaica, to repeal several acts, and clauses of acts, respecting slaves, and for the better Order and Government of Slaves, and for other Purposes; commonly called the Consolidated Act . . . London: Printed for B. White, and Son, Fleet-Street; J. Sewell, Cornhill; R. Faulder, New-Bond-Street; and J. Debrett, and J. Stockdale, Piccadilly, 1788.

Acts of Assembly Passed in the Charibbee Leeward Islands From 1690, to 1730. London: 1734.

Acts of Assembly, passed in the Island of Barbadoes, From 1648, to 1718. London: Printed by order of the Lords Commissioners of Trade and Plantations, 1732.

Acts of Assembly passed in the island of Jamaica; from 1681, to 1737, inclusive. London: printed, by order of the Lords Commissioners of Trade and Plantations, by Thomas Baskett and Robert Baskett, Printers to the King's Most Excellent Majesty, 1743.

Acts of Assembly, passed in the island of Jamaica, from the year 1681 to the year 1769 inclusive. In two volumes. Vol. 2. Kingston, Jamaica: Printed by Alexander Aikman, 1787.

Acts Passed in the Island of Barbados From 1643–1762, Inclusive . . . London: Printed for Richard Hall, 1764.

Africanus, Joannes Leo. *A Geographical Histories of Africa* . . . Translated by John Pory. London, 1600. British Library G. 4258.

An Abridgement of the Acts of assembly, passed in the island of Jamaica: from 1681, to 1737, inclusive. London: Printed by order of the Lords Commissioners of Trade and Plantations, by Thomas Baskett and Robert Baskett, printers to the King's Most Excellent Majesty, 1743.

An Abridgement of the Laws in Force and Use in Her Majesty's Plantations; (Viz.) Of Virginia, Jamaica, Barbadoes, Maryland, New-England, New-York, Carolina, &c. London: Printed for John Nicholson at the King's-Arms in Little Britain, R. Parker, and R. Smith, under the Royal-Exchange, and Benj. Tooke at the Middle-Temple-Gate in Fleetstreet, 1704.

Anon. *The Female Monster or, The second part of the world turn'd topsy turvey. A satyr.* London: Printed and sold by B. Bragg, in Avemary-Lane, 1705.

Anon. *Great Newes from Barbados, or a True and Faithful Account of the Grand Conspiracy of the Negroes.* London, 1676.

Bacon, Francis. *The Works of Lord Bacon with an introductory essay, and a portrait.* Vol. 1. London, 1871.

"Barbados, 1651. The Charter of Barbados." In *Laws of the Island of Barbados. Made and Enacted since the Reducement of the Same, unto the Authority of the Common-wealth of England* (1654).

Baxter, Richard. *A Christian Directory, or, A sum of practical theologie and cases of conscience directing Christians how to use their knowledge and faith, how to improve all helps and means, and to perform all duties, how to overcome temptations, and to escape or mortifie every sin: in all four parts.* London: Printed by Robert White for Nevill Simmons, 1673.

Behn, Aphra. *Oroonoko: Or, The Royal Slave A True History.* 1688. In *Aphra Behn: Oroonoko, The Rover, and Other Works.* Edited by Janet Todd. London: Penguin Books, 1992.

Best, George. *A True Discourse of the Late Voyages of Discoverie for finding of a passage to Cathaya, by the North-Weast, Under the Conduct of Martin Frobisher General. Devided into three Bookes . . .* London, 1578. 3 vols.

Blackstone, William. *Commentaries on the laws of England.* Oxford: Clarendon, 1766.

Bracton, Henry de. *On the Laws and Customs of England 1240–1260.* 4 vols. Translated by S. E. Thorne. Cambridge, MA: Harvard University Press, 1968.

Branagan, Thomas. *The Penitential Tyrant; or, slave trader reformed* 2nd ed. New York: Printed and sold by Samuel Wood, no. 362 Pearl-Street, 1807.

Broughman, Henry. *An Inquiry into the Colonial Policy of the European Powers.* Vol. 2. Edinburgh, 1803.

Browne, Thomas. *Pseudodoxia Epidemica: Or, Enquiries into very many received Tenents and commonly presumed Truths.* London: Printed by T.H. for E.Dod, 1646.

Burke, Edmund. *Sketch of a Negro Code.* 1792. In *Slavery, Abolition, and Emancipation: Writings in the British Romantic Period,* vol. 2 of *The Abolition Debate.* Edited by Peter J. Kitson. London: Pickering & Chatto, 1999.

Burton, Richard. *A View of the English Acquisitions in Guinea, and the East-Indies, with An Account of the Religion, Government, Wars, Strange Customs, Beasts, Serpents, Monsters, and other Observables in those Countries: together with a description of the Isle of St. Helena and the Bay of Sculdania where the English usually refresh in their voyages to the Indies: intermixt with pleasant relations and enlivened with picture.* London: Printed for Nathaniel Crouch, 1686.

Clarkson, Thomas. *An Essay on the Slavery and Commerce of the Human Species, particularly the African, translated from a Latin dissertation, which was honoured with the first prize in the University of Cambridge, for the year 1785, With Additions.* London: printed by J. Phillips, George-Yard, Lombard-Street, and sold by T. Cadell, in The Strand, and J. Phillips, 1786.

———. *An Abstract of the Evidence delivered before a Select Committee of the House of Commons in the Years 1790, and 1791 . . .* London: Printed by James Phillips, George Yard, Lombard Street, 1791.

———. *The True State of the Case, Respecting the Insurrection at St. Domingo.* Ipswich, 1792.

———. *History of the Rise, Progress, and Accomplishment of the Abolition of the Slave-Trade, By the British Parliament.* Vol. 1. London: Printed for Longman, Hurst, Rees, and Orme, 1808.

———. *Negro Slavery: Argument that the Colonial Slaves are Better off than the British Peasantry/answered from the Royal Jamaica Gazette.* Birmingham, 1824.

Coke, Sir Edward. *The First part of the Institutes of the Laws of England, or, A commentary upon Littleton: not the author only, but of the law itself. Tenth Edition.* London: Printed by William Rawlins, and Samuel Roycroft, assigns of Richard Atkins and Edward Atkins, Esquires. And are to be sold by Charles Harper at the Flower-de-Luce against St. Dunstan's Church in Fleet-Street and J. Walthoe in Vine-Court Middle-Temple, adjoining to the Cloysters, 1703.

Coleridge, Samuel Taylor. Samuel Taylor Coleridge to Robert Southey, [February 1808], in *Unpublished Letters of Samuel Taylor Coleridge* (2 vols.). Edited by Earl Leslie Griggs. London, 1932. 1:395.

Columbus, Christopher. *The Journal of Christopher Columbus (during his first voyage, 1492–93) and documents relating the voyages of John Cabot and Gaspar Corte Real.* London, 1893.

The Complete Geographer: or, the Chorography and Topography of all the known parts of the earth . . . London, 1709.

Cugoano, Ottobah. *Thoughts and sentiments on the evil and wicked traffic of the slavery and commerce of the human species, humbly submitted to the inhabitants of Great-Britain, by Ottobah Cugoano, A Native of Africa.* London, 1787.

The Debate on a Motion for the Abolition of the Slave-Trade, in the House of Commons, on Monday the second of April, 1792, reported in detail. London, 1792.

Dickson, William, LL.D. *Mitigation of Slavery, In Two Parts. Part 1, Letters and Papers of the Late Hon. Joshua Steele.* London, 1814.

Edmondson, William. *A Letter of Examination to All who have assumed the place of Overseers of the Flock, &c..* London, 1672.

Edwards, Bryan. *The History Civil and Commercial, of the British Colonies in the West Indies. In two volumes.* 2 vols. Dublin: Luke White, 1793.

Engels, Frederick. *The Condition of the Working Class in England.* New York: J. W. Lovell Co., 1887.

Equiano, Olaudah *The Interesting Narrative of the Life of Olaudah Equiano Or, Gustavus Vassa, The African.* 1789. Edited by Shelly Eversley. New York: Random House, 2004.

Falconbridge, Alexander. *An Account of the Slave Trade on the Coast of Africa.* London, 1788.

Foot, Jesse. *A Defence of the planters of the West-Indies; compromised in four arguments . . .* London: Printed for J. Debrett, opposite Burlington-House, Piccadilly, 1792.

Fox, George. "For the Governor of Barbadoes, with his Council and Assembly, and all others in power, both civil and military, in this Island; from the people called Quakers." *Journal of George Fox.* London, 1891.

Godwyn, Morgan. *The Negro's & Indians advocate, suing for their admission to the church, or, A persuasive to the instructing and baptizing of the Negro's and Indians in our plantations shewing that as the compliance therewith can prejudice no mans just interest, so the* willful neglecting and opposing of it, is no less than a manifest apostacy from the Christian faith: to which is added, a brief account of religion in Virginia. London: Printed for the author, by J.D., 1680.

Goldsmith, Oliver. *History of the Earth and Animated Nature in Eight Volumes* Vol. 2. Dublin: Printed by James Williams, 1776–1777.

Hacket, Thomas. *A Summarie of the Antiquities, and wonders of the Worlde, abstracted out of the sixteen first bookes of the excellente historiographer Plinie, wherein may be seene the wonderful workes of God in his creatures.* Imprinted at London by Henry Denham, for Thomas Hacket, and are to be solde at his shop in Lumbert Streate, 1566. Unpaginated.

Hakluyt, Richard, and Edmund Goldsmid, eds. *The Principal Navigations, Voyages, Traffiques and Discoveries of the English Nation, 1598–1600.* 16 vols.

Herbert, Sir Thomas. *Some yeares travels into divers parts of Asia and Afrique. Describing especially the two famous empires, the Persian and Great Mogull: weaved with the history of these later times. As also, many . . . kingdoms in the Orientall India, and other parts of Asia; together with the adjacent Iles . . . With a revival of the first discoverer of America.* London: Printed by Richard Bishop for Jacob Blome and Richard Bishope, 1638.

Hoare, Prince. *Memoirs of Granville Sharp, esq.* London, 1820.

Indagines, Johannes ab. *Briefe introductions, both natural, pleasaunte, and also delectable unto the art of chiromancy, or manuel diuination, and physiognomy with circumstances upon the faces of the signes . . . Written in Latin tonge, by John Indagines, prieste. And now lately translated into Englishe, by Fabian Withers.* London, 1558.

Jobson, Richard. *The Golden Trade, or, A Discovery of the River Gambia and the Golden Trade of the Aethiopians: Also, the commerce with a great blacke merchant, called Buckor Sano, and his report of the houses covered with gold, and other strange observations for the good of our owne countrey; set down as they were collected in travelling, part of the yeares, 1620 and 1621.* London: Printed by Nicholas Okes, and are to be sold by Nicholas Bourne, dwelling at the entrance of the Royall Exchange, 1623.

The Laws of Barbados Collected in One Volume, by William Rawlin of the Middle-Temple, London, Esquire. And Now Clerk of the Assembly of the Said Island. London, 1699.

Laws of Jamaica: Comprehending all the Acts in Force, passed between the thirty-second year of the reign of King Charles the Second, and the thirty-third year of the Reign of George the Third, The . . . Vol. 2. Jamaica, 1792.

Laws of Jamaica, pass'd by the governours, council and assembly in that island, and confirm'd by the Crown. 1716.

Leslie, Charles. *A New and Exact Account of Jamaica, from the Earliest Accounts, to the Taking of Porto Bello by Vice-Admiral Vernon in thirteen letters from a gentleman to his friend . . . in which are briefly interspersed, the characters of its governors and lieutenant governors.* London: Printed for J. Hodges, 1739.

Ligon, Richard. *A True and Exact History of the Island of Barbados.* 1657. Edited by David Smith. E-text 2012, 3d ed.

Long, Edward. *History of Jamaica. Or, general survey of the antient and modern state of that island: with reflections on its situation, settlements, inhabitants, . . . In three volumes.* London: Printed for T. Lowndes, 1774.

Mandeville, Sir John. *The Voyages and Travailes of Sir John Mandeville Knight Wherein is set downe the way to the Holy Land, and to Jerusalem . . .* London, 1625.

Marees, Pietre de. "A description and historicall declaration of the golden Kingdome of Guinea, otherwise called the golden coast of Myna . . ." translated by G. Artic Dantise, in *Purchas and his Pilgrimes.* London, 1625.

More, Hannah. *Slavery, a Poem. By Hannah More.* London: Printed to T. Cadell, in the Strand, 1788.

More, Thomas. *Utopia.* 1516. Translated and introduced by Paul Turner. New York: Penguin Books, 1965.

Münster, Sebastian. *A Treatyse of the Newe India by Sebastian Münster.* Translated by Richard Eden. London, 1553. Unpaginated.

Newton, John. *The Journal of a Slave Trader (John Newton), 1750–1754, with Newton's Thoughts upon the African Slave Trade.* Edited, with an introduction, by Bernard Martin and Mark Spurrell. London: Epworth, 1962.

Preston, William. *A Letter to Bryan Edwards, Esquire, containing observations on some passages of his History of the West Indies.* London: Printed for J. Johnson, No. 72, St. Paul's Church-Yard, 1795.

Prince, Mary. *The History of Mary Prince: A West Indian Slave.* 1831. Edited by Sara Salih. London: Penguin, 2000.

Raleigh, Sir Walter. *The Discovery of Guiana, and The Journal of the Second Voyage thereto by Sir Walter Raleigh.* 1595. London, Paris, New York & Melbourne: Cassel & Company, Limited, 1887.

Ramesey, William. *Mans Dignity and Perfection Vindicated. Being some serious thoughts on that Commonly Received Errour touching the Infusion of the Soule of Man. . . .* London, 1661.

Ramsay, James. *An Essay on the Treatment and Conversion of the African Slaves in the British sugar colonies.* Dublin: Printed for T. Walker, C. Jenkin, R. Marchbank, L. White, R. Burton, P. Byrne, 1784.

Raynalde, Thomas. *The Byrth of Mankynde, Otherwise Named the Womans Booke.* London, 1560.

Robertson, Robert. *A Letter to the Right Reverend the Lord Bishop of London, from an Inhabitant of His Majesty's Leeward-Caribbee-Island.* London, 1730.

Shakespeare, William. *The Tempest.* 1623. New York: Signet Classics, 1998.

Sharp, Granville. *A Representation of the Injustice and Dangerous Tendency of Tolerating Slavery . . .* London, 1769.

Sloane, Hans. *A Voyage to the Islands of Madera, Barbados, Nieves, S. Christophers and Jamaica, with the natural history of the Herbs and Trees, four-footed beasts, fishes, birds, insects, reptiles, &c. of the last of those islands; to which is prefix'd, an introduction, wherein is an account of the inhabitants, air, waters, diseases, trade, &c. of that place, with some relations concerning the neighbouring continent, and islands of America. Illustrated with figures of the things described, which have not been heretofore engraved. In large copper-plates as big as the life.* 2 vols. London: Printed by B.M. for the author, 1707–1725.

Swinburne, H. *A Brief Treatise of Testaments and Last Wills.* 1590. New York: Garland, 1978.

Thicknesse, Philip. *A Year's Journey through France and Part of Spain.* 2 vols.Vols. 1 & 2. London: Printed for and sold by W. Brown, 1778.

Topsell, Edward, *The Historie of foure-footed beastes Describing the true and Lively Figure of every beast . . .* London, 1607.

Tryon, Thomas. *Friendly advice to the gentlemen-planters of the East and West Indies In Three Parts.* London, 1684.

Woods, Joseph. *Thoughts on the slavery of the negroes.* London: Printed and sold by James Phillips, George-Yard, Lombard-Street, 1784.

Secondary Sources

Agamben, Giorgio. *State of Exception.* Translated by Kevin Attell. Chicago: University of Chicago Press, 2005.

Amussen, Susan Dwyer. *Caribbean Exchanges: Slavery and the Transformation of English Society, 1640–1700.* Chapel Hill: University of North Carolina Press, 2007.

Anderson, Clare. *Legible Bodies: Race, Criminality and Colonialism in South Asia.* New York: Berg, 2004.

Banks, Taunya Lovell. "Dangerous Woman: Elizabeth Key's Freedom Suit—Subjecthood and Racialized Identity in Seventeenth-Century Colonial Virginia." *Akron Law Review* 41 (2008): 799–837.

Barclay, Jenifer. "'The Greatest Degree of Perfection': Disability and the Construction of Race in American Slave Law." In "Locating African American Literature," edited by Rhonda Thomas and Angela Naimou. Special issue, *South Carolina Review* 46, no. 2 (Spring 2014): 27–43.

———. "Mothering the 'Useless': Black Motherhood, Disability and Slavery." *Women, Gender, and Families of Color* 2, no. 2 (Fall 2014): 115–40.

Barker, Clare, and Stuart Murray. "Disabling Postcolonialism: Global Disability Cultures and Democratic Criticism." *Journal of Literary and Cultural Disability Studies* 4, no. 3 (2010): 219–36.

Barnes, Colin. *Cabbage Syndrome: The Social Construction of Dependence.* Lewes: Falmer, 1990.

———. "Disability Studies: New or Not-So-New Directions." *Disability and Society* 4, no. 4 (1999): 577–80.

———, and Michael Oliver. *The New Politics of Disablement.* Tavistock: Palgrave Macmillan, 2012.

Baynton, Douglas. "Disability and the Justification of Inequality in American History." In *The New Disability History,* edited by Paul Longmore and Lauri Umansky, 33–57. New York: New York University Press, 2001.

Beckles, Hilary. *Natural Rebels: A Social History of Enslaved Black Women in Barbados.* New Brunswick, NJ: Rutgers University Press, 1989.

———. "Plantation Production and White 'Proto-Slavery': White Indentured Servants and the Colonisation of the English West Indies, 1624–45." *Americas* 41, no. 3 (January 1985): 21–45.

———. "A 'Riotous and Unruly Lot': Irish Indentured Servants and Freemen in the English West Indies, 1644–1713." *William and Mary Quarterly* 47, no. 4 (October 1990): 503–22.

———. "The Slave Drivers' War: Bussa and the 1816 Barbados Slave Rebellion." *Boletín de Estudios Latinoamericanos y del Caribe* 39 (December 1985): 85–110.

———. *White Servitude and Black Slavery in Barbados, 1627–1715.* Knoxville: University of Tennessee Press, 1989.

Bell, Richard. "Slave Suicide, Abolition and the Problem of Resistance." *Slavery and Abolition* 33, no. 4 (2012): 525–49.

Bennett, Michael. "Inoculation of the Poor against Smallpox in Eighteenth-Century England." In *Experiences of Poverty in Late Medieval and Early Modern England and France,* edited by Anne M. Scott, 199–223. Burlington, VT: Ashgate, 2012.

Billings, Warren M. "The Case of Fernando and Elizabeth Key: A Note on the Status of Blacks in Seventeenth-Century Virginia." *William and Mary Quarterly,* 3d ser., 30, no. 3 (July 1973): 467–74.

Blackburn, Robin. *The American Crucible: Slave, Emancipation, and Human Rights.* London: Verso, 2013.

———. *The Making of New World Slavery: From the Baroque to the Modern, 1492–1800.* New York: Verso, 1997.

Block, Sharon. *Colonial Complexions: Race and Bodies in Eighteenth-Century America.* Philadelphia: University of Pennsylvania Press, 2018.

Boose, Lynda E. "The Getting of a Lawful Race." In *Women, "Race," and Writing in the Early Modern Period,* edited by Margo Hendricks and Patricia Parker, 35–54. New York: Routledge, 1994.

———. "Scolding Brides and Bridling Scolds: Taming the Woman's Unruly Member." *Shakespeare Quarterly* 42, no. 2 (Summer 1991): 179–213.

Boster, Dea H. *African American Slavery and Disability: Bodies, Property, and Power in the Antebellum South, 1800–1860.* New York: Routledge. 2013.

———. "An 'Epeleptick' Bondswoman: Fits, Slavery, and Power in the Antebellum South." *Bulletin of the History of Medicine* 83, no. 2 (Summer 2009): 271–301.

Boucher, Philip P. *Cannibal Encounters: Europeans and Island Caribs, 1492–1763.* Baltimore: Johns Hopkins University Press, 1992.

Brammall, Kathryn M. "Monstrous Metamorphosis: Nature, Morality, and the Rhetoric of Monstrosity in Tudor England." *Sixteenth Century Journal* 27, no. 1 (Spring 1996): 3–21.

Braude, Benjamin. "The Sons of Noah and the Construction of Ethnic and Geographical Identities in the Medieval and Early Modern Periods." In "Constructing Race." Special issue, *William and Mary Quarterly* 54, no. 1 (January 1997): 103–42.

Bronstein, Jamie L. *Caught in the Machinery: Workplace Accidents and Injured Workers in Nineteenth-Century Britain.* Stanford, CA: Stanford University Press, 2008.

Brown, Christopher Leslie. *Moral Capital: Foundations of British Abolitionism.* Chapel Hill: University of North Carolina Press, 2006.

Brown, Kathleen. *Good Wives, Nasty Wenches, and Anxious Patriarchs: Gender, Race, and Power in Colonial Virginia.* Chapel Hill: University of North Carolina Press, 1996.

———. "Native Americans and Early Modern Concepts of Race." In *Empire and Others: British Encounters with Indigenous Peoples, 1600–1850,* edited by Martin Daunton and Rick Halpern, 79–100. Philadelphia: University of Pennsylvania Press, 1999.

Brown, Vincent. *The Reaper's Garden: Death and Power in the World of Atlantic Slavery.* Cambridge, MA: Harvard University Press, 2008.

———. *Surviving Slavery in the British Caribbean.* Philadelphia: University of Pennsylvania Press, 2017.

Browne, Simone. "Digital Epidermalization: Race, Identity and Biometrics." *Critical Sociology* 36, no. 1 (January 2010): 131–50.

Brueggmann, Brenda Jo. "Interlude 1: On (Almost) Passing." In *Lend Me Your Ear: Rhetorical Constructions of Deafness,* 81–100. Washington, DC: Gallaudet University Press, 1999.

———. "'It's So Hard to Believe that You Pass': A Hearing-Impaired Student Writing on the Borders of Language." In *Lend Me Your Ear: Rhetorical Constructions of Deafness,* 50–80. Washington, DC: Gallaudet University Press, 1999.

Brune, Jeffrey A., and Daniel J. Wilson, eds. *Disability and Passing: Blurring the Lines of Identity.* Philadelphia: Temple University Press, 2013.

Bucher, Bernadette. *Icon and Conquest: A Structural Analysis of the Illustrations of de Bry's Great Voyages.* Translated by Basia Muller Gulati. Chicago: University of Chicago Press, 1981.

Buckley, Roger Norman. *Slaves in Red Coats: The British West India Regiment.* New Haven, CT: Yale University Press, 1991.

Buisseret, David, ed. *Jamaica in 1687: The Taylor Manuscript at the National Library of Jamaica.* Kingston: University of the West Indies Press, 2008.

Burch, Susan, and Michael Rembis, eds. *Disability Histories.* Urbana: University of Illinois Press, 2014.

Burnard, Trevor. *Mastery, Tyranny, and Desire: Thomas Thistlewood and His Slaves in the Anglo-Jamaican World.* Chapel Hill: University of North Carolina Press, 2004.

Burton, Jonathan, and Ania Loomba, eds. *Race in Early Modern England: A Documentary Companion.* London: Palgrave Macmillan, 2007.

Bush, Barbara. "African Caribbean Slave Mothers and Children: Traumas of Dislocation and Enslavement Across the Atlantic World." *Caribbean Quarterly* 56, no. 1/2 (March–June 2010): 69–94.

———. "Defiance or Submission? The Role of the Slave Woman in Slave Resistance in the British Caribbean." *Immigrants and Minorities* 1, no. 1 (1982): 16–38.

———. "Hard Labour: Women, Childbirth and Resistance in British Caribbean Slave Societies." *History Workshop Journal* 36 (1993): 83–99.

———. *Slave Women in Caribbean Society, 1650–1838*. Bloomington: Indiana University Press, 1990.

Butler, Judith. *Bodies that Matter: On the Discursive Limits of "Sex."* London: Routledge, 1993.

Byrd, Alexander. *Captives and Voyagers: Black Migration Across the Eighteenth-Century British Atlantic World*. Baton Rouge: Louisiana State University Press, 2008.

———. "Eboe, Country, Nation, and Gustavus Vassa's *Interesting Narrative*." *William and Mary Quarterly* 63, no.1 (2006): 123–48.

Carey, Brycchan, and Peter J. Kitson. Introduction. In *Slavery and the Cultures of Abolition: Essays Marking the Bicentennial of the British Abolition Act of 1807*, edited by Brycchan Carey and Peter J. Kitson, 1–10. Woodbridge, UK: Boydell & Brewer, 2007. Carretta, Vincent. *Equiano the African: Biography of a Self-Made Man*. Athens: University of Georgia Press, 2005.

———. "Response to Paul Lovejoy's 'Autobiography and Memory: Gustavus Vassa, alias Olaudah Equiano, the African.'" *Slavery and Abolition* 28, no. 1 (2007): 115–19.

Chaplin, Joyce E. "Natural Philosophy and an Early Racial Idiom in North America: Comparing English and Indian Bodies." *William and Mary Quarterly*, 3d ser., vol. 54, no. 1 (January 1997): 229–52.

———. "Race." In *The British Atlantic World, 1500–1800*, edited by David Armitage and Michael J. Braddick, 154–72. New York: Palgrave Macmillan, 2002.

———. *Subject Matter: Technology, the Body, and Science on the Anglo-American Frontier, 1500–1676*. Cambridge, MA: Harvard University Press, 2001.

Clark, Stuart. *Thinking with Demons: The Idea of Witchcraft in Early Modern Europe*. New York: Oxford University Press, 1997.

Clavin, Matt. "Race, Rebellion, and the Gothic: Inventing the Haitian Revolution." *Early American Studies* 5, no. 1 (Spring 2007): 1–29.

Cole, Anna, and Anna Haebich. "Corporal Colonialism and Corporeal Punishment: A Cross-cultural Perspective on Body Mortification." In "Body Modification," edited by Jessica Cadwallader and Samantha Murray. Special issue, *Social Semiotics* 17, no. 3 (2007): 293–311.

Colley, L. *Britons: Forging the Nation, 1707–1837*. New Haven, CT: Yale University Press, 1996.

Cover, Robert. "Violence and the Word." *Yale Law Journal* 95, no. 8 (July 1986): 1601–29.

Craton, Michael. *Testing the Chains: Resistance to Slavery in the British West Indies*. Ithaca, NY: Cornell University Press, 1982.

Crenshaw, Kimberlé. "Demarginalizing the Intersection of Race and Sex: A Black Feminist Critique of Antidiscrimination Doctrine, Feminist Theory, and Antiracist Politics." *University of Chicago Legal Forum* 140 (1989): 139–67.

Cunningham, Karen. *Imaginary Betrayals: Subjectivity and the Discourses of Treason in Early Modern England*. Philadelphia: University of Pennsylvania Press, 2011.

Curran, Andrew S. *The Anatomy of Blackness: Science and Slavery in an Age of Enlightenment*. Baltimore, MD: John Hopkins University Press, 2011.

Daston, Lorraine, and Katherine Park. *Wonders and the Order of Nature, 1150–1750.* New York: Zone Books, 1998.

Davis, David Brion. *Inhuman Bondage: The Rise and Fall of Slavery in the New World.* Oxford: Oxford University Press, 2006.

———. *The Problem of Slavery in Western Culture.* New York: Oxford University Press, 1999.

Davis, Lennard J. *Bending Over Backwards: Disability, Dismodernism and Other Difficult Positions.* New York: New York University Press, 2002.

———. "Crips Strike Back: The Rise of Disability Studies." *American Literary History* 11, no. 3 (1999): 500–512.

———. *Enforcing Normalcy: Disability, Deafness, and the Body.* New York: Verso, 1995.

Davis, Natalie Zemon. "Judges, Masters, Diviners: Slaves' Experience of Criminal Justice in Colonial Suriname." *Law and History Review* 29, special issue 4 (November 2011): 925–84.

Davis, Robert C. *Holy War and Human Bondage: Tales of Christian-Muslim Slavery in the Early Modern Mediterranean.* Santa Barbara, CA: Praeger/ABC-CLIO, 2009.

Dawson, Mark S. "First Impressions: Newspaper Advertisements and Early Modern English Body Imaging, 1651–1750." *Journal of British Studies* 50, no. 2 (April 2011): 277–306.

Dayan, Joan. "Legal Slaves and Civil Bodies." *Napantla: Views from South* 2, no.1 (2001): 3–39.

Delbourgo, James. *Collecting the World: Hans Sloane and the Origins of the British Museum.* Cambridge, MA: Harvard University Press, 2017.

———. *Slavery in the Cabinet of Curiosities: Hans Sloane's Atlantic World.* British Museum, 2007. http://www.britishmuseum.org/pdf/delbourgo%20essay.pdf. Accessed 7 January 2013.

De Mel, Neloufer. "Playing Disability, Performing Gender: Militarised Masculinity and Disability Theatre in the Sri Lankan War and its Aftermath." In *Disability in the Global South: The Critical Handbook,* edited by Shaun Grech and Karen Soldatic, 99–116. Cham, Switzerland: Springer International, 2016.

Diptee, Audra. *From Africa to Jamaica: The Making of an Atlantic Slave Society, 1775–1807.* Gainesville: University Press of Florida, 2012.

Dorsey, Joseph C. "Women without History: Slavery and the International Politics of *Partus Sequitur Ventrem* in the Spanish Caribbean." *Journal of Caribbean History* 28, no. 2 (1994): 165–207.

Downs, Jim. *Sick from Freedom: African-American Illness and Suffering during the Civil War and Reconstruction.* New York: Oxford University Press, 2012.

Drescher, Seymour. *Econocide: British Slavery in the Era of Abolition.* Pittsburgh, PA: University of Pittsburgh Press, 1977.

Dubois, Laurent. *Avengers of the New World: The Story of the Haitian Revolution.* Cambridge, MA: Harvard University Press, 2004.

Dunn, Richard S. *Sugar and Slaves: The Rise of the Planter Class in the English West Indies, 1624–1713.* Chapel Hill: University of North Carolina Press, 1972.

Dunthorne, Anna. "How to Approach a Monster: A Comparison of Different Approaches in the Historiography of Early Modern Monster Literature." *History Compass* 6, no. 4 (July 2008): 1107–20.

Eliav-Feldon, Miriam. *Renaissance Imposters and Proofs of Identity*. New York: Palgrave Macmillan, 2012.

Erevelles, Nirmala. "Crippin' Jim Crow: Disability, Dis-location, and the School-to-Prison Pipeline." In *Disability Incarcerated: Imprisonment and Disability in the United States and Canada*, edited by Liat Ben-Moshe, Chris Chapman, and Allison C. Carey, 81–99. New York: Palgrave Macmillan, 2014.

———. *Disability and Difference in Global Contexts: Enabling a Transformative Body Politic.* New York: Palgrave Macmillan, 2011.

Erickson, Peter. "Representations of Blacks and Blackness in the Renaissance." *Criticism* 35, no. 4. (1993): 499–528.

Everill, Bronwen. *Abolition and Empire in Sierra Leone and Liberia.* New York: Palgrave Macmillan, 2013.

Fanon, Frantz. *Black Skin, White Masks.* [1952] London: Pluto Press, 1986.

Fergus, Claudius. "The Bicentennial Commemorations: The Dilemma of Abolitionism in the Shadow of the Haitian Revolution." *Caribbean Quarterly* 56, no. 1/2 (March–June 2010): 139–58.

———. "'Dread of Insurrection': Abolitionism, Security, and Labor in Britain's West Indian Colonies." *William and Mary Quarterly*, 3d ser., 66, no. 4, Abolishing the Slave Trades: Ironies and Reverberations (October 2009): 757–80.

Ferrar, Ada. *Freedom's Mirror: Cuba and Haiti in the Age of Revolution*. Cambridge: Cambridge University Press, 2014.

Fett, Sharla. *Recaptured Africans: Surviving Slave Ships, Detention, and Dislocation in the Final Years of the Slave Trade.* Chapel Hill: University of North Carolina Press, 2018.

Fick, Carolyn. *The Making of Haiti: The Saint Domingue Revolution from Below.* Knoxville: University of Tennessee Press, 1990.

Finkelstein, Vic. *Attitudes and Disabled People: Issues of Disablement.* New York: World Rehabilitation Fund, 1980.

Fisher, Linford. "Atlantic Indian Slavery and Indian Middle Passages." Paper presented at the Annual Conference of the Association of Caribbean Historians, Nassau, Bahamas, 19 May 2015.

———. "'Dangerous Designes': The 1676 Barbados Act to Prohibit New England Indian Slave Importation." *William and Mary Quarterly*, 3d ser., 71, no. 1 (January 2014): 99–124.

———. *The Indian Great Awakening: Religion and the Shaping of Native Cultures in Early America.* Oxford: Oxford University Press, 2012.

———. "'Why Shall Wee Have Peace to Bee Made Slaves?' Indian Surrenderers During and After King Philip's War." *Ethnohistory* 64, no. 1 (January 2017): 91–114.

Fissel, Mary. *Vernacular Bodies: The Politics of Reproduction in Early Modern England.* New York: Oxford University Press, 2004.

Follet, Richard. "Heat, Sex, and Sugar: Pregnancy and Childbearing in the Slave Quarters." *Journal of Family History* 28, no. 4 (October 2003): 510–39.

Forde, Maarit, and Diana Paton, eds. *Obeah and Other Powers: The Politics of Caribbean Religion and Healing.* Durham, NC: Duke University Press, 2012.

Foucault, Michel. *Discipline and Punish: The Birth of the Prison.* Translated by Alan Sheridan. New York: Vintage Books, 1995.

Franklin, John Hope, and Loren Schweninger. *Runaway Slaves: Rebels on the Plantation.* New York: Oxford University Press, 1999.

Freedman, Paul. "The Medieval Other: The Middle Ages as Other." In *Marvels, Monsters, and Miracles: Studies in the Medieval and Early Modern Imaginations,* edited by Timothy S. Jones and David A. Sprunger, 1–24. Kalamazoo: Medieval Institute, 2002.

Friedman, John Block. *The Monstrous Races in Medieval Art and Thought.* Cambridge, MA: Harvard University Press, 1981.

Fritze, Ronald H. "Herbert, Sir Thomas, First Baronet (1606–1682)." In *Oxford Dictionary of National Biography.* Oxford University Press, 2004. www.oxforddnb.com. Accessed 2 November 2014.

Fryer, Peter. *Staying Power: The History of Black People in Britain.* London: Pluto Press, 1984.

Fuentes, Marisa J. *Dispossessed Lives: Enslaved Women, Violence, and the Archive.* Philadelphia: University of Pennsylvania Press, 2016.

Gabel, S., and S. Peters. "Presage of a Paradigm Shift? Beyond the Social Model of Disability Toward Resistance Theories of Disability." *Disability and Society* 9, no. 6 (October 2004): 585–600.

Garland, Robert. *The Eye of the Beholder: Deformity and Disability in the Graeco-Roman World.* 2nd ed. London: Bristol Classic Press, 2010.

Garland-Thomson, Rosemarie. "Disability and Representation." *PMLA* 120, no. 2 (March 2005): 522–27.

———. "Disability, Identity, and Representation: An Introduction." In *Rethinking Normalcy: A Disability Studies Reader,* edited by Tanya Titchkosky and Rod Michalko, 63–74. Toronto: Canadian Scholars' Press, 2009.

———. "Feminist Disability Studies." *Signs* 30, no. 2 (2005): 1555–87.

———. "Staring at the Other." *Disability Studies Quarterly* 25, no. 4 (Fall 2005): np.

Gaspar, David Barry. "With a Rod of Iron: Barbados Slave Laws as a Model for Jamaica, South Carolina, and Antigua, 1661–1697." In *Crossing Boundaries: Comparative History of Black People in Diaspora,* edited by Darlene Clark Hine and Jacqueline McLeod, 343–66. Bloomington: Indiana University Press, 1999.

Ghai, Anita. *(Dis)embodied Form: Issues of Disabled Women.* New Delhi: Har-Anand, 2003.

Gilroy, Paul. *The Black Atlantic: Modernity and Double Consciousness.* London: Verso, 1993.

Gleeson, Brendan. *Geographies of Disability.* London: Routledge, 1999.

Goetz, Rebecca Anne. *The Baptism of Early Virginia: How Christianity Created Race.* Baltimore, MD: Johns Hopkins University Press, 2012.

Goffman, Erving. *Stigma: Notes on the Management of Spoiled Identity.* Canada: Simon & Schuster, 1986.

Goldberg, Johnathan. *Tempest in the Caribbean.* Minneapolis: University of Minnesota Press, 2004.

Gomez, Michael. *Exchanging Our Country Marks: The Transformation of African Identities in the Colonial and Antebellum South.* Chapel Hill: University of North Carolina Press, 1998.

Goodley, Dan. *Disability Studies: An Interdisciplinary Introduction.* London: Sage, 2011.

Gordon, Avery. *Ghostly Matters: Haunting and the Sociological Imagination.* Minneapolis: University of Minnesota Press, 2008.

Goveia, Elsa V. *The West Indian Slave Laws of the 18th Century.* [Barbados]: Caribbean Universities Press, 1970.

Grech, Shaun. "Colonialism Is Not a Metaphor! Disability, the Global South and Decolonising Eurocentric Disability Studies." *Social Identities: Journal for the Study of Race, Nation, and Culture* 21, no. 1 (2015): 6–21.

———. "Disability, Poverty and Development: Critical Reflections on the Majority World Debate." *Disability and Society* 24, no. 6 (2009): 771–84.

———. "Recolonising Debates or Perpetuated Coloniality? Decentring the Spaces of Disability, Development and Community in the Global South." *International Journal of Inclusive Education* 15 (2011): 87–100.

Greenblatt, Stephen. *Marvelous Possessions: The Wonder of the New World.* Chicago: University of Chicago Press, 1991.

Greene, Jack P. "Changing Identity in the British Caribbean: Barbados a Case Study." In *Colonial Identity in the Atlantic World, 1500–1800,* edited by Nicholas Canny and Anthony Pagden, 213–65. Princeton, NJ: Princeton University Press, 1989.

Groebner, Valentin. *Defaced: The Visual Culture of Violence in the Late Middle Ages.* New York: Zone Books, 2004.

———. *Who Are You? Identification, Deception, and Surveillance in Early Modern Europe.* Translated by Mark Kyburz and John Peck. New York: Zone Books, 2007.

Guyatt, Mary. "The Wedgwood Slave Medallion: Values in Eighteenth-Century Design." *Journal of Design History* 13, no. 2 (2000): 93–105.

Hahn-Rafter, N. *Creating Born Criminals.* Chicago: University of Illinois Press, 1997.

Haley, Alex. *Roots: The Saga of an American Family.* [1963] 30th ann. ed. New York: Vanguard Books, 2007.

Hall, Douglas. *In Miserable Slavery: Thomas Thistlewood in Jamaica, 1750–86.* Barbados: University of West Indies Press, 1999.

Hall, Kim F. *Things of Darkness: Economies of Race and Gender in Early Modern England.* Ithaca, NY: Cornell University Press, 1995.

Hall, Neville. "The Judicial System of Plantation Society: Barbados on the Eve of Emancipation." In *Le passage de la société esclavagiste à la société post-esclavagiste au 19e siècle* (Point-à-Pitre, Guadaloupe: Colloque d'histoire antillaise, 1971), 1:38–70.

Handler, Jerome S. "Custom and Law: The status of enslaved Africans in seventeenth-century Barbados." *Slavery and Abolition* 37, no. 2 (2016): 233–55.

———. "Diseases and Medical Disabilities of Enslaved Barbadians, From the Seventeenth Century to around 1838, Part I." *Journal of Caribbean History* 40 (2006): 1–38.

———. "Diseases and Medical Disabilities of Enslaved Barbadians, From the Seventeenth Century to around 1838, Part II." *Journal of Caribbean History* 40 (2006): 177–214.

———. "Escaping Slavery in a Caribbean Plantation Society: Maronage in Barbados, 1650s-1830s." *Nieuwe West—Indische Gids—New West Indian Guide* 71, no. 3/4 (1997): 183–225.

———. "Slave Medicine and Obeah in Barbados, circa 1650–1834." *Nieuwe West—Indische Gids—New West Indian Guide* 74 (2000): 57–60.

———. "Slave Revolts and Conspiracies in Seventeenth-Century Barbados." *Nieuwe West—Indische Gids—New West Indian Guide* 56, no. 1–2 (1982): 5–42.

———. *The Unappropriated People: Freedman in the Slave Society of Barbados.* 1974. Reprinted with a foreword by Melanie J. Newton. Kingston: University of the West Indies Press, 2009.

Hannaford, Ivan. *Race: The History of an Idea in the West.* Baltimore, MD: John Hopkins University Press, 1996.

Hartman, Saidiya. "The Belly of the World: A Note on Black Women's Labors." *A Critical Journal of Black Politics, Culture, and Society* 18, no. 1 (2016): 166–73.

———. *Lose Your Mother: A Journey Along the Atlantic Slave Route.* New York: Farrar, Straus & Giroux, 2007.

Heuman, Gad. Introduction. In "Out of the House of Bondage: Runaways, Resistance, and Marronage in Africa and the New World," edited by Gad Heuman. Special issue, *Slavery and Abolition* 6, no. 3 (1985): 1–8.

———. "Runaway Slaves in Nineteenth-Century Barbados." In "Out of the House of Bondage: Runaways, Resistance, and Marronage in Africa and the New World," edited by Gad Heuman. Special issue, *Slavery and Abolition* 6, no. 3 (1985): 95–111.

———, ed. *Out of the House of Bondage: Runaways, Resistance and Marronage in Africa and the New World.* London: Frank Cass, 1986.

Higman, Barry W. *Slave Populations of the British Caribbean, 1807–1834.* Baltimore, MD: John Hopkins University Press, 1984.

Hochschild, Adam. *Bury the Chains: The British Struggle to Abolish Slavery.* London: Pan-Macmillan Press, 2007.

Hogarth, Rana A. *Medicalizing Blackness: Making Racial Difference in the Atlantic World. 1780–1840.* Chapel Hill: University of North Carolina Press, 2017.

Holt, Thomas C. "Marking: Race, Race-Making, and the Writing of History." *American Historical Review* 100, no. 1 (February 1995): 1–20.

Honouring the Truth, Reconciling the Future: Summary of the Final Report of the Truth and Reconciliation Commission of Canada. June 2015. https://web-trc.ca/.

Inikori, Joseph E. *Africans and the Industrial Revolution in England: A Study of International Trade and Economic Development.* Cambridge: Cambridge University Press, 2002.

Innes, Joanna. "The King's Bench Prison in the Later Eighteenth Century: Law, Authority and Order in a London Debtor's Prison." In *An Ungovernable People: The English and Their Law in the Seventeenth and Eighteenth Centuries*, edited by John Brewer and John A. Styles, 250–98. New Brunswick, NJ: Rutgers University Press, 1981.

Jackson, Shona N. *Creole Indigeneity: Between Myth and Nation in the Caribbean*. Minneapolis: University of Minnesota Press, 2012.

James, C. L. R. *The Black Jacobins: Toussaint L'Ouverture and the Saint Domingo Revolution*. 1963. New York: Random House, 1989.

James, Marlon. *The Book of Night Women*. New York: Riverhead Books, 2009.

Jeffreys, Mark. "The Visible Cripple (Scars and Other Disfiguring Displays Included)." In *Disability Studies: Enabling the Humanities*, edited by Sharon L. Snyder, Brenda Jo Brueggermann, and Rosemarie Garland-Thomson, 31–39. New York: Modern Language Association, 2001.

Johnson, Sara E. *The Fear of French Negroes: Transcolonial Collaboration in the Revolutionary Americas*. Berkeley: University of California Press, 2012.

Jones, Cecily. *Engendering Whiteness: White Women and Colonialism in Barbados and North Carolina, 1627–1865*. Manchester: Manchester University Press, 2014.

Jordan, Winthrop. *White Over Black: American Attitudes Toward the Negro, 1550–1812*. Chapel Hill: University of North Carolina Press, 1968.

Kennedy, Stefanie. "'Let Them Be Young and Stoutly Set in Limbs:' Race, Labor, and Disability in the British Atlantic World." In "Disability and Colonialism: (Dis)encounters and Anxious Intersectionalities." Special issue, *Social Identities* 21, no. 1 (2015): 37–52.

———, and Melanie J. Newton. "The Hauntings of Slavery: Colonialism and the Disabled Body in the Caribbean." In *Disability and the Global South: The Critical Handbook*, edited by Shaun Grech and Karen Soldatic, 379–91. New York: Springer Science+Business Media, 2016.

Kermode, Jenny, and Garthine Walker, eds. *Women, Crime, and the Courts in Early Modern England*. London: University College London, 1994.

Kidd, Colin. *The Forging of Races: Race and Scripture in the Protestant Atlantic World, 1600–2000*. Cambridge: Cambridge University Press, 2006.

Kiple, Kenneth F. *The Caribbean Slave: A Biological History*. Cambridge: Cambridge University Press, 1984.

Kleege, Georgina. "Disabled Students Come Out: Questions without Answers." In *Disability Studies: Enabling the Humanities*, edited by Sharon L. Snyder, Brenda Jo Brueggemann, and Rosemarie Garland-Thomson, 308–16. New York: Modern Language Association, 2002.

Kleinman, Arthur, Veena Das, and Margaret Lock, eds. *Social Suffering*. Berkeley: University of California Press, 1997.

Koot, Christian J. *Empire at the Periphery: British Colonists, Anglo-Dutch Trade, and the Development of the English Atlantic, 1621–1713*. New York: New York University Press, 2011.

Kopelson, Heather Miyano. *Faithful Bodies: Performing Religion and Race in the Puritan Atlantic*. New York: New York University Press, 2015.

Krise, Thomas W., ed. *Caribbeana: An Anthology of English Literature of the West Indies, 1657–1777*. Chicago: Chicago University Press, 1999.

Kristeva, Julia. *Powers of Horror: An Essay on Abjection*. New York: Columbia University Press, 1982.

Kriz, Kay Dian. "Curiosities, and Transplanted Bodies in Hans Sloane's 'Natural History of Jamaica.'" *William and Mary Quarterly* 57, no. 1 (January 2000): 35–78.

Kupperman, Karen Ordahl. "Presentment of Civility: English Reading of American Self-Presentation in the Early Years of Colonization." In "Constructing Race." Special issue, *William and Mary Quarterly* 54, no. 1 (January 1997): 193–228.

Laquer, Thomas. "The Cultural Origins of Popular Literacy in England, 1500–1850." *Oxford Review of Education* 2, no. 3 (1976): 255–75.

Lazarus-Black, Mindie. "John Grant's Jamaica: Notes Towards a Reassessment of Courts in the Slave Era." *Journal of Caribbean History* 27, no. 2 (1 January 1994): 144–59.

Lees, Lynn Hollen. *The Solidarities of Strangers: The English Poor Laws and the People, 1700–1948*. Cambridge: Cambridge University Press, 1998.

Lindfors, Bernth, ed. *Africans on Stage: Studies in Ethnological Show Business*. Bloomington: Indiana University Press, 1999.

Lindsay, Tom. "'Which First Was Mine Own King': Caliban and the Politics of Service and Education in *The Tempest*." *Studies in Philosophy* 113, no. 2 (Spring 2016): 397–423.

Linebaugh, Peter, and Marcus Rediker. *The Many-Headed Hydra: Sailors, Slaves, Commoners, and the Hidden History of the Revolutionary Atlantic*. Boston: Beacon, 2000.

Longman, Paul K., and Lauri Umansky, eds. *The New Disability History: American Perspectives*. New York: New York University Press, 2001.

Loomba, Ania. *Shakespeare, Race, and Colonialism*. Oxford: Oxford University Press, 2002.

Lovejoy, Paul E. "Autobiography and Memory: Gustavus Vassa, alias Olaudah Equiano, the African." *Slavery and Abolition* 27, no. 3 (2006): 317–47.

———. "Issues of Motivation—Vassa/Equiano and Carretta's Critique of the Evidence." *Slavery and Abolition* 28, no 1 (2007): 121–25.

Lowe, Kate. "The Stereotyping of Black Africans in Renaissance Europe." In *Black Africans in Renaissance Europe*, edited by Thomas F. Earle and Kate Lowe, 17–47. Cambridge: Cambridge University Press, 2005.

Lund, Roger. "Laughing at Cripples: Ridicule, Deformity and the Argument from Design." *Eighteenth-Century Studies* 39, no. 1 (Fall 2005): 94.

MacGregor, Arthur. "Sloane, Sir Hans, Baronet (1660–1753)." In *Oxford Dictionary of National Biography*. Oxford University Press, 2004. www.oxforddnb.com. Accessed 5 April 2014.

Martinez, Jenny S. *The Slave Trade and the Origins of International Human Rights Law*. New York: Oxford University Press, 2012.

———. "The Slave Trade on Trial: Lessons of a Great Human-Rights Law Success." *Boston Review* (September/October 2007): 12–17.

Martínez, Maria Elena. "The Black Blood of New Spain: Limpieza de Sangre, Racial Violence, and Gendered Power in Early Colonial Mexico." *William and Mary Quarterly*, 3d ser., 61, no. 3 (July 2004): 479–520.

————. *Genealogical Fictions: Limpieza de Sangre, Religion, and Gender in Colonial Mexico.* Stanford, CA: Stanford University Press, 2008.

Mbembe, Achille. "Necropolitics." Translated by Libby Meinties. *Public Culture* 15, no. 1 (2003): 11–40.

McElligott, Jason. "Crouch, Nathaniel [Robert Burton] (c. 1640–1725?)." *Oxford Dictionary of National Biography.* Oxford University Press, 2004. www.oxforddnb.com. Accessed 2 November 2014.

McRuer, Robert. *Crip Theory: Cultural Signs of Queerness and Disability.* New York: New York University Press, 2006.

————, and Abby L. Wilkerson. Introduction. In "Desiring Disability: Queer Theory Meets Disability Studies," edited by Robert McRuer and Abby L. Wilkerson. Special issue, *GLQ: A Journal of Lesbian and Gay Studies.* 9, no. 1–2 (2003): 1–23.

Meekosha, Helen. "Contextualizing Disability: Developing Southern/Global Theory." Keynote address, 4th Biennial Disability Studies Conference. Lancaster University, UK, September 2008, 1–20.

————. "Decolonising Disability: Thinking and Acting Globally." *Disability and Society* 26, no. 6 (2011): 667–82.

————. *The Mystery of the Eye and the Shadow of Blindness.* Toronto: University of Toronto Press, 1998.

————, and A. Jakubowicz. "Disability, Participation, Representation, and Social Justice." In *Disability and the Dilemmas of Education and Justice.* Edited by Carol Christensen and Fazal Rizvi, 79–95. Philadelphia: Open University Press, 1996.

Metzler, Irina. "Disability in the Middle Ages: Impairment at the Intersection of Historical Inquiry and Disability Studies." *History Compass* 9, no. 1 (2011): 45–60.

Michalko, Rod. *The Difference that Disability Makes.* Philadelphia: Temple University Press, 2002.

Miller, Gordon L. "The Fowls of Heaven and the Fate of the Earth: Assessing the Early Modern Revolution in Natural History." *Worldviews* 9, no. 1 (2005): 57–81.

Millet-Gallant, Ann. *The Disabled Body in Contemporary Art.* New York: Palgrave Macmillan, 2010.

Mintz, Sidney. *Sweetness and Power: The Place of Sugar in Modern History.* New York: Penguin Books, 1985.

Molineux, Catherine. *Faces of Perfect Ebony: Encountering Atlantic Slavery in Imperial Britain.* Cambridge, MA: Harvard University Press, 2012.

Morgan, Gwenda, and Peter Rushton. "Visible Bodies: Power, Subordination and Identity in the Eighteenth-Century Atlantic World." *Journal of Social History* 39, no. 1 (2005): 39–64.

Morgan, Jennifer L. *Laboring Women: Reproduction and Gender in New World Slavery.* Philadelphia: University of Pennsylvania Press, 2004.

———. "Partus Sequitur Ventrem: Law, Race, and Reproduction in Colonial Slavery." *Small Axe* 22, no. 1 (March 2018): 1–17.

———. "'Some Could Suckle Over Their Shoulder:' Male Travelers, Female Bodies, and the Gendering of Racial Ideology, 1500–1770." *William and Mary Quarterly*, 3d ser., 54, no. 1 (January 1997): 167–92.

Morgan, Kenneth. 'Long, Edward (1734–1813)." *Oxford Dictionary of National Biography.* Oxford University Press, 2004. www.oxforddnb.com. Accessed 17 May 2015.

Morgan, Philip D., and Andrew Jackson O'Shaughnessy. "Arming Slaves in the American Revolution." In *Arming Slaves: From Classical Times to the Modern Age,* edited by Christopher Leslie Brown and Philip D. Morgan, 180–208. New Haven, CT: Yale University Press, 2006.

Morrison, Toni. *Beloved.* New York: Plume, 1987.

Müller, Patrick. "'The Impediment that Cannot Say Its Name': Stammering and Trauma in Selected American and British Texts." *Anglia: Zeitschrift für englische Philologie* 130, no. 1 (April 2012): 54–74.

Muskateem, Sowandé M. *Slavery at Sea: Terror, Sex, and Sickness in the Middle Passage.* Urbana: University of Illinois Press, 2016.

Muyinda, Herbert. "Negotiating Disability: Mobilization and Organization among Landmine Survivors in Late Twentieth-Century Northern Uganda." In Burch and Rembis, *Disability Histories*, 98–115.

Nelson, Camille A. "American Husbandry: Legal Norms Impacting the Production of (Re)productivity." *Yale Journal of Law and Feminism* 19, no. 1 (2007–8): 1–48.

Nelson, Charmaine A. "'Ran Away from Her Master . . . a Negro Girl Named Thursday': Examining Evidence of Punishment, Isolation, and Trauma in Nova Scotia ad Quebec Fugitive Slave Advertisements." In *Legal Violence and the Limits of the Law,* edited by Amy Swiffen and Joshua Nichols, 68–91. London: Routledge, 2017.

Newman, Simon P. "Reading the Bodies of Early American Seafarers." *William and Mary Quarterly* 55, no. 2 (January 1998): 59–82.

Newton, Melanie J. *The Children of Africa in the Colonies: Free People of Color in Barbados in the Age of Emancipation.* Baton Rouge: Louisiana State University Press, 2008.

———. "The King v. Robert James, a Slave, for Rape: Inequality, Gender, and British Slave Ameliorations, 1823–1834." *Abolition* 33, no. 1 (2012): 583–610.

———. "Returns to a Native Land: Indigeneity and Decolonization in the Anglophone Caribbean." *Small Axe* 17, no. 2 (July 2013): 108–22.

Nicholson, Bradley J. "Legal Borrowing and the Origins of Slave Law in the British Colonies." *American Journal of Legal History* 38 (1994): 42.

Nielsen, Kim E. *A Disability History of the United States.* Boston: Beacon, 2012.

Niro, Brian. *Race.* New York: Palgrave Macmillan, 2003.

Nixon, Rob. "Caribbean and African Appropriations of *The Tempest.*" *Critical Inquiry* 13 (1987): 557–78.

Oldfield, J. R. *Chords of Freedom: Commemoration, Ritual and British Transatlantic Slavery.* Manchester: Manchester University Press, 2007.

Oliver, Michael. "Conductive Education: If It Wasn't So Bad It Would Be Funny." *Disability, Handicap and Society* 4, no. 2 (1989): 197–200.

———. *The Politics of Disablement*. London: MacMillan, 1990.

Olmos, M. F., and L. Paravisini-Gerbert, *Creole Religions of the Caribbean: An Introduction from Vodou and Senteria to Obeah and Espiritismo*. New York: New York University Press, 2003.

Ospina, Maria, and Liz Dennett. *Systematic Review on the Prevalence of Fetal Alcohol Spectrum Disorders*. Alberta, Canada: Institute of Health Economics, 2013.

Palmié, Stephan. "Toward Sugar and Slavery." In *The Caribbean: A History of the Region and Its Peoples*, edited by Stephan Palmié and Francisco A. Scarano, 131–48. Chicago: University of Chicago Press, 2011.

Parshall, Peter. "Great Knowledge: Albercht Dürer and the Imagination." *Art Bulletin* 95, no. 3 (September 2013): 393–410.

Paton, Diana. *No Bond but the Law: Punishment, Race, and Gender in Jamaican State Formation, 1780–1870*. Durham, NC: Duke University Press, 2004.

———. "Obeah Acts: Producing and Policing the Boundaries of Religion in the Caribbean." *Small Axe* 13, no. 1 (2009): 1–18.

———. "Punishment, Crime, and the Bodies of Slaves in Eighteenth-Century Jamaica." *Journal of Social History* 34, no. 4 (2001): 923–54.

Patterson, Orlando. "Slavery and Slave Revolts: A Socio-Historical Analysis of the First Maroon War Jamaica, 1655–1740 Part 1." *Social and Economic Studies* 19, no. 3 (1970): 289–325.

———. *Slavery and Social Death: A Comparative Study*. Cambridge, MA: Harvard University Press, 1982.

Perry, Amanda T. "A Traffic in Numbers: The Ethics, Effects, and Affect of Mortality Statistics in the British Abolition Debates." *Journal of Early Modern Cultural Studies* 12, no. 4 (2012): 78–104.

Phillips, Caryl. *Cambridge*. 1991. New York: Vintage International, 1993.

Pierrot, Grégory. "'Our Hero': Toussaint Louverture in British Representations." *Criticism* 50, no. 4 (Fall 2008): 581–607.

Pike, Ruth. *Linajudos and Conversos in Seville: Greed and Prejudice in Sixteenth- and Seventeenth-Century Spain*. New York: Peter Lang, 2000.

Popova, Svetlana, Shannon Lange, Dennis Bekmuradov, Alanna Mihic, and Jürgen Rehm. "Fetal Alcohol Spectrum Disorder Prevalence Estimates in Correctional Systems: A Systematic Literature Review." *Canadian Journal of Public Health/Revue Canadienne de Sante'e Publique* 102, no. 5 (September/October 2011): 336–40.

Practor, Howard S. *Colonial British Caribbean Newspapers: A Bibliography and Directory*. Westport, CT: Greenwood Press, 1990.

Pratt, Mary Louise. *Imperial Eyes: Travel Writing and Transculturation*. 3d ed. New York: Routledge, [1992] 2008.

Prude, Jonathan. "To Look upon the 'Lower Sort': Runaway Ads and the Appearance of Unfree Laborers in America, 1750–1800." *Journal of American History* 78 (June 1991): 124–59.

Puckrein, Gary A. *Little England: Plantation Society and Anglo-Barbadian Politics, 1627–1700.* New York: New York University Press, 1984.

Rankin, Jim, Patty Winsa, and Hidy Ng. "Unequal Justice: Aboriginal and Black Inmates Disproportionately Fill Ontario Jails." *Toronto Star*, 1 March 2013. www.thestar.com/news/insight/2013/03/01/unequal_justice_aboriginal_and_black_inmates_disproportionately_fill_ontario_jails.html. Accessed 10 June 2015.

Rattansi, Ali. *Racism: A Very Short Introduction.* New York: Oxford University Press, 2007.

Rediker, Marcus. *The Slave Ship: A Human History.* New York: Viking, 2007.

Roberts, Justin. *Slavery and the Enlightenment in the British Atlantic, 1750–1807.* New York: Cambridge University Press, 2013.

Rugemer, Edward B. "The Development of Mastery and Race in the Comprehensive Slave Codes of the Greater Caribbean during the Seventeenth Century." *William and Mary Quarterly* 70, no. 3 (July 2013): 429–58.

Ryden, David Beck. *West Indian Slavery and British Abolition, 1783–1807.* New York: Cambridge University Press, 2010.

Salih, Sarah. "Filling Up the Space between Mankind and Ape: Racism, Speciesism and the Androphilic Ape." *Ariel* 38, no. 1 (2007): 95–111.

———. Introduction. In *The History of Mary Prince: A West Indian Slave* [1831], edited by Sarah Salih, vii–xxxii. Toronto: Penguin Books, 2000.

———. "Putting Down Rebellion: Witnessing the Body of the Condemned in Abolition-era Narratives." In *Slavery and the Cultures of Abolition: Essays Marking the Bicentennial of the British Abolition Act of 1807*, edited by Brycchan Carey and Peter J. Kitson, 64–86. Woodbridge, UK: Boyndell & Brewer, 2007.

Samuels, Ellen. "Examining Millie and Christine McKoy: Where Enslavement and Enfreakment Meet." *Signs: Journal of Women in Culture and Society* 37, no. 11 (2011): 53–81.

Scarry, Elaine. *The Body in Pain: The Making and Unmaking of the World.* Oxford: Oxford University Press, 1985.

Schiebinger, Londa. "Why Mammals Are Called Mammals: Gender Politics in Eighteenth-Century Natural History." *American Historical Review* 98, no. 2 (April 1993): 382–411.

Seed, Patricia. *To Love, Honor, and Obey in Colonial Mexico: Conflicts over Marriage Choice, 1574–1821* Stanford, CA: Stanford University Press, 1998.

Shakespeare, Tom. "The Social Model of Disability: An Outdated Ideology?" *Research in Social Science and Disability* 2 (2002): 9–28.

———, and Nicholas Watson. "The Social Model of Disability." In *The Disability Studies Reader*, 4th ed., edited by Lennard J. Davis, 214–21. New York: Routledge, 2013.

Sharpe, Andrew N. "England's Legal Monsters." *Law, Culture and the Humanities* 5 (2009): 100–130.

Sharples, James. "Hearing Whispers, Casting Shadows: Jailhouse Conversation and the Production of Knowledge during the Antigua Slave Conspiracy Investigation in 1736." In *Buried Lives: Incarcerated in Early America*, edited by Michele Lise Tarter and Richard Bell. Athens: University of Georgia Press, 2012.

Shaw, Jenny. *Everyday Life in the Early English Caribbean: Irish, Africans, and the Construction of Difference*. Athens: University of Georgia Press, 2013.

Sheller, Mimi. *Consuming the Caribbean: From Arawaks to Zombies*. New York: Routledge, 2003.

Sheridan, Richard. *Doctors and Slaves: A Medical and Demographic History of Slavery in the British West Indies*. New York: Cambridge University Press, 1985.

Sherry, M. "(Post)colonizing Disability." In "Intersecting Gender and Disability Perspectives in Rethinking Postcolonial Identities." Special issue, *Wagadu* 4 (2007): 10–22.

Shildrick, Margrit. *Embodying the Monster: Encounters with the Vulnerable Self*. London: Sage, 2002.

———. "Maternal Imagination: Reconceiving First Impressions." *Rethinking History* 4, no. 3 (2000): 243–60.

Shyllon, F. O. *Black Slaves in Britain*. New York: Published for the Institute of Race Relations by Oxford University Press, 1974.

Siebers, Tobin. "Disability as Masquerade." *Literature and Medicine* 23, no. 1 (Spring 2004): 1–22.

———. "A Sexual Culture for Disabled People." In *Sex and Disability*, edited by Robert McRuer and Anna Mollow, 37–53. Durham, NC: Duke University Press, 2012.

Smallwood, Stephanie E. *Saltwater Slavery: A Middle Passage from Africa to American Diaspora*. Cambridge, MA: Harvard University Press, 2007.

Smedley, Audrey. *Race in North America: Origin and Evolution of a Worldview*. 3d ed. Boulder, CO: Westview, 2007.

Smith, Cassander. *Black Africans in the British Imagination: English Narratives of the Early Atlantic World*. Baton Rouge: Louisiana State University Press, 2016.

Smith, David Chan. "Brief Introduction to *A True and Exact History of the Island of Barbados*, by Richard Ligon ([1657] E-text." 3d ed., 2012, i–xxxix.

Smith, Mary-Antoinette, ed. *Thomas Clarkson and Ottobah Cugoano: Essays on the Slavery and Commerce of the Human Species*. Peterborough, ON: Broadview, 2010.

Snyder, Christina. *Slavery in Indian Country: The Changing Face of Captivity in Early America*. Cambridge, MA: Harvard University Press, 2010.

Snyder, Terri L. *The Power to Die: Slavery and Suicide in British North America*. Chicago: University of Chicago Press, 2015.

Socolow, Susan. *The Women of Colonial Latin America*. Cambridge: Cambridge University Press, 2000.

Spierenburg, Pieter. *The Spectacle of Suffering: Executions and the Evolution of Repression: From a Preindustrial Metropolis to the European Experience*. Cambridge: Cambridge University Press, 2008.

Spillers, Hortense J. *Black, White, and in Color: Essays on American Literature and Culture*. Chicago: University of Chicago Press, 2003.

Stagg, Kevin. "Representing Physical Difference: The Materiality of the Monstrous." In *Social Histories of Disability and Deformity*, edited by Kevin Stagg and David M. Turner, 19–38. New York: Routledge, 2006.

Stiker, Henri-Jacques. *A History of Disability*. Translated by William Sayers. Ann Arbor: University of Michigan Press, 2009.

Stolcke, Verena. "Invaded Women: Gender, Race, and Class in the Formation of Colonial Society." In *Women, "Race," and Writing in the Early Modern Period*, edited by Margo Hendricks and Patricia Parker, 272–86. New York: Routledge, 1994.

Swaminathan, Srividhya. "Developing the West Indian Proslavery Position after the Somerset Decision." *Slavery and Abolition* 24, no. 3 (2003): 40–60.

Sweet, James H. "The Iberian Roots of American Racist Thought." In "Constructing Race." Special issue, *William and Mary Quarterly* 54, no. 1 (January 1997): 143–66.

Taylor, Clare. "Planter Comment upon Slave Revolts in 18th Century Jamaica." *Slavery and Abolition: A Journal of Slave and Post-Slave Studies* 3, no.3 (1982): 243–53.

Thomas, Carol. *Sociologies of Disability and Illness: Contested Ideas in Disability Studies and Medical Sociology*. London: Palgrave Macmillan, 2007.

Thomas, Hugh. *The Slave Trade: The Story of the Atlantic Slave Trade, 1440–1870*. New York: Simon & Schuster Paperbacks, 1997.

Thomas, Keith. *Man and the Natural World: Changing Attitudes in England, 1500–1800*. New York: Penguin Books, 1984.

Thornton, John. *Africa and Africans in the Making of the Atlantic World, 1400–1800*. 2d ed. Cambridge: Cambridge University Press, 1998.

———. "War, the State, and Religious Norms in 'Coromantee' Thought: The Ideology of an African American Nation." In *Possible Pasts: Becoming Colonial in Early America*, edited by Robert Blaire St. George. Ithaca, NY: Cornell University Press, 2000.

Titchkosky, Tanya. *Reading and Writing Disability Differently: The Textured Life of Embodiment*. Toronto: University of Toronto Press, 2007.

Tomlins, Christopher. *Freedom Bound: Law, Labor, and Civic Identity in Colonizing English America, 1580–1865*. New York: Cambridge University Press, 2010.

———. "Transplants and Timing: Passages in the Creation of an Anglo-American Law of Slavery Histories of Legal Transplantations." *Theoretical Inquiries in Law* 10, no. 289 (2009): 389–421.

Trouillot, Michel-Rolph. *Silencing the Past: Power and the Production of History*. Boston: Beacon, 1995.

Turner, David M. Introduction. In *Social Histories of Disability and Deformity*, edited by Kevin Stagg and David M. Turner, 1–16. New York: Routledge, 2006.

———. *Disability in Eighteenth Century England: Imagining Physical Impairment*. New York: Routledge, 2012.

Turner, Katherine. "Thicknesse, Philip (1719–1792)." In *Oxford Dictionary of National Biography*. Oxford University Press, 2004. www.oxforddnb.com. Accessed 23 February 2015.

Turner, Mary. *Slaves and Missionaries: The Disintegration of Jamaican Slave Society, 1787–1834*. Chicago: University of Illinois Press, 1982.

Turner, Sasha. "Home-Grown Slaves: Women, Reproduction, and the Abolition of the Slave Trade, Jamaica 1788–1807." *Journal of Women's History* 23, no. 3 (Fall 2011): 39–62.

———. *Contested Bodies: Pregnancy, Childrearing, and Slavery in Jamaica*. Philadelphia: University of Pennsylvania Press, 2017.

Twinnam, Ann. *Purchasing Whiteness: Pardos, Mulattos, and the Quest for Social Mobility in the Spanish Indies.* Stanford, CA: Stanford University Press, 2015.

Vaughan, Alden T. "Caliban in the 'Third World': Shakespeare's Savage as Sociopolitical Symbol." *Massachusetts Review* 29, no. 2 (1998): 289–313.

———, and Virginia Mason Vaughan. "Before Othello: Elizabethan Representations of Sub-Saharan Africans." *William and Mary Quarterly,* 3d ser., 54, no. 1 (January 1997): 19–44.

———, and Virginia Mason Vaughan. *Shakespeare's Caliban: A Cultural History.* Cambridge: Cambridge University Press, 1991.

Waldstreicher, David. "Reading the Runaways: Self-Fashioning, Print Culture, and Confidence in Slavery in the Eighteenth-Century Mid-Atlantic." *William and Mary Quarterly,* 3d ser., 56, no. 2, African and American Atlantic Worlds (April 1999): 243–72.

Walker, Garthine. *Crime, Gender, and Social Order in Early Modern England.* New York: Cambridge University Press, 2003.

———. "Everyman or a Monster? The Rapist in Early Modern England, c. 1600–1750." *History Workshop Journal* 76:1 (October 2013): 5–31.

———. "Imagining the Unimaginable." *Journal of Family History* 41, no. 3 (July 2016): 271–93.

Walvin, James. Introduction. In *Slavery and British Society, 1776–1846,* edited by James Walvin. Baton Rouge: Louisiana State University Press, 1982.

———. "The Slave Trade, Quakers, and the Early Days of British Aboltion." In *Quakers and Abolition,* edited by Brycchan Carey and Geoffrey Plank. Urbana: University of Illinois Press, 2014.

Watson, Alan. *Roman Law and Comparative Law.* Athens: University of Georgia Press, 1991.

———. *Slave Laws in the Americas.* Athens: University of Georgia Press, 1989.

Weaver, Karol. *Medical Revolutionaries: The Enslaved Healers of Eighteenth-Century Saint Domingue.* Urbana: University of Illinois Press, 2006.

Wendell, Susan. *The Rejected Body: Feminist Philosophical Reflections on Disability.* New York: Routledge, 1996.

———. "Unhealthy Disabled: Treating Chronic Illnesses as Disabilities." *Hypatia* 16, no. 4 (Fall 2001): 17–33.

Westhauser, Karl E. "Revisiting the Jordan Thesis: 'White over Black' in Seventeenth-Century England and America." *Journal of Negro History* 85, no. 3 (2000): 112–22.

Wheatley, Edward. "Medieval Constructions of Blindness in France and England." In *The Disability Studies Reader,* 3d ed., edited by Lennard J. Davis, 63–76. Chicago: University of Illinois Chicago, 2010.

Wheeler, Roxann. *The Complexion of Race: Categories of Difference in Eighteenth Century British Culture.* Philadelphia: University of Pennsylvania Press, 2000.

Whitford, David. "A Calvinist Heritage to the 'Curse of Ham': Assessing the Accuracy of a Claim about Racial Subordination." *Church History and Religious Culture* 90, no. 1 (2010): 25–45.

Williams, Eric. *Capitalism and Slavery.* Chapel Hill: University of North Carolina Press, 1944.

Williams, Gareth. "Representing Disability: Some Questions of Phenomenology and Politics." In *Exploring the Divide: Illness and Disability,* edited by Colin Barnes and Geof Mercer, 1194–212. Leeds: Disability Press, 1996.

Williamson, Samantha. *Poverty, Gender and Life Cycle under the English Poor Law, 1760–1834.* Woodbridge UK: Boydell & Brewer, 2011.

Wilson, Kathleen. "The Performance of Freedom: Maroons and the Colonial Order in Eighteenth-Century Jamaica and the Atlantic Sound." *William and Mary Quarterly,* 3d ser., 66, no. 1 (January 2009): 45–86.

Wood, Betty. "Godwyn, Morgan (bap. 1640, d. 1685x1709)." *Oxford Dictionary of National Biography.* Oxford University Press, 2004. www.oxforddnb.com.. Accessed 5 April 2014.

———. *Slavery in Colonial America, 1619–1776.* Lanham, MD: Rowman & Littlefield, 2005.

Wood, Marcus. *Blind Memory: Visual Representations of Slavery in England and America.* New York: Routledge, 2000.

Woodbridge, Linda. *Vagrancy, Homelessness, and English Renaissance Literature.* Urbana: University of Illinois Press, 2001.

Young, Hershini Bhana. *Haunting Capital: Memory, Text, and the Black Diasporic Body.* Lebanon, NH: University Press of New England, 2005.

———. "Inheriting the Criminalized Black Body: Race, Gender, and Slavery in Eva's Man." *African American Review* 39, no. 3 (Fall 2005): 377–93.

Zola, Irving Kenneth. *Missing Pieces: A Chronicle of Living with a Disability.* Philadelphia: Temple University Press, 1982.

Index

Sloane, Hans, 59, 111
smallpox, 120
social rescue language, 140
Spanish colonie, or Briefe chronicle of the acts and gestes of the Spaniards in the West Indies, called the new world, The, 20
speech impediments, 122–23
Staying Power: The History of Black People in Britain, 13
suicide, 122
Swinburne, 56

Tacky's War, 1760, 52, 128, 135–36, 149, 164
Tempest, The, 13, 23–24
Tharp, John, 115
Thicknesse, Philip, 26, 149, 151
Thistlewood, Thomas, 57–58, 62, 66, 114
Thoughts on the Slavery of the Negroes, 139
Topsell, Edward, 21, 26
Towrson, William, 28
Treatise of the Newe India, A, 18
True and Exact History of the Island of Barbados, 29, 117
True Discourse of the late voyages of discoverie, for the finding of a passage to Cathaya by the Northweast, A, 22
Tryon, Thomas, 132–35

van Senden, Caspar, 21
violence, 4, 31; of colonization, 9–10; constant threat of, 12; disabling, of slavery, 7, 132–34; discursive, 5, 11; against laborers, 32–33; psychological wounding and masquerade of runaway advertisements and, 122–24; sexual, 54–60, 134; spectacle of, 60–66; systematized racist, 6; towards corpses, 66
voices of disability, 10–11
Voyages and travailes of Sir John Mandevile knight, The, 19

Walpole, Robert, 149
Wedgwood, Josiah, 143–44
Weinrich, Martin, 13
Wheatley, Phillis, 153
Wilberforce, William, 76–77, 141, 148
Willoughby, Francis, 43
women, African: childbirth by, 15–16, 87, 155–59; maternal inheritance and, 15–16, 33–34, 55; monstrosity of, 27–28, 38, 155–59; narratives of deformed, 28–31, 36–37; physical health of, 87–88; portrayed as simultaneously beautiful and repulsive, 18, 30; skin color and, 22
Wood, Marcus, 143
Wood, Sampson, 69–70
Woods, Joseph, 139, 143, 151

Year's Journey, A, 149
Young, Hershini Bhana, 69

Zong massacre (1781), 158

STEFANIE HUNT-KENNEDY is an associate professor at the University of New Brunswick.

The University of Illinois Press
is a founding member of the
Association of University Presses.

———————————————————

University of Illinois Press
1325 South Oak Street
Champaign, IL 61820-6903
www.press.uillinois.edu